"[E]ngaging scenes of the times keep the pages turning as this historical romance . . . swirls energetically through angst and disclosure."

—PUBLISHERS WEEKLY

"Sarah E. Ladd has written a story sure to warm your heart even on the coldest day."

—LAURIE ALICE EAKES, AUTHOR OF *A RELUCTANT COURTSHIP*

"Readers will cheer for the determined heroine and the flawed hero in this engaging story of redemption, set in the lush English countryside. Sarah E. Ladd is quickly establishing herself as a rising star in Regency romance."

—DOROTHY LOVE, AUTHOR OF *CAROLINA GOLD*

ACCLAIM FOR
The Heiress of Winterwood

"If you are a fan of Jane Austen and *Jane Eyre*, you will love Sarah E. Ladd's debut."

—USATODAY.COM

"My kind of book! The premise grabbed my attention from the first lines and I eagerly returned to its pages. I think my readers will enjoy *The Heiress of Winterwood*."

—JULIE KLASSEN, BEST-SELLING, AWARD-WINNING AUTHOR OF
THE TUTOR'S DAUGHTER

"Oh my, what an exquisite tale! With clarity and grace, Sarah E. Ladd has penned a timeless regency that rises to the ranks of Heyer and Klassen, a breathless foray into the world of Jane Austen with very little effort . . . *and* very little sleep."

—JULIE LESSMAN, AWARD-WINNING AUTHOR OF
THE DAUGHTERS OF BOSTON AND WINDS OF CHANGE SERIES

"This debut novel hits all the right notes with a skillful and delicate touch, breathing fresh new life into standard romance tropes."

—ROMANTIC TIMES, 4 STARS

"Captivated from the very first page! *The Heiress of Winterwood* marks Sarah E. Ladd as a rising Regency star sure to win readers' hearts!"

—LAURA FRANTZ, AUTHOR OF
THE COLONEL'S LADY AND LOVE'S RECKONING

"A delight from beginning to end, *The Heiress of Winterwood* is a one-of-a-kind Regency that kept me sighing with joy, laughing, crying, and even biting my nails when the occasion called for it! A whirlwind of emotions captured in an exciting tale of intrigue, kidnapping, and bittersweet love. This is Ms. Ladd's debut? I can't wait to see what she writes next! Remember the name, Sarah E. Ladd, because I'm sure you will be seeing much more from this talented author."

—MARYLU TYNDALL, BEST-SELLING AUTHOR OF
VEIL OF PEARLS AND THE SURRENDER TO DESTINY SERIES

"Ladd's charming Regency debut is enhanced with rich detail and well-defined characters. It should be enjoyed by fans of Gilbert Morris."

—LIBRARY JOURNAL

"This adventure is fashioned to encourage love, trust, and faith especially in the Lord and to pray continually, especially in times of strife."

—CBA RETAILERS + RESOURCES

The
HEADMISTRESS
of
ROSEMERE

The

HEADMISTRESS

of

ROSEMERE

SARAH E. LADD

THOMAS NELSON
Since 1798

NASHVILLE   DALLAS   MEXICO CITY   RIO DE JANEIRO

Published in Nashville, Tennessee, by Thomas Nelson. Thomas Nelson is a registered trademark of Thomas Nelson, Inc.

Thomas Nelson, Inc., titles may be purchased in bulk for educational, business, fund-raising, or sales promotional use. For information, please e-mail SpecialMarkets@ThomasNelson.com.

Scripture quotations are taken from the King James Version of the Bible.

Library of Congress Cataloging-in-Publication Data

Ladd, Sarah E., author.
  The Headmistress of Rosemere / Sarah E. Ladd.
    pages cm. — (Whispers on the Moors ; 2)
  ISBN 978-1-4016-8836-3 (trade paper : alk. paper) 1. Young women—Fiction.
2. Girls' schools—Fiction. 3. London (England)—Fiction. 4. Christian fiction.
5. Love stories. I. Title.
  PS3612.A3565H43 2013
  813'.6—dc23   2013025256

Printed in the United States of America

13 14 15 16 17 18 RRD 6 5 4 3 2 1

I lovingly dedicate this novel to my parents, Ann and Wayne. Thank you for going on this journey with me and for believing in my dreams.

There was no doubt in William Sterling's mind. He was being followed.

He was an easy target—now more than ever.

He knew better than to travel at such a late hour in the moors, when midnight's haze shrouded the moon's gray light and the new-fallen snow gave the illusion of an even terrain.

An owl's mournful cry sliced the night's uncomfortable silence, and with a sharp click of his tongue, William urged his mount into a faster gait.

He'd avoided the main road that leads directly to Eastmore Hall's iron gate, for it was too broad. Too exposed. He chose, instead, the cart path leading from Darbury's town square to Wainslow Peak. For although it was narrow and masked with snow, he'd be hidden.

The thoroughbred beneath him pranced and skittered to the

left, tossing his magnificent head in tenacious indignation. William regarded the horse's caution. Perhaps the stubborn beast was wiser than he was.

He could dismount and lead Angus back to Eastmore Hall on foot. Considering the ice and wind, it would be less treacherous. But the walk would be long and would slow his pace considerably. As quickly as he had the thought, the memory of the two suspicious men who'd been eyeing him at Griffin's End Inn came back.

No, he needed the protection of Eastmore Hall. Now.

William tightened his knees against the animal's sides and cast yet another glance over his shoulder. "Ya!"

In spite of the frigid air, perspiration trickled down his temples. Time seemed sluggish in the uncertainty. He crested Wainslow Peak, which was little more than a shallow hill with outcroppings of ancient stone, and circled his horse in the clearing next to Sterling Wood. He filled his lungs with the bitterly cold air and scanned the shadowed landscape.

The snow-covered grass swept down to the valley of the River Thaughley. The moon's waning light fell on Rosemere School for Young Ladies—his tenant.

If only Eastmore Hall were that close.

With a jerk of his gloved hand, he tipped his wide-brimmed hat low and turned his mount toward home. Without warning, a great, dark horse catapulted from the cover of the ash and birch trees and skidded, blocking the path and sending up a cloud of snow and earth. Plumes of white breath spewed from the horse's nostrils. Angus reared up, his frantic, high whinny piercing the eerie silence. With the strength afforded by shock, William tightened his legs around the horse's girth and pitched forward. He whipped his head around, searching for a pass to break free from the stony crags caging him. But instead of finding an exit, he faced another man on horseback.

"Get off the horse, Sterling."

Pulse hammering, William licked his lips and tugged the reins, circling his frenzied horse, desperate for escape. Every sordid incident that had led to this moment flashed before him in vivid detail. Remorse would do nothing now, not with a pistol pointed straight at his chest.

"I said dismount!"

William lurched around. A third pistol barrel challenged him. *Surrounded.*

Muttering, William slid from the saddle and planted his top boots in the swirling snow. If he were a praying man, now would be the time to employ such a plea. But he was beyond such saving.

William released the reins and raised both hands in the air.

The first man stepped toward him, pistol pointed. "Introductions not necessary, are they, Sterling? I daresay you know why we are here."

William shifted as the man wearing a caped coat stepped closer. He forced his voice to be low. "I have little money on me, if that is what you've come for."

"It's not your money I've come for. It's Captain Rafertee's money."

Perspiration stung William's eyes. "I have given Rafertee my note of hand. We agreed on the terms. I have three months left to provide the funds, and I will."

The man smirked and called over his shoulder to the men behind him, "Three months, lads. What do we think about that? Seems like an awfully long time to me."

The men snickered. William clenched his teeth as the pistol pressed against the wool fabric of his greatcoat.

The stranger's gravelly voice was as threatening as the pistol. "I got concerned, you understand. You left London in a hurry. Secretly, as if to avoid us. Why, you didn't even say farewell. And you've been gone for so long." A sneer cracked the man's face, and the moon's light fell on his crooked teeth.

The pounding in William's head intensified. The men behind his accuser cackled.

"We need to remind this fine gentleman that the captain won't take kindly if his money's not there when he sets foot on land again after all those months at sea. And it's my job to make sure the captain stays happy."

The man grabbed William's coat, yanked a button free, and ripped his leather pouch from the safety of his person. Without glancing down at his prize, the stranger tossed the leather packet to one of his partners.

William's attacker leaned in closer. His breath reeked of ale. If it had been only the one man, William would have taken a chance and fought—he could hold his own in a brawl. But with three, experience affirmed he'd stand little chance. A man standing behind the others walked over and slapped Angus's hindquarters and shouted, sending the animal off into the black of night.

Without a horse, William was at their mercy. He pressed his lips together and looked toward the stirring clouds.

Tonight I will meet my maker.

The gun dug into his belly. Chest heaving, William forced himself to look at his assailant. He knew not the man's identity, but he knew one thing with certainty: Rafertee cavorted with the darkest sort. The most dangerous, evil men.

William should know, for he had done the same.

William shifted. "All my money is in there. I've nothing else to give you. If you kill me, you'll never get the rest of it. What would Rafertee have to say then?"

The man's low, wide-brimmed hat shadowed his eyes. "Consider our visit a reminder. Either the good captain gets his money or you die." A sardonic laugh oozed from the man's unkempt face. "Just so you are fully aware, I'll be the one who has the pleasure of carrying out that order."

Without another word, the man's balled fist slammed into William's gut, stealing the wind from his lungs and hurling him backward. He lost his footing on the moor's icy carpet, and the sudden jolt hurled him back against a rocky crag. Before he could regain his balance, someone grabbed his coat and a fist slammed into his jaw. He fell. His head struck rock. He moved to stand, but as he did, one of the cloaked figures kicked his middle.

William collapsed, his cheek flat against the snow. A form approached, but William did not move. He could not move, even if he so desired.

"Three months, Sterling."

Another sharp kick thrust white stars across his vision, curling him in agony. His breath came in jagged gasps and burned like fire.

The voices were muffled. William could no longer decipher their words. A tunnel of sound whirred around him. Then the ground beneath him trembled as he heard the horses' hooves thunder off.

You're alive.

William lay still on the icy ground and groaned. The voices in his head were taunting him louder than his attackers and were impossible to ignore.

Considering the sorry state of you, you should be grateful.

Then all was still, quiet, save for the whistle of the wind through barren branches. William assessed his condition, limb by limb. Nothing appeared to be broken, but one eye was swelling shut and salty blood covered his lips.

After several attempts, William managed to roll over onto his knees. Fresh snow had begun to fall and had accumulated on his coat. He shook his arms and it scattered.

He attempted a whistle, hoping that by a miracle Angus would hear, but his upper lip was beyond such a task. So he waited and listened for any indication that his horse had not abandoned him.

He heard nothing, save for the mournful *too-wit* call of the owls on a distant moor.

He shouted as loud as his lungs would allow, "Angus!"

Nothing.

Head throbbing, ribs aching, he winced at the pain of simply breathing. He scanned his surroundings, disoriented. Had he been a more attentive estate master, he would know exactly how far he was from home. He'd be familiar with every tree. Every stump. Every vale. But in his confusion, he wasn't sure. As he turned, he noticed the black outline of chimneys rising above snow-covered trees.

Rosemere.

Heavy snow had ridden in on the sharp easterly wind. William reached for his hat, which had fallen in the attack, and slapped it against his leg. His left eye was now swollen shut. Something warm trickled down his cheek, but his muscles ached too severely to try to wipe it away.

The familiar sound of hoofbeats clicked toward him and stopped.

Panic seized him. He scrambled under the shelter of a low bush, then turned and saw not Rafertee's men but Angus enter the clearing and toss his head.

Perhaps he would be able to return to Eastmore after all.

But when he stood, the ground beneath him spun and he staggered. He managed to put one foot in front of the other, but after two attempts to mount the horse, it became clear he'd never be able to ride the animal, not in his state. He looked back down to Rosemere, barely able to make out the tiny stable that sat just inside the courtyard wall. Did he have any other choice?

2

Patience Creighton clutched her loosely woven shawl tightly around her neck with one hand and lifted her lantern above her head with the other.

"Is he . . . dead?"

Not waiting for her manservant, George, to respond, Patience knelt next to the stranger's battered form and winced at the sight of his swollen, purple eyelid and the dried blood on his lips.

"No, not dead." George's ever-present scent of leather signaled that he'd drawn near. "Yet."

With a trembling hand, Patience reached out to touch the man's chest, hesitant, as if with one touch he would spring to life and grab her. But her shivering fingertips landed on the damp, rough wool of his caped greatcoat, and he did not so much as wince.

"Who is he?" she asked, her eyes not leaving the still form.

"'Tis William Sterling. Do you not recognize him?"

Her landlord's name was the last name she expected to hear. "Surely not William Sterling of Eastmore Hall?"

"Aye. One and the same."

Shocked, Patience lifted the lantern higher and leaned down, squinting to make out his features in the flickering light. Mr. Sterling's hatless head rested against the dirt floor. A deep gash marred his forehead, and stubble darkened his square jaw. "Where did you find him?"

"Right here. Came down to do my morning duties, like I always do, and here he was, sprawled out on the stable floor, looking just as you see him now." The manservant knelt next to her. "His horse was in the courtyard, right outside the stable, saddled. Charlie is tending to him."

A sharp gust of wind curled in through the half-open door, slamming the door against the side of the wooden stable wall and pelting them with stinging sleet.

Patience gave Mr. Sterling's shoulder a gentle push, hoping for a response, but none came. His breath appeared so shallow that she wondered if he was still breathing. "We must get him out of the cold. Mary has a fire started in the kitchen. Quickly now."

George nudged her aside and leaned down to loop his arms under William Sterling and called to the stable boy. "Charlie, get over 'ere and help me!"

"Shh, George!" Patience waved her hands in an attempt to keep the manservant quiet. She cast an anxious glance over her shoulder to the dark house. The last thing she needed was for Rosemere's twenty-nine impressionable young students to wake and see a half-dead man being carried from the stable.

Hysteria would ensue for months.

"We mustn't wake the girls." Patience stood and tightened her thin shawl around her. "Take him in through the kitchen, and we will figure out what to do there."

Leaving George and Charlie to carry their visitor, Patience scurried from the stable and took the path to the kitchen entrance at the back of the house, the harsh wind nearly pinching the breath from her lungs.

Patience burst through the door. Mary, the aging housekeeper, looked up expectantly, her face already flushed from tending the fire. "Well? What is it?"

Patience hung her shawl on a hook, her pulse still racing from the morning's disruption. "It's Mr. Sterling from Eastmore Hall. He's unconscious. Must have been thrown from his horse." She glanced at the blaze flickering in the grate. "We are going to need hot water and linens."

Patience did not wait for Mary's response. She went to the shelf next to the wide stone fireplace where they kept her father's wooden medicine chest. Reaching up with both hands, she slid the oblong box off the shelf and tucked it beneath her arm.

Mary grabbed an armful of linen strips from a chest. "Where are you going to put him?"

Patience bit her lip as she struggled to balance a jar of ointment on top of the teak chest. She hesitated. It was imperative that none of the girls be aware of the man's presence, and George, strong as he was, would never be able to carry a man up the stairs to a proper bedchamber. She nodded toward a narrow hallway that led to the manservant's small quarters. "In George's room."

Just then, Charlie flung open the door and rushed in, prancing eagerly from foot to foot as he held the door open. George was carrying the limp William Sterling over one broad shoulder. "Where do you want 'im?"

Patience pointed toward the corridor. "Put him in your room until we can figure out a better arrangement."

Patience grabbed one of Mary's candles with her free hand and followed Charlie and George to the small bedchamber. The candlelight flickered odd shapes on the walls and slanted ceiling. Patience's heart thumped in an erratic cadence as George sat Mr.

Sterling's unresponsive body on the straw mattress and peeled the soggy coat from his broad shoulders.

She set the medicine chest on the bureau. "Has he woken yet?"

George's response was none too quiet. "Hasn't made a peep."

Patience pushed her long braid over her shoulder and knelt down, positioning her candle to illuminate the man's face. Years had passed since she last encountered Mr. Sterling, but now, in the candlelight, she recognized his straight nose. The cleft in his chin. And yet, the sight before her made her cringe, for he was almost unrecognizable. His left eye was bruised and swollen shut. Dried blood and dirt crusted his lips and whiskered chin. A thick lock of dirty light brown hair swept over his forehead, and his head drooped forward in complete unresponsiveness.

Patience stood and reached for a blanket at the foot of the bed. "We must get him warm. Mary, fetch water and a compress."

George let Mr. Sterling roll back against the pillow and lifted his legs onto the bed. Patience draped the blankets over him, noting how his boots hung off the bed's end. She could not recall the last time she had seen Mr. Sterling. He may very well be the school's landlord, but he never called—his steward had attended to all matters related to the property and buildings. He never attended church. She did not doubt he paid calls to town, but she rarely had cause to leave Rosemere. Indeed, she would have had difficulty recognizing him even by the light of day when he was well, let alone in his current state.

She felt Mary at her elbow, leaning in to look. "Merciful heavens. Master Sterling looks dead."

Patience drew a shaky breath, then pressed her lips together. This man, whether he was their landlord or a common vagabond, needed their help. And as the woman in charge of the school, she would see that he received it.

"Mary, where is that compress? And get the hartshorn from Father's medicine box, will you?"

Patience sat down on the bed as gently as if it had been a bed of nails and leaned closer to study the marks on his face. "What do you suppose happened? Do you think he was thrown from his horse?"

George gave a coarse huff. "Not with that lip."

Patience's stomach churned as the meaning of his words sank in. George needn't expand on his thoughts for her to understand. The thought of a man being beaten in such a manner in such close proximity to their school! To her girls!

Mary returned, carrying a pan of water, and handed her the vial.

"Thank you. Hold that candle close, will you?"

Mary positioned herself behind Patience's shoulder.

Forcing her hands to stay steady, Patience uncorked the bottle and held it under the man's nose, giving him the full effect of its vapors.

With his next inhale, William Sterling only grimaced. Hardly the response she had hoped for. Patience exchanged the small bottle for Mary's compress.

The damp linen felt warm and heavy in her hand. She brushed Mr. Sterling's hair from his forehead, but at the sight of more blood, pulled her hand away.

The gash on his forehead appeared more serious than she had thought. Much more serious than any injury she could recall on school grounds. "Do you think you should call after the surgeon?"

George leaned in close to get a better look, squinting to see in the faint light. "And leave you and the young ladies alone with a man in the house?"

Patience shook her head. "Mr. Sterling is hardly a threat, George, not in this condition. I think we are quite safe."

George shifted hesitantly. "As you wish, Miss." The thud of his boots signaled his departure.

Patience returned her attention to Mr. Sterling. She was close to him—closer than she had been to any man in years, with the exception of her brother or father. She wiped her hands on the flannel folds of her robe, as if doing so would give her any more right to be tending to such a task. She had a great deal of experience tending to the accidental bumps and bruises of her girls, but never on a man—and never wounds of such magnitude. Cold still clung to his form, the scent of frost and earth lacing every breath she took. Her hands suddenly felt clumsy, Mary's compress felt more like a stone than a damp cloth. She bit her lip and bent over the man, unsure of where—of how—to start.

With cautious movements she touched the compress to his wind-burned cheek and wiped spots of dirt away. She moved upward to his temple, then to his forehead, near the gash, and at the touch, icy blue eyes flew open. Mr. Sterling sat up in bed, the force nearly knocking Patience to the floor.

She gasped and jumped up, pitching back as if he were a snake preparing to strike.

Mr. Sterling frowned, and his eyes darted about the room. He was as an animal, stuck between fight and flight. His light hair clung to his damp face, and his eyes narrowed on her. Cold. Unwavering.

He blurted out a single, breathless word: "Isabelle!"

Heart pounding, Patience approached the bed, forcing her voice to be quiet. Low. Soothing, as if she were talking to one of her students who had awoken from a nightmare. "You've been injured, Mr. Sterling. Please, lie back down."

He stared at her, his glare boring into her as if he were either reading her thoughts or spying on her soul. Then, as quickly as he had awoken, the expression in his eyes went absent. Hollow. His wild gaze darted from her to Mary and then back to her before he slumped back down on the bed, his head against the pillow.

She released the breath she'd been holding and cast a hesitant glance at Mary, whose complexion had grown ashen at the dramatic display. As timid as a lamb, Patience sat back down, lifted the compress, and pressed it to his face. This time his black eyelashes fluttered but remained closed. He merely groaned.

"Well," Patience whispered, "'tis no doubt. Whatever happened was significant indeed."

Mary, who was never short of opinions, drew a chair closer and continued to hold the candle high. "*Tsk*. You know what they say about 'im. Roguish man."

Patience flung Mary a warning glance. She would not tolerate such open judgment from her staff. But had she not shared the same thought? She'd heard the stories. The rumors.

Sitting on the side of the bed, she turned her attention back to her patient. He carried with him a scent of moorland and horse, and as she leaned closer still, the scent of ale clung to him. Patience pressed her lips together. Perhaps the stories *were* true.

But rumors or not, this man needed tending. With a gentle touch she pressed the cloth to the damaged skin, softly whisking away traces of dirt and blood.

Mary whispered, "Who do you suppose is Isabelle?"

Patience paused, the linen cloth hanging in midair. No doubt *those* stories of him were true as well. "I cannot say."

As she touched her cloth to the area around the wound on his forehead, he recoiled. His eyes again opened, but this time he looked at her for but a moment before attempting to sit.

Alarmed, she stood and pressed her hand on his shoulder. Even in his weakened state, his corded muscles twitched beneath the fine linen of his billowy sleeve. "No, no. Please, lie down. You've been thrown from your horse."

He shook off her hand and sat up, grimacing. He touched his face, then looked at the blood on his hand.

Patience cleared her throat. "You are at Rosemere, sir."

He ignored her and moved to swing his legs over the side of the bed, but at the movement, he grabbed his ribs protectively and swayed to the left.

Patience lunged forward to offer support if he should lose his balance. "Please be still. Our man has gone for the surgeon and—"

"No." His voice, gritty as stone, stopped hers. "No surgeon."

She wanted to argue. Surely he knew he was in no condition to leave, that he needed tending to. She noticed Mary had a dram of brandy in her hand. She took the glass and said, "Here, drink this. It will warm you."

He did not protest, but when the glass touched his split lip, he flinched and handed the glass back to her. "Rosemere?"

"Y-yes, sir."

His eyes narrowed on her. "Where's Edmund Creighton?"

Patience stiffened at the mention of her father's name. "My father died six months ago."

One eyebrow raised as far as the gash on his forehead would afford. "Rawdon Creighton, then?"

"My brother is in London."

It was in that moment when Patience realized Mr. Sterling knew not who she was. And why should he? Why should a man of his position know the name of a headmaster's daughter?

Feeling more confident, she ignored the sting of the slight and pushed a stray lock of hair from her face. "I am Patience Creighton, sir. Rawdon Creighton's sister and current headmistress of Rosemere."

His blank look betrayed him. "Of course. Miss Creighton." He studied her face for a moment, making little effort to hide his confusion. A frown creased his face when he adjusted his position. "I apologize for the intrusion."

"Do not apologize." Patience placed the compress in his

dirt-smudged hand and clasped her hands behind her back. "I am more concerned about your well-being than the earliness of the hour."

Awkward silence pinned them for a time, but when Mr. Sterling attempted to stand, Patience moved closer. At first it was her intention to take his arm to steady him, but then she thought better of such an intimate action.

"Is my horse here?" he muttered.

"We found a saddled horse in the courtyard."

"Good."

She drew a sharp breath as he put both feet on the floor. "But you are injured, sir. And it is still too dark . . . at least wait for the sun to rise—"

But he was already standing, and his unstable steps swayed him closer to her. Then, as quickly as his arrival had interrupted the dawn's peace, he stumbled through the door of the bedchamber and was gone.

Patience wondered if she had seen a spirit, a vapor perhaps, but one glance at Mary's big eyes confirmed that she had just seen their landlord—in the flesh. She stared at the empty space where the man had been, shocked at both the surprise of the bloody visitor and the gruffness of his demeanor. She hurried to the window and watched him limp through the deepening snow toward the stable and disappear into the dark building.

Inside her, a battle raged. How she wanted to go back to the warmth of her bed. Forget that Mr. Sterling had been here. Forget the sight of blood. But the thought of the man—any man—who had moments ago been barely coherent and now was outside, preparing to leave, pecked at her conscience.

She gathered Mr. Sterling's forgotten greatcoat, ignored Mary's protest, and stepped out into the predawn's gray light.

Patience raced through the courtyard toward the stable,

stepping in the footprints left by Mr. Sterling's much larger boots to prevent snow from getting in her thin slippers. Shivering, she arrived at the stable as Mr. Sterling was leaving, followed by Charlie, who looked every bit the boy he was.

Patience had to almost shout to be heard over the wind sweeping off the moors. "I must object, Mr. Sterling."

He either didn't hear her or he ignored her, fumbling to place the toe of his boot in the stirrup. She watched, helpless, as his first attempt to mount his horse failed.

"At least don your coat," Patience pleaded, extending the damp wool garment in his direction. "You are sure to catch your death."

On his second attempt, Mr. Sterling succeeded to mount the skittish animal. She could not see his face as he circled the large animal around. Realizing he would not be swayed, she backed away from his horse, coat still in her arms, to avoid getting trampled.

"I will send George to see that you arrived home safely," she called.

"Thank you, but no need." And with that William Sterling gave his horse a kick. But instead of taking the lane to the main road, he whirled his horse and thundered down the path through the moors. She frowned. Why on earth would he elect to take the narrow rutted path instead of the wide main road, especially in this light?

The pounding of hooves faded as Patience and Charlie stood together looking out at the moors until the horse and rider had disappeared.

Charlie's youthful voice broke the silence. "Miss Creighton, his coat!"

Patience, still not sure what to make of the early morning's happenings, had all but forgotten about the soggy garment in her arms. She turned to the boy. "Well, it appears that the excitement for this morning has passed. Dear George will return with the surgeon to find no patient." She offered Charlie a smile, adjusted the coat in one arm, and gave the stable boy a quick squeeze around his shoulders with the other. "We'll sort this out later. Thank you for your help. Go get some rest before breakfast."

He smiled at her and nodded before running back to the warmth of his quarters in the stable.

Patience looked over her shoulder, past the hedge, and out to where the early-morning mist still blanketed the moorland. She had never been frightened in Darbury, but then, never had she heard of anyone being attacked on the moors. Could such a thing have happened? In their tranquil village? A shiver shook her, and she scurried back to the warmth of the kitchen.

Inside, Mary waited with a pinched expression. "What, did he not take his coat?"

Patience hung the coat on a hook to dry near the now-blazing fire. "He was in a hurry to be free from Rosemere, it would seem."

Mary huffed. "Likely he was up to no good. You know the Sterlings."

"Actually, I do not." Patience moved closer to the fire, rubbing the chill from her arms and soaking in the warmth. "And may I remind you, neither do you. For all we know, he was indeed thrown from his horse."

"Did you see that split lip? That's not from—"

"Mary!" Patience found it easier to scold than to acknowledge that she might share a similar thought. "We shall give Mr. Sterling the benefit of the doubt and pray that his mount has the good sense not to throw his master." Silence hung heavy in the wake of the rare rebuke, and Patience, tired after the unexpected crisis, pressed a hand to her forehead. At least none of the girls had wandered down to the kitchen and seen their guest, and if she could have her way, they never would find out about him.

"Let us not speak of this to the rest of the staff. Especially not to the girls." Patience headed for her bedchamber.

"And your mother? Mrs. Creighton? Will we be telling her?"

Mary's words froze Patience to the spot. She wanted to pretend that the words had never been uttered, but instead she forced confidence to her voice. "In light of my mother's health, let us not tell her of this visit."

"Very well, Miss. You go on. I'll clean up and wait for George and Mr. Wilson to arrive."

Normally Patience would stay and wait to greet the surgeon herself, but something else equally as important weighed on her mind. Rawdon. Her brother. As the school's legal owner, he must be informed of this.

Not wanting to wake any of her sleeping students, Patience opted to take the servants' staircase from the kitchen to the west wing. The stairs were old and uneven in this part of the house, so she lifted her candle high to illuminate all of the bows and gaps.

Her head throbbed. She could recall a time not so long ago when there was nothing more romantic than the idea of a handsome, injured stranger being brought to their doorstep in the midst of a snowy dawn. Especially when that stranger was as dashing and wealthy as Mr. William Sterling. Her days of impressionable youth were long behind, and yet, she could hardly deny that the sight of him, attractive despite his wounds, awoke a long-forgotten dream within her. She was curious about him, much more curious than she ought to be, considering her circumstances.

She quickly rebuked herself. She needed to focus on maintaining order in the school to which she had dedicated her life, not spin childish fantasies about a man who was not even aware of her existence.

At least that is what she attempted to convince herself of.

At the top of the stairs, Patience paused. The hallway, which in her youth seemed endless, was only a narrow corridor with rooms off of both sides and a sitting area at the end with a wide bay window overlooking the courtyard and stable. No matter how softly she stepped, the old floor creaked and groaned under her weight. Not wishing to wake her mother, she tiptoed down the corridor, paused at the door to her mother's room, then went across the hall to her own.

Once in her bedchamber, Patience placed the candle on the narrow writing desk and sat down. Her body screamed for the rest and warmth afforded by her bed, but her mind raced with her thoughts. She took up a quill and spread a fresh piece of paper before her. Surely with news of a predawn visitor and violence on the moors, Rawdon would return. Since his sudden departure six months ago, she had received but two letters: one announcing that he had arrived in London and another saying that he had been detained. He claimed he was needed in London to settle their father's business interests following his death. There had been no further explanations. At first she had expected his return daily. But now she didn't know when he would return. *If* he would return.

Patience loved the school—and her young charges within its walls. It had been her home since the day she was born. But the heavy weight of seeing to all the details alone wore on her. She set her lips, angry that her brother had abandoned her. She dipped her quill in ink and pressed the tip to the paper.

She would tell him just that.

3

William winced as he drew each breath. But at least the relentless cold somewhat numbed his pain and called his attention away from the throbbing on his face and the aching in his ribs.

The black branches and restless fog seemed in constant movement around him, blurring in and out of focus. Even Angus seemed to sense his master's weary state, for his gait was unusually slow. Every one of the beast's footfalls racked William's frame.

Rosemere was just more than a mile from Eastmore Hall. The ride should be an easy one, for dawn's light was making everything familiar.

Snow started to fall yet again, gently and dreamlike at first, with fluffy white flakes floating down in the morning's budding light. The spicy scent of cold and ice surrounded him, and the frosty grass crunched beneath Angus's hooves. But even though the worst of the storm had passed, the winds, angry and wild, continued to make their presence known. He dared not wish for calmer weather, for despite the bitter bite, the discomfort fit his crime. Did he not bring this—the beating and all associated with it—upon himself?

He could almost hear his father's voice in the silent morning.

A fool and his money, be soon at debate, which after with sorrow, repents him too late.

When had he become the fool his father warned him about? The sheer magnitude of his loss made him feel sick, lost.

Gambling. Thousands of pounds gone, and by his own deed. Once the wealthiest man for miles, now beaten as a warning to pay a debt he could not pay. And he could blame no one else.

It was his fault. His own reckless fault.

He pulled Angus to a halt as he again crested Wainslow Peak. Before him, veiled in the pale light of morning, stretched Sterling land. At its center stood Eastmore Hall, a majestic stone testament to his family's steadfast spirit. How arduously his father had tried to instill in him a keen business sense. A sharp eye for numbers. An ambitious spirit. But those traits had seemed to pass on to his younger brother, Graham, not to him. How many times had his father rebuked William's impulsive nature, his tendency for mischief?

His father had invested all in husbandry, stating repeatedly that it was what Eastmore must invest in if it were to remain in this part of England. But William had never been interested in sheep. Or farming. He'd been interested in naught but horses. The faster the animal, the stronger the beast, the more they fascinated him.

As a young man with coins in his pocket and an eye for misguided adventure, he and his chums rarely lacked for exploits. But his actions had been foolish—youthful escapades. His pattern had not turned self-destructive until his heart paid the price for his folly. *Isabelle.*

He'd given his heart to her, and she'd matched him with her restlessness, her wildness of spirit. But it was her betrayal, her sudden disappearance, that broke his soul and hurled him down the path to his ruin. How he had tried to bury the pain under any diversion. He'd gambled on one too many horses—and lost. The money he owed might as well be a king's ransom.

Regret pressed upon him, aching far more than the wounds marring his face and his body. In the depth of his self-loathing but two choices remained: He could turn his back on his inheritance, sell Eastmore Hall and the land associated with it, pay his debt, and lead a poor but free life. Or he could try for luck one last time. That option beamed brighter, called louder. He was a gambling man, was he not? One not easily intimidated by loss or ruin. The higher the stakes, the higher his interest and the more he invested. He would right past wrongs and restore Eastmore Hall to its former glory, or he would accept his demise. He needed time. Three months. *Until Captain Rafertee returned.*

And a little bit of good fortune would hurt none.

The morning dawned gray and contrary. A quick glance through the latticed panes of Patience's bedchamber window confirmed that a generous dusting of snow covered the grounds of Rosemere, and by the look of the low-hanging clouds and wispy fog, more might be looming.

Within the school's stone walls, the sleeping house was springing to life. An hour or so had passed since their early-morning visitor's departure. The scents of strong coffee, hot chocolate, and baking bread filled the corridors, and the excited chatter of girls going about their morning routines resounded.

If she pressed her eyes shut, Patience could imagine that things were as they had always been, back when her father was living. But try as she might, the simple act of closing her eyes and pretending did not change the fact that her father was gone.

Or that her mother could not cope with the loss of him.

Or that her brother had deserted them when she needed his help the most.

As Mary helped her dress in a somber gray mourning gown, similar to the ones she had worn every day since her father died, Patience contemplated the mysterious visit from Mr. William Sterling. The tales she had heard of him, passed on in hushed tones in the village, rang rich with mystery and extravagance. But the man who'd lain in George's bed that morning was hardly the man embodied in those stories. He'd seemed rough. Harsh.

Maybe even dangerous.

And yet . . . intriguing.

The memory of that bold expression in his ice-blue eyes refused to leave her alone. Perhaps it was the lure of things unknown. Of things beyond the walls of Rosemere. Of a world—a life—she would never know or understand. Or simply the thrill of possible romance.

Patience looked out the window and glanced down at the snow drifts that hugged the skeletons of rose bushes and shrubs. Had he made it home to Eastmore? Had he but stayed at Rosemere as she'd prompted, he'd be safe and warm. But then she'd likely have had another predicament, for how would she keep even one of her twenty-nine charges from discovering his presence?

She determined to think of it no more. What was done was done, and as soon as she stepped down those stairs, she would not have a moment of solitude until night once again fell on the moors.

She would have it no other way.

Patience sent Mary on her way to finish preparing breakfast for the girls, fastened her father's pocket watch on a chain about her neck, and tucked a stray ebony lock of hair beneath her ivory comb before stepping into the corridor. After securing her door, she stepped across the way to her mother's. She hesitated before placing her hand on the door's brass handle. Truth be told, she would need more energy to face her mother than she needed for all the pupils waiting below.

Every morning was the same. She'd greet her mother with all the enthusiasm she could muster, but she never knew what to expect. Some days were better than others, and Patience allowed herself on those days to hope that perhaps her mother's zest for life was returning. But then there were the other days, when grieving tears robbed her mother of speech, and she could barely rise from her bed.

Patience forced a smile to her face, brightness to her eyes, and tapped on the door. "Mother?"

She waited. No response came.

"Mother, are you awake?"

Still silence.

Patience turned the handle and stepped inside Margaret Creighton's dark room. Light filtered through the drawn curtains, barely bright enough to illuminate her mother's figure still abed.

Patience sighed. 'Twould be one of those days.

With determined steps, she went to the window and pulled back the brocade fabric in one sweep. Silver brightness reached to the corners of the chamber, reviving the space and soliciting protests from her mother.

"Patience! What are you doing? Close those coverings at once."

"It's time to rise. We've much to do today."

"I am not well." Her thin voice was muffled beneath the pile of quilts and coverlets. "Let me be."

Patience ignored her mother's tone, refusing to allow her to continue on in such a fashion. "Mother, you must." With a quick scan of the room, she noted she was not the first to try to wake her. It had been Mary, no doubt, who had left a tray of tea on the writing desk, the steam still curling from the tiny pot. She poured her mother a cup and took it to her. "Drink this."

With a *tsk*, her mother pushed her hand away. "Do you not hear me? I am unwell."

Patience swallowed the resentment swelling within her—the response had become their daily ritual. "You must at least try to get up."

"Why?" Her mother sat up in a huff, her graying hair hanging limply about her face from beneath her sleeping cap. "Why should I?"

Patience returned the rejected tea to the tray and moved to the wardrobe. She was so weary of the same conversation day after day. "I will give you twenty-nine sound reasons why you must get up, and they are all downstairs, waiting to learn." Patience pulled a black muslin mourning dress and stays from the wardrobe and held them in front of her.

Her mother only huffed. "That was your father's vision, not mine."

"Well then, that leaves us with one option, does it not?" Patience slipped the dress over her arm and returned to the bed. "We should close the school. But seeing that you and I have nowhere else to go, and we rely on the school's income to live on month after month, we would have no choice but to move to the poor house."

"How can you be so unfeeling?" Tears filled her mother's eyes, and Patience immediately regretted her bluntness. But how long could she continue to allow her mother to stay in bed, swathed in her misery, refusing to live her life?

Patience sat next to her mother on the bed, set the gown and stays aside, and took her mother's hand in hers. "No words could describe how much I miss Father. But he would want us to move forward and continue the work he started. It would break his heart to see you in such despair. Please, you must try."

Patience reached for a linen handkerchief on the small rosewood table next to the bed. "You need to get out of bed. Let's go downstairs for breakfast today. Louisa has been struggling with her French. Perhaps you could spend time with her. It might brighten your spirits."

"I do wish Rawdon would return. What could possibly be keeping him from us?"

Patience drew a sharp breath and demonstrated control over every muscle in her face to keep from showing her frustration. *Rawdon. Always Rawdon.*

Her mother's refusal to accept that her brother had abandoned them offended Patience. How could her mother not see what he had done? And yet, day after day, she spoke of him as if his return were imminent.

Patience, too, had anticipated his return—initially. But it had become clear that he had no such plans. This meant the responsibilities of running the school fell to her. How she wanted to remind her mother of this detail. The memory of Rawdon's departure was enough to ignite Patience's own temper.

But Patience kept her opinion of Rawdon to herself—her mother would never hear it. "Rawdon has been gone for six months. We have heard from him only twice. I think you should prepare yourself for the fact that—"

"Don't you dare!" Her mother's voice shook with sudden intensity. The older woman's pale eyes narrowed and filled with tears. "He will soon return and set all to right. You shall see."

He will set all to right? Patience bit back a retort. No matter how hard she had worked these many months to keep the school running efficiently, her effort, ignored by her mother, seemed little more than a whisper on the wind.

4

Feeling exhausted even before the day was truly under way, Patience carefully closed her mother's door and let the brass handle slip from her fingers. She sighed. She would give anything to have her mother back, the mother she remembered. The mother who was full of life, full of overflowing love. Margaret Creighton was but a shell of the woman who occupied so many of Patience's fondest memories.

Lost in her own torrent of thoughts, Patience was startled when Cassandra Baden, fellow teacher and dear friend, turned the corner from the servants' stairs.

"Patience!" exclaimed Cassandra, face flushed, brown eyes wide. "You must tell me quickly, and you must tell me every detail. What happened this morning? I heard a man's voice, I heard Mary fussing, and I thought—"

Alarmed that someone else knew of their surprise visitor and petrified that her mother would hear, Patience grabbed Cassandra's hand and pulled her to a cushioned bench in the sitting area at the corridor's end. "Shh!"

"But what happened? I do not under—"

With a wave of her hand, Patience silenced Cassandra, and then, once certain they were alone, she leaned close. "Was he loud? Do you think the girls heard?"

Scrunching her face in thought, Cassandra shook her head. "I do not think so. Who was he?"

Patience chewed her lip. "It . . . it was Mr. Sterling."

Cassandra frowned. "Mr. William Sterling? Here?"

Patience paused to consider her words—and how much she would reveal of her suspicion about what had really happened. "Apparently he was out riding and had an accident and took shelter in our stable. George found him while tending to his morning duties."

"Was he injured?"

Patience unwillingly recalled the man's blood-stained lips, swollen eye, and gashed forehead. And as much as she tried to deny it, she remembered the feel of strong muscle beneath his woven shirt when she tried to force him to be still. "He had cuts and bruises, was unconscious for a time, but as soon as he regained his senses, he left."

Patience could interpret the expressions shadowing her friend's face without her friend uttering a sound. Time had made them closer than sisters. "I know what you are thinking. It wasn't the least bit romantic, Cassandra Baden." Patience spoke the words to convince Cassandra as well as herself. "He was abrupt, almost rude. And he reeked of spirits."

Cassandra's smile vanished, as if she'd just gotten caught up with her childish romantic fantasies.

Patience sat up straighter. "You know how such men are. He will no doubt send his steward out to collect our rent at the end of the month as always, and we shall not hear from him again."

"I suppose you are right," Cassandra said, glancing at the door to Mrs. Creighton's bedchamber. "I take it you did not tell your mother?"

Patience shook her head. "No, and I think we should not speak of it. Such stories will only lead to rumors and tall tales, neither of which we need. George, Mary, and Charlie are the only ones who saw him. At least I *think* they are the only ones."

"And Mr. Rawdon Creighton? Will you inform him of the visit?"

Patience stiffened, hearing her brother's name for the second time that morning. She knew of Cassandra's relationship with her brother. In fact, Rawdon had confided in Patience his plans to propose marriage to her pretty friend. But days after he made that bold statement, their father died. And on the dreary August morning after the funeral, a somber Rawdon departed for London, declaring that he needed to settle business for their father.

He never returned.

Patience believed he had betrayed them both, and yet Cassandra continued to defend him, very much like his own mother.

Patience fixed her eyes on the floor's broad wooden planks. Their father, whether she liked it or not, had named Rawdon, not her, as the one who was to care for the school. "I wrote to him and explained the situation this morning. George will post it today."

"Surely after such news he will return to Darbury." Wistful hopefulness haunted her friend's tone, who then said, with forced gaiety, "But the next time there is such a happening, I expect you to come get me. I am starved for excitement." She stood and reached to pull Patience to her feet. "Have you had breakfast?"

Patience looked at her mother's door—again. In the past, the Creighton family ate breakfast in the privacy of their family dining room instead of the dining hall with the staff and students. It had been part of their effort to maintain life as a normal family unit—as normal a family life as could be had in a house shared with dozens of students and a full teaching staff. But with her father dead, her brother out of town, and her mother indisposed, it seemed silly to take breakfast alone. "No."

"Then come and eat with the teachers in the dining hall."

Patience didn't protest as her friend nudged her along the narrow corridor and down the stairs. With each step toward the dining hall, the comforting sounds and scents of morning intensified. She took a deep breath, appreciating the scent of jams and rolls, coffee and tea.

The dining hall was in the oldest part of Rosemere. Exposed beams ran the width of the airy room. A fire blazed in the wide stone fireplace, its cheery crackle helping to combat the cool chill seeping in the broad paned windows. The stone floor felt cold to Patience through the thin soles of her kidskin boots. She looked out the windows at the bleak moors, stretched out broad and desolate, and found herself grateful for the welcoming warmth of the wood fire.

She always liked the sound of the children's chatter. Many institutions similar to Rosemere forbade talking during meals. But her father had hardly been one to follow convention. He'd believed camaraderie among the students was important for a well-rounded education, and he always allowed—nay—encouraged the interaction.

Six long wooden tables flanked with equally long benches filled the large room. At the farthest table sat the teachers. The girls were seated at the other tables according to their age, each one dressed in the school gown of blue muslin with gray trim, white stockings, and half boots made of black kid leather. At the closest table were the youngest girls—ages six to eight. Patience put a hand on the shoulder of young Miss Charlotte Allenham and leaned in close. "Has that tooth come loose yet?"

The plump girl turned her flaxen head and flashed a broad, toothless smile.

"Well!" exclaimed Patience. "Very becoming."

She patted Miss Georgiana Mussy's shoulder and smoothed the thick mahogany braid of Miss Emma Simmons. These girls were more than her students. Yes, she took great pride in overseeing their education, but she'd also found strength—and distraction—in the busy happenings of their everyday lives.

For today at least, she resolved to put her troubles aside and enjoy her day.

L

A voice, familiar yet distant, pulled William from slumber.

"What in blazes happened to you?"

William jerked his head around to look at Lewis and moved to rub his hand over his face, but when he touched his mouth, searing pain catapulted him upright, bringing back the memory of the previous night. He groaned, more from the recollection than the pain.

Lewis, in heavy boots, thumped across the bedchamber's wooden floor and stopped at the foot of the bed. Even with his eyes pressed shut, William could picture Lewis McOwen, Eastmore Hall's groom, standing, arms folded across his chest in customary fashion, an incredulous expression on his long face.

Most men of William's situation would never allow their head groom in their bedchamber. But ever since his financial situation crumbled, William had been forced to dismiss the majority of his house staff. His most trusted servant, Lewis, not only filled the role of groom but also that of footman, valet, coachman, and even, on one very desperate situation, maid.

William's body ached and his head throbbed. "Go away."

"I will not go away. Or have you forgotten?" William could hear boots stomp around the bed and move to the window. "Mr. Bley will be here within the hour to assess the horses."

"Blast!" William sank deeper against his pillow.

"Judging by the looks of you, you have had other things on your mind." Lewis opened the curtains, and the light may as well have been fashioned from daggers, so sharp was the glow. "You'd best be about things." Lewis retrieved William's discarded boots and waistcoat from the floor. "Remember, Mr. Bley said he must be back in Darbury to meet the noon coach. You'll not have much time."

William drew a deep breath, the simple action sending a blade through his side. Of course Lewis was right. Lewis was always right.

William slowly opened his good eye. "Had a rough night."

"*Humph.* Looks like."

"No, not that sort of rough night," William sputtered, annoyed at the inference. "It was Rafertee's men."

"Ah." Lewis's expression sobered, and he settled in a chair opposite the bed. He just looked at William, waiting for the story.

William preferred a reprimand to silence. But this was Lewis's way. And Lewis had borne witness to many, if not most, of his mistakes. Always patient, Lewis remained silent.

William frowned. *Anything* but silence.

Although Lewis was but a hired man at Eastmore Hall, William's relationship with him had been longstanding, so much so that the boundaries that would normally separate servant and master had blurred. Both men came of age on Eastmore's moors, William, the master's son, and Lewis, the head groom's son. Despite William's father's annoyance, the boys spent much time together, bound by their passion for horses. The friendship, such as it was, survived the deaths of both their fathers and had even lasted through William's wild and turbulent years. With his money nearly gone—along with his comrades—Lewis was one of the few who had remained loyal. Which made verbalizing the details of the ambush that much more difficult.

"So what happened?"

With great effort—and pain—William rolled over and sat up, grimacing and protectively supporting his ribs, and relayed the story of his late-night visit to the inn and his ride across the moors. "When I came to, I could barely see, so I decided to wait out the snowstorm in the Rosemere stable. I apparently lost consciousness and woke up in a bed inside Rosemere."

Lewis raised his eyebrows. "The girls' school?"

"Yes."

Lewis chuckled and scratched the back of his head. "Well, I'll be."

William brushed his disheveled hair from his forehead. "Were you aware that Mr. Creighton died and Rawdon Creighton is in London?'

"Yes."

"And that Creighton's daughter is running the school?

"Uh-huh."

William stopped short of asking for more details about Miss Patience Creighton, although of all the aforementioned, the memory of her burned most vividly in his mind. But the details of the visit were so hazy, he almost doubted his recollection. Had he simply imagined her? Perhaps she was nothing more than a lovely illusion, a vaporous angel, brought into being by several blows to the head.

Lewis pushed himself up from the padded chair. "Best get yourself cleaned up. Can't meet Bley looking like that." The tone of his voice held the familiar lilt. "He might get the wrong impression." On his way out the door, he called back over his shoulder, "I'll send Martha up with water and coffee. Strong coffee. Oh, and I almost forgot." He pulled a letter from inside his coat and tossed it on the bed. "Arrived yesterday."

William eyed the letter. Even at a distance he could make out his brother's unmistakable handwriting. He would read Graham's letter later, after the conversation with Bley.

William stood from his bed with slow, deliberate movements. His eye throbbed, his lip stung, and with every breath a sharp pain pierced his side. Everything within him screamed to crawl back to the comfort of the wide bed and remain still until the pain subsided. But he'd anticipated Mr. Bley's visit for a week. If he was to restore Eastmore Hall to what it had been, this was the first step. He had to persuade Bley to purchase a foal sired by Slaten. He needed the money—now more than ever.

William shuffled to the wardrobe and opened the door. He may no longer have the funds of a country gentleman, but at least he could *appear* as if he did. After Martha brought hot water and coffee, he gingerly washed his face and decided to forgo shaving. He dressed in buckskin breeches fashioned by Weston's in London and top boots polished with the most reflective gleam. He took great pains with his cravat, carefully folding and tying the billowing white linen, an art he had been forced to master after he dismissed his valet. He fastened the buttons on his tan single-breasted waistcoat and then pulled on his dark green kerseymere tailcoat. Once dressed, he stood back and assessed his reflection in the looking glass.

He never did care for pretentious clothing—his interest had always been more in sport—but when his funds had flowed freely, he'd spared no expense to look every bit the part. All the money he had spent on such luxuries now seemed a frivolous waste, especially when he hadn't a sixpence to scratch with. From the neck down, he was immaculate. From the neck up, he looked like a bloke who'd been bested in a bout of boxing.

He combed his fingers through his hair, gingerly removing tangles and debris, noting the need for a haircut. But then he reminded himself that Bley was not coming to see him. He was coming to see Slaten.

Slaten. If it were possible to blame anyone besides himself for his current situation, it might be the horse . . . although it could hardly be the animal's fault, for his downfall began years before. When Isabelle broke their engagement, gambling on horses became William's profession, taking him to the heights of glory and the depths of ruin. But luck had always returned . . . a faithful, if fickle, companion.

He'd taken Slaten, an accomplished racer, for payment of a debt. At the time he had considered it an even—if not advantageous—exchange. The animal was well-known for his wild, competitive nature, which translated to success on a course. But William's efforts to pad his pocketbook were dashed well over a year ago. William had used the last of his money to enter the horse in a prestigious race. But when the horse stumbled mid-race over another horse that had taken a spill, Slaten permanently damaged a tendon in his leg, bringing his racing days to an end. It was at that moment when all was lost.

William lifted the coffee to his wounded lip, but the housekeeper's steaming beverage did little to soothe William's wounds or his spirit. Lewis was right. Bley would not be in Darbury long. He would have this one opportunity to get Bley to speak for Slaten's unborn offspring. So today he would push through anything, any pain.

He had to.

Before leaving the house, William instructed Martha to light fires and open the main visiting rooms. Heating the rooms was expensive, but in the event Mr. Bley should enter Eastmore Hall, William needed to at least give the impression he was a man of sizable means.

William walked the path from Eastmore Hall to the L-shaped stable, a relatively new structure fashioned of stone and timber. He avoided looking back at Eastmore. Even as recently as a year ago, the stately home boasted the most incredibly manicured landscape in the county.

That, too, was gone. Shameful.

William pulled back the door to the stable. The tension in his back eased. Surrounded by the things that made him comfortable, he finally drew a deep breath. Familiar scents of straw and hay were balanced in the air. In the stall straight ahead, Angus, looking no worse after their early-morning ride, whinnied at William's entrance, tossing his chestnut mane.

"There you are." William stepped closer, propped his hands on his hips, and stared at the animal.

The gelding puffed air and nudged at William's pocket.

The horse knew his master too well.

"You didn't think I'd forget, did you?"

Angus nudged again, and William reached his gloved fingers into his pocket and extended a carrot.

Lewis stood at the far end of the stable's wide center aisle, brushing Slaten's glossy raven coat. Although a fine specimen of horseflesh, Slaten was far too feisty for his own good. For the safety of the other horses, they kept the stallion separate as much as possible. His lean muscles twitched as he adjusted his footing and swung his striking black head around as William approached.

"Making him beautiful, are you, Lewis?"

Lewis stopped the grooming and let the brush hang at his side. "Not hard to do, and this cheeky sweetgoer knows it."

William knelt and ran his hand over the career-ending bulge on the horse's leg—the result of significant scar tissue from the tendon injury. He tried—for the millionth time—to push the memory of that horrific day from his mind. At least the animal survived the tumble, and he could still find hope in the fact that the horse might help him recover from his losses. Yet this would not be a quick fix—or a sure one.

William stood and patted the horse's sleek neck, then walked over to the farthest stall to check on the mother. With any luck,

Mr. Bley would decide to buy the foal based only on the impressive racing qualifications of its parents. "Is the mare ready?"

"Yes."

"The glow of motherhood suits her," he joked.

Lewis did not look up from his task. "Bley should arrive at any time. The letter said he'd leave Bradwell in the morning. Should put them here about ten, weather permitting."

William flicked his pocket watch. "Quarter of." He snapped it closed and heard the sound of hooves on the gravel path outside. William's heart thudded. The arriving carriage had to be that of Mr. Bley. This was his chance to begin to set things to right. He pulled his hat low over his forehead in an attempt to conceal the marks on his face and straightened his coat. He bent over to brush the dust off his boots.

As confidently and nonchalantly as he could, William strolled out of the stable and saw a carriage pulled by four magnificent chestnuts rolling to a stop. A door swung open.

William sucked in a deep breath, reminding himself that he had the advantage. He was not acquainted with Mr. Bley personally, but he knew how men like Mr. Bley—wealthy, carefree, and bored—thought.

Mr. Bley jumped down, looking every bit as William had expected. He appeared to be about William's age with a tall, athletic build. He was well-dressed in a caped overcoat of charcoal wool and shiny Hessian boots. A wide red band circled his beaver hat, and a gloved hand gripped an ornately carved cane.

Mr. Bley would, no doubt, expect to be greeted by a butler—or a footman, at the very least. William had to act as if he happened to be nearby as the carriage rumbled up. No doubt Bley knew William was purse-pinched—everyone did—but William needed to keep the rumors low. This was a game of pretenses, a battle of charades that he intended to win.

"Ho, there!" he called as Mr. Bley turned to assess Eastmore Hall. "Adrian Bley?"

The man turned. "Indeed!" He headed toward William. He seemed startled as he drew close enough to see William's face, and then his eyes crinkled in amusement. He gave a burst of good-natured laughter. "By jove, good man, what happened to you? A mill gone poorly?"

William forced a chuckle. "Afraid so."

Mr. Bley stepped closer, propped his hands on his hips, and studied William's face. "Well, I'd hate to see the sorry bloke what tangled with you, to be sure. Heard you were a bit of a bruiser, Sterling. And see, here are the marks to prove it."

William tried to apply as light a tone to his voice as possible, although with every grin his lip throbbed and with every laugh his ribs ached. It was easy enough to blame his appearance on a sparring match not gone in his favor. "'Tis the price a bloke pays for a bit of fun, am I right?"

Bley laughed, rich and deep.

William pretended not to notice how the man assessed his coat. His boots. At least in that he could be confident.

As if on cue, Lewis led Slaten from the stable. From the corner of his eye, William saw Bley's expression transform from skepticism to greedy approval in mere seconds. William walked to the horse, took him by the bridle, and circled him around for a better view.

Bley knelt down to take a close look at the bulging disfigurement on the animal's lower leg. "So this is the injury that felled the mighty Slaten. Happened at Newmarket, did it not?"

William smoothed Slaten's glossy mane. "He was a length behind another horse going into a turn. That horse took a spill, and Slaten here took a tumble over him." William rubbed the horse's corded neck. "He'll not race again, but I daresay his offspring will."

Bley circled the animal, pausing to lift a foreleg and look at the teeth. "And how did you come to own him?"

"Won in a wager."

Bley chortled. "You don't say."

"Indeed. When he came to my stable, he had already won at Weatherby's and Staxton. But for all of his success, he was still young. I am of the belief that he was raced too early and with too little training."

Bley stepped back and crossed his arms across his chest. "I saw him race at Staxton."

William raised an eyebrow. "Did you, now?"

"Bloody fast. Never seen anything quite like him. Tried to buy him myself at the time, but the owners would not part with him. Was shocked to hear about his tumble."

"I had never seen him race when I won him—had only his reputation to go on. Then the first race I entered him in, the accident happened." William stopped short of revealing that he had every last farthing he owned invested in that race, and when his horse did not even finish, he had nothing left.

The man looked around the grounds. "Where's the mare?"

William signaled Lewis, who led out the bay mare from another section of the stable, her stomach swollen, her gait slow.

"How much longer until she foals?"

Slaten tossed his black mane and sniffed the air, and William paused to steady him before responding. "No longer than a month." He watched for any indication in the man's expression as to whether he had any interest in speaking for the unborn horse. The sooner William could get a buyer and a down payment, the better—and safer—he would feel. "I'd say no more than two weeks."

"And your price?"

William named the figure.

Bley whistled low and nodded. "I'd want the foal weaned from the mother as soon as possible. I want the trainer of my choosing to get ahold of it early on."

William stepped back to give Bley room to circle the mare. Bley's reputation as a horseman was legendary. William stood by silently as the man ran his hands down the legs, studied the face, the mouth, and did all manner of other assessments. He then returned to the stallion.

After what felt like a span of time much longer than necessary, the man finally walked toward William. "You say this will be his first offspring?"

William nodded. "Yes. He's not been sired outside of Eastmore Hall. I have two other mares with foal."

Bley nodded. "I'll consider it and get back with you."

Disappointment battled optimism. William had hoped that Bley would agree to purchase the foal or at least give a strong indication of his intention. He needed money. Quickly. But he knew Bley's type. He would have to wait until the idea struck the man's fancy.

And wait he would.

5

William had never seen such green eyes.

At least he was almost certain he recalled seeing green eyes.

He thought about the unexpected Miss Creighton as he steered Angus down the worn path from Eastmore to Rosemere—just as he had during many of the waking moments that filled the two days since he saw her last. The snow had melted in the afternoon's weak sunlight, and even at their slow pace, mud splashed on his boots and Angus's legs.

William tightened the reins as a hare hopped onto the path. Angus seemed unusually skittish, but William could hardly blame him. The events after the encounter with Rafertee's men were a blur. He possessed only a vague recollection of how he managed to get into the Rosemere stable and what transpired after, but gradually snippets returned. Hushed voices. A damp cloth. A thick black braid. A kind smile.

Patience Creighton.

Had he known such a lovely creature lived at Rosemere, he would have taken more interest in his tenant.

Eastmore Hall had many tenants, but the relationship between Eastmore Hall and Rosemere was longstanding and unique. Most of Eastmore's tenants were farmers. His family traditionally provided the tenants with a cottage, and in turn they would share profits from the harvest. But the terms with Rosemere had always been different. A massive dwelling in its own right, Rosemere had been built by his great-great grandfather as a gift for William's grandmother upon her wedding. But over time the gray building had fallen into disrepair and was no longer needed by the family, so his father oversaw the repairs and let it to Edmund Creighton as a school. William's father, who cared deeply about the success of his tenants, had taken great interest in the school's growth and even funded projects. But since his death, the relationship had grown cold. As it stood, his steward had been the one to manage the lease, visiting periodically and seeing to necessary repairs and any problems that would arise. The Creightons had been model tenants, which kept them out of his affairs.

But the recent event had changed that.

He pulled Angus to a stop in front of the ornate iron fence that marked the grounds of the school.

Rosemere was an impressive structure, with a three-story stone façade, a parapet lining the roof, and several ornate chimneys disappearing into the low-hanging, shifting clouds. Large mullioned windows flanked the aged doors.

A sharp wind screeched through the bare elms guarding the gate. William hesitated. He could turn around and pretend the humiliating situation had never happened. Even if the inhabitants of Rosemere told every citizen of Darbury of his misadventure, what harm could come of it?

A reputation once lost was lost forever.

Or so his father used to warn.

William doubted many people in Darbury knew the extent of his ruin, of his self-imposed misfortune, and if his recent difficulty had not reached them yet, it likely would not. With his steward gone, he needed to foster this relationship. Personally. The rent paid by the school was the most substantial he collected. He could not afford to lose the school as a tenant. Besides, by all propriety, he should thank Miss Creighton for the kindness she showed and smooth any ill will or dampen any misconceptions. And the sooner he got it over with, the better.

William dismounted and pushed open the ancient gate, its hinges squeaking in protest. Whether it was the thickening clouds or the lateness of the hour, evening seemed to descend early, blanketing the ground with frigid purple light. Leafless shrubbery lining the drive caught on the folds of his caped greatcoat, and the wind, equally as intent, whipped raw and vicious around his head. A sudden giggle caught his ears, and then a girl's shout. He looked to see a group of girls beyond the stable dressed in dark coats, their faces hidden by matching bonnets. He stayed to the far side of the drive lest they take notice of him. He did not need to have a gaggle of girls staring at the wounds still marring his face.

A young boy, probably nine or ten, did notice him and came trotting from around the west end of the building. "Take your horse, sir?"

William pulled his tall hat tight and kept his eyes down, but not before recognizing that this was the boy who had attempted to hold Angus steady while he had mounted in his hasty departure. He tossed the child the reins. "Thank you."

The boy led Angus around the back, and William walked up to the house, taking the lion-shaped iron knocker in his hand and letting it fall heavily against the wooden door. A servant answered— an older man with thick white hair and rheumy brown eyes. At the sight of his wounds, the old man's eyes opened wide. "Mr. Sterling."

This man knows who I am.

William entered the large entrance hall paneled with dark wood. At the far end of the room, a roaring fire bathed the foyer in warmth, and the large mullioned windows flanking the doors filled the room with the evening's fading light. The scent of bread mingled with smoke from the fire teased him. The sound of a pianoforte met his ears. At the far opposite corners of the room, two symmetrical and intricately carved staircases disappeared to the upper floors.

William placed his coat and hat in the servant's outstretched hands. He followed the man down a narrow hall. Now that he was here, curiosity took hold. Vague recollections surfaced of being inside Rosemere as a boy with his father. William stepped into the study, almost relieved to see that Miss Creighton was real—and not at all imagined.

She sat in a wingback chair, a young girl with long mahogany hair and startling blue eyes on her lap.

Gentle light from the fire seemed to soften Miss Creighton's expression. Her hair was no longer in a careless braid but was swept tidily away from her face and atop her head. Her eyes were not as brilliant by the light of day but larger than he had recalled.

William cleared his throat. "I hope I am not intruding."

"Of course not, Mr. Sterling. It is a pleasure to see you." She whispered in the child's ear, and in a flash of muslin and ribbon, the little girl promptly hopped from her lap. Miss Creighton stood and placed a hand on the child's shoulder and nudged her out from behind her. "Allow me to present Miss Emma Simmons."

The child made him nervous, for what was one to say to a child, let alone a girl? Not knowing what else to do, William bowed to the little person. "How do you do, Miss Simmons."

The girl curtsied, but when her gaze landed on William's lip, she stood frozen for several seconds, mouth agape, eyes fastened on his lip.

Miss Creighton gathered some papers from the table. "Emma, why don't you take your word cards into the morning room? I believe Miss Baden is in there with the others."

The little girl seemed oblivious to her guardian's direction. Her attention was fixed boldly on William's face. "What happened to your eye?"

Miss Creighton's dismay at the innocent question far outweighed his own discomfort. She blurted out, "Emma! It is not polite to ask such things!"

But the young Miss Simmons seemed too concerned about his eye to hear.

"It's fine, Miss Creighton, really." William knelt down on one knee. "See, it isn't that bad. It should be better soon. Doesn't hurt a bit." But her small face scrunched in disbelief. He scrambled for an answer appropriate to say to such a small person. "I fell from my horse."

Emma's tiny eyebrows drew together. "Naughty horse."

Miss Simmons's emphatic disapproval almost brought a laugh to his lips. "It was not the horse's fault. I should have been more careful."

He could see that his answer did not satisfy her, so he stood up, ignoring the jabbing pain in his side that still plagued him. "Do you ride, Miss Simmons?"

The little girl's blue eyes grew big, and she moved her head slowly from side to side. "No, sir."

"What!" he exclaimed, finding that once the initial shock of conversing with a child wore off, he was almost enjoying this discussion. "You do not ride at all? Not even that plump black pony I passed in the pasture on my ride here today?"

She giggled and shook her head again. "That is Violet."

"Violet, the pony," he repeated. "Well then, you must learn to ride before you can decide if an animal is naughty or not, for a good rider should always be in control."

Miss Creighton, face flushing in dismay, put her hands on the girl's shoulders. "Off with you, Emma, to Miss Baden."

The little girl hesitated and then whispered to her headmistress.

Miss Creighton leaned down to hear. "Yes, you may visit Delilah, but only after you have finished your cards. Mind you do not forget your cap and gloves."

The girl gathered the cards from Miss Creighton, casting inquisitive glances toward William during the process, then scurried from the room, her untethered tresses bouncing against her back with every step.

Once she was gone, William said, "I know who Violet is, but who is Delilah?"

Miss Creighton did not remove her gaze from the door until the sound of footsteps could no longer be heard from the hall. "The girls have a pet goat."

"A goat?"

Miss Creighton walked over to the desk and adjusted a stack of paper. "A troublesome, cantankerous creature, really, who causes more mischief than not. But the girls are quite fond of her. Delilah has been a permanent fixture here for at least the last ten years, probably more."

With an extended hand, Patience offered him a seat next to the fire. Its warmth begged him to draw near. As he sat on a tufted chair cushion, the heat wrapping around him like a blanket, he felt his tension relax. He looked back at Miss Creighton and noticed the softness in her expression, the kindness in her eyes. She *was* as he remembered. Not an angel. Not an illusion. But an exquisite sight to behold. He'd hardly be a man if he did not notice how the early-evening light filtering through the west window caught on the contour of her cheek.

"Would you care for tea?"

William shook his head, reminding himself of his purpose here. "Thank you, but I must forgo your offer. My visit will be brief."

"As you wish." She crossed back across the room, sat in a chair opposite him, and folded her slender hands atop the thick fabric of her gray skirt. She assessed him with expectant eyes.

He cleared his throat and touched two fingertips, still cold from the ride, to his lip. "I apologize for my appearance."

"Not at all. On the contrary, Mr. Sterling, it relieves my mind to see you. I was quite worried about you after you departed."

He felt an unexpected warmth. How long had it been since anyone had shown any concern for him? "I appreciate your concern, Miss Creighton, but as you can see, I am on the mend."

"I'm glad to hear it."

The honeyed timbre of her voice, combined with the awkwardness of their circumstances, made his mind go blank. He stood and turned toward the window. "I wanted to thank you for your assistance. It must have been quite a shock to receive a visitor in such a state."

Her answer was as diplomatic as any her father would have given. "You are always welcome at Rosemere, Mr. Sterling, regardless of your condition."

Before he could open his mouth to speak, the door swung open, and a young woman with nut-brown hair and dressed in a blue pinafore came in.

"Patience, I—" The intruder snapped her mouth shut when she spied him. Her hand flew to her throat, and her face reddened to the color of the coral trim on her gown. "Oh, I'm terribly sorry, I'll come back la—"

"Nonsense." Miss Creighton stood and waved her in. "Mr. Sterling, allow me to present Miss Baden, one of our teachers here at Rosemere."

William offered a stiff bow. "Miss Baden. My pleasure."

She stared at him, her light brown eyes unblinking, before returning the greeting with a quick curtsy. She then turned back to Miss Creighton. "It is Louisa. She is having trouble with her French again, and you said that you have a book you wanted her to read."

"Ah, yes." Miss Creighton turned to the bookcase and pulled a worn brown book from a shelf. She flipped through the pages before handing it to Miss Baden. "Have her start here. She should have no problem with it at all. Tell her I will hear her this evening before bed."

Miss Baden took the book, tucked it under her arm, dropped a curtsy, and hurried from the room. Miss Creighton returned to her seat, and William struggled to remember what they had been discussing.

Miss Creighton's expression was calm, as if she were accustomed to such interruptions. "As you were saying, Mr. Sterling?"

He resettled himself and attempted to recall exactly what he had said. So many thoughts went through his head. So many thoughts to convey. But her closeness and the nearly constant activity were distractions. He cleared his throat. "Perhaps I will take a cup of tea, Miss Creighton."

She smiled as if pleased and stood to pull the cord behind the desk.

He used the time to gather his thoughts. "I did also want to let you know of a few changes. Normally I would have had such a conversation with your father or your brother, but do I remember correctly? Did you not say your brother is away?"

A twitch jumped in her cheek. "Rawdon is in London." The inflection of her voice lowered. She looked at the floor.

His desire to refrain from overstepping his boundaries overruled his curiosity. "Well then, am I to assume you are the proper person with whom I should discuss business matters?"

"Yes, sir, that is correct. I am the headmistress now."

William pushed his fingers through his hair. This sort of business had normally been handled by another. And never, in his wildest imagination, would he have anticipated discussing such matters with a woman. But Miss Creighton's quiet confidence boosted his resolve to continue.

"I trust, then, you are accustomed to dealing with Mr. Livingstone."

"Your steward. Of course. He was last here about a month ago."

William nodded. "He has been relieved of his duties. For the time being, I will be handling all affairs with Rosemere. Personally."

A hint of a frown crossed her face.

Did she disapprove of his decision? Or perhaps doubt his ability? His confidence already shaken, he did not want to appear weak in front of a tenant, especially one who was such a beautiful woman, so he hastened to add, "Until arrangements for a new steward can be made."

Her frown dissipated. "Well then, I shall look forward to working with you on—"

The door flew open again. This time an older woman with a white smock over her black dress stepped in. She didn't bother to look in his direction. "Dinner's going to be late, Miss Creighton. George has gone to Fletcher's to fetch the—"

"Mary, please." Miss Creighton jumped to her feet, a flush coloring her cheeks at the sudden intrusion. "We have a guest."

The woman turned, looked down a hawk nose, her expression pinched, and made no effort to hide an obvious repulsion to the marks on his face.

He adjusted his position uncomfortably under the woman's scrutiny. Was this woman a servant? A teacher?

The woman drew in a sharp breath. "I'll come back."

After she left, William, more amused than offended, said,

"Well, Miss Creighton, 'tis a wonder indeed that you are ever able to complete a thought! This appears to be a busy room."

She smiled. "Well, with twenty-nine students, five teachers, four servants, and my mother, there is rarely a dull moment."

He tapped his fingers on his knee before jumping to his feet. "I can see you are busy, Miss Creighton. I'll not keep you from your duties."

"But your tea, Mr. Sterling. Surely you will want to warm yourself before going out again into the cold."

He shook his head. He did want to stay in her company, but he did not wish to be a nuisance. "Perhaps another time. I've no wish to detain you, and I have another tenant to visit before darkness falls completely. I've only come by to thank you for your kindness and to inform you of Livingstone's absence."

Even without the benefit of the tea, William departed from Rosemere with a strange feeling of warmth and a persistent suspicion that there was more to Miss Creighton than what he might have assumed. He reminded himself of the necessity of maintaining focus and keeping his goal steadfastly in front of him, for the last time he allowed his heart and mind to be occupied by a woman, his ruination followed. But even with that sharp reminder, he felt certain that the interesting Miss Creighton would not be far from his thoughts.

6

Later that evening, with a candlestick in hand, Patience climbed the staircase to the east wing, as she did every night before the clock struck eight. The candle's glow cast long, bending shadows on the worn stairs.

Visiting the youngest students at Rosemere was a habit she had started four years ago when young Emma Simmons came to live at the school.

Emma was not yet four years old and would cry lonely, heart-wrenching tears nightly. She was the youngest student ever to live at Rosemere, and during those first difficult weeks, Patience had been the only one who could console her. Over time, visits to the bedchamber of the youngest students had become a nightly ritual. Patience would read a story or verse to the girls and tuck them each into bed with a kiss and a prayer. It was normally a relaxing time, when the day would slow and evening would slip into night. It signaled her last task of the day, and afterward Mary would always have a cup of tea waiting for her.

But tonight, as she drew closer to the sleeping chamber shared by the five girls, her heart felt odd. Restless. Her days flew by at such a blinding pace that she rarely had time to pause and reflect. She barely had time to sort her thoughts.

This day, on the surface, had passed in all normalcy. Lessons were taught, meals were planned, letters had been written. She'd completed her tasks with regular efficiency. Even though those tasks could be difficult, they brought her meaning and purpose. But then, toward the end of the day, she had received their most unusual visitor again, and ever since, her mind seemed slow, her thoughts sluggish.

Mr. William Sterling. What an unusual character he was proving to be. For years they'd lived in close proximity, more strangers than neighbors. In truth, until their meeting after his accident, he'd likely been oblivious to her existence. And her awareness of him was limited to the girlhood whispers she had shared with schoolmates about his mysterious reputation and handsome presence.

But in recent years he had rarely crossed her mind, save for the fact that he had been absent from her father's funeral. And now, not once but twice he had been in her home. And both times he had left behind thoughts of something she had assumed was long buried. What would it be like to have a suitor, especially one as handsome and strong as William Sterling? She could not deny that he was handsome. Despite his wounds, his blue eyes were sharp and alert. His jaw was strong and determined.

And why, after all this time, should a visit from him unnerve her so? Any childhood inclination to think him romantic and exciting should be squelched by a more mature assessment of his less-than-proper behavior, or at least the accompanying rumors.

This afternoon he'd presented himself as well-spoken and self-assured. Not at all gruff and harsh like the man they had found unconscious. And yet, she wondered, who was Isabelle? And why should he call her name while in such a state? Undoubtedly, she must be far from the type of women who dwelled in Darbury—someone much more fashionable. Elegant.

She made her way down the darkened corridor, her only distraction the quiet chatter of girls behind closed paneled doors and the muted patter of feet on wooden floors. When she opened the door to the youngest students' room, she heard a circling of "hushes" and the delightful melody of little-girl giggles.

She relaxed. This is what she needed to focus on. This, and not on a silly romantic notion of a stranger.

Patience smiled at her little girls, all gathered by the fire, their stocking feet poking out from the hems of their plain, white muslin gowns. The scent of lavender water from recent baths hung sweetly in the air. Their cheeks, rosy and fresh, glowed with smiles, and their eyes held the glimmer of promised secrets and shared dreams.

Patience stood in the room and propped her hands on her hips. "And what are you girls giggling at, I wonder?"

Henny clasped a hand over her mouth and giggled, her brown eyes bright. "Emma said that Delilah ate one of Mr. George's gloves."

The girls covered their mouths and dissolved into laughter.

Emma drew her knees up to her chest. "She did! She did! And Mr. George was so cross with Delilah." She clapped her hands over her face. "Poor Mr. George."

Patience could not help but smile at the child's account of the goat. She could not quite understand why the stubborn goat was such a source of amusement for the girls, for the animal was always raising havoc for George and Charlie. But the wilder the goat's antics, the broader their amusement.

Patience took her seat in a straight-back wooden chair next to the fire, and the girls gathered around her. Emma. Georgiana. Charlotte. Louisa. Henny.

Once they were settled, Patience clasped her hands in her lap. "And what shall I read to you tonight?"

"The Mrs. Teachum book!" cried Louisa, leaning forward, her dark eyes wide with anticipation. The other girls agreed, so Patience sifted through a basket next to her chair of worn novels and pulled a copy of *The Governess*. She had read this book to the girls so many times she was certain they would tire of it, but instead, they clamored for it. But it was no surprise that the girls would love the story of the adventures of nine young girls at a school much like Rosemere.

Patience opened to the story "An Account of a Fray, Begun and Carried on for the Sake of an Apple: In Which Are Shown the Sad Effects of Rage and Anger."

Patience read with animated voice and dramatic inflection, and the girls, as usual, reacted to the argument the students were having over apples and the ensuing altercation.

At the end, when the students in the story were reprimanded for their anger and maliciousness, her own students grew somber. Patience closed the book and placed it on her lap. "And what of these young ladies? What can you learn from their misfortune?"

"Do not argue," piped Henny.

Charlotte said, "Be nice."

Patience nodded. "You are so right. We must be kind to those around us, even when they do something to hurt or upset us." She leaned forward and lowered her voice. "You girls have a special bond with one another. There will be times when you will be frustrated with one another, like the girls in the story with the apple. But you must control your temper." She turned to Louisa. "If you are upset with one of the other girls, what should you do?"

"Forgive them."

"You are correct." She looked at their faces, so sweet and

innocent. "And what if it is hard to forgive someone? What should you do?"

"Pray to God for help." Louisa's timid answer warmed her.

They were learning the truths that were so important. Her father would have been proud.

"Oh, you girls are all kind, and I know I can trust you not to argue and fight like the girls in the book. Always remember, we all get angry. What is important is that you handle your anger appropriately. Now, to bed with you."

The girls scurried up into their beds, and Patience stoked the fire before pulling extra quilts from the wardrobe. Before leaving, she pressed a kiss on each girl's forehead, heard their prayers, and tucked an extra quilt around each one to guard against the cold February night.

The last child was Emma. The other four girls came from sound families and spent holidays in their own loving homes, but Emma was different.

Patience tucked the quilt around the girl's tiny frame. Emma motioned for her to lean closer. "Do you think that man's eye is better yet?" she whispered.

Patience sat down on the edge of the bed, leaning close so as not to disturb the other girls. "It will probably take a few more days to heal."

Emma frowned, clearly dissatisfied with the response. "Naughty horse."

Patience smoothed the child's hair from her face. "I sincerely doubt the horse intended to throw Mr. Sterling."

Emma wrinkled her nose. "Do you think it hurts him?"

"I am sure it is not pleasant, but he is on the mend. He told me as much himself." She pressed a kiss to the child's forehead, offered a smile, and took up her candlestick. "How thoughtful of you to be concerned for the welfare of others. Sweet dreams, my darlings."

Patience pulled the door closed behind her. Once again, Rosemere was as silent as the grave.

And her mind was free to roam.

ℒ

William slumped in his chair, a goblet of claret balanced in his hand.

Night had fallen. Darkness—and a bone-chilling cold—blanketed Eastmore Hall's paneled library. The dying glow from the fire played on the goblet's intricate cuts and angles. He nudged his booted foot closer to the fire and stared unblinking into the weak flame.

He touched his healing lip, then rubbed a hand across his sideburn and over his chin. He was distracted. Why could he think of little else besides Miss Creighton? Of the curve of her neck, the slope of her nose? His conversation with the blue-eyed little girl at the school kept coming back to him, and the memory of the hall's warmth toyed with his mind.

He had not wanted to leave Rosemere.

The realization shocked him as much as it confused him. He would have been quite content to stay in Miss Creighton's company for as long as the day and the evening would allow. But she had obvious responsibilities that were far more important than humoring a man that she no doubt regarded as little more than her landlord. His attempt to offer simple gratitude for a kind gesture had resulted in more questions he could not readily answer.

Eastmore Hall had once been welcoming and inviting, much like Rosemere. His mother had seen to that. But since her death, and then that of his father, the estate property had been on a sharp decline.

William pulled his brother's letter from his waistcoat, unfolded it, and strained to read it in the dim light. The letter was short but good-natured. Graham, a captain in His Majesty's navy and away most of the time, asked William to watch over his wife and daughter. They lived but a short ride away, at Winterwood Manor, just on the other side of Sterling Wood. He would ride out to Winterwood soon to check on Amelia and little Lucy, for he owed his brother that much and more. Life had taken the brothers in opposite directions. Graham had enjoyed much success. But William, despite his privilege and opportunity, had floundered. It was Graham who had started William on the path to confronting his wrongs and failures instead of hiding them.

Not even a year ago, when William did manage to spend time in Eastmore Hall, the house was never still. Servants were busy at all hours. Guests at all times. The gatherings within Eastmore's walls had been legendary. But as his funds dwindled, so did his comrades. And as the friends' departures left empty spaces in his routines, condemning silence moved in. One by one his friends had left him, and now he was alone in a massive estate, with most of the rooms under dusty white sheets, a skeleton crew, and barely enough funds to keep fires going in a few rooms.

He could handle the loneliness during the day. When the weather was fine and he could escape out of doors, where isolation was by choice, he could imagine that everything was as it had been. Time flew past when he was working with his horses. With his steward dismissed, he found that he actually enjoyed calling on his tenants—especially when the tenant was Miss Creighton.

At night, all was different.

How desperately he wanted to be able to place blame on someone other than himself. To pretend that his poor decisions had been the result of an external force. But how could he deny his folly? He'd been a slave to the gaming tables and the pursuit of adventure.

If only *she* would have stayed.

He tossed the dark purplish wine against the back of his throat, ignoring the burning as it slid down.

Normally he would force his mind to think of anything else. Horses. Racing. Cards. But with the dull physical pain and his overwhelming loneliness, he would allow his mind to go there.

Just this once.

He closed his eyes and leaned his head against the back of the tufted chair. So much of the last eight years had been lived in a foggy haze of drink. She was the one aspect he could recall with pinpoint precision, as if he had seen her the previous night instead of the eight years it had actually been. How vividly he recalled the brilliant luster of her mahogany hair. The sway of her hips when she walked. The tinkling of her carefree laugh. The brush of her breath as she would lean in dangerously close to whisper in his ear.

Isabelle.

He had loved her to the point of obsession. And she had led him to believe that her affection matched his. She had been as foolish as he, her interests as worldly, her vanity as broad. Her impulsive lust for life was intoxicating. She'd swept him along in her whirlwind, captivating him and entrancing him. He would have given her the world had she but asked. But Isabelle was of a wild, untamed nature, carefree and restless. He should have heeded the warning.

His memory lingered on the day he proposed. Isabelle accepted, and his future seemed bright and boundless. But a few days later he received a letter from her, communicating her regret and stating that her heart belonged to another. She departed Darbury before he could confront her. He had not seen nor heard from her since.

William had demanded answers from her former guardian, her uncle and the local vicar, Thomas Hammond, but the old man would give no information, only repeat her request for privacy.

William had searched for her for months. She had wanted to disappear, and she succeeded. William never knew what became of her, and that fact drove him to the point of madness. Time had dulled the searing ache, but the dawdling presence of her betrayal still stung. He had given her his heart, and she had taken it. And to this day, a hole marked the empty space where it should be. She was out there, living her life. Somewhere. And his inability to accept that fact, coupled with his tendency toward impulsive behavior, had spiraled him downward.

He rubbed his hand down his face, wincing not at the pain from his still-swollen lip and jaw, but from the twinge of emotion knotted in his chest. He deserved what he was getting. How could he deny it? He had a choice to make when she left, and instead of choosing to put his life back together and fight, he chose to bury himself in mindless, destructive pursuits. He had become a virtual prisoner in the halls that gave him the wealth to live the destructive life he had chosen.

Why his thoughts should turn to Miss Creighton, he did not know. Was it her mannerism that reminded him of another?

Or was it true admiration of a person who had embraced family responsibility?

Or was it purely loneliness?

He indulged in one long swig of claret, dampening the effects of painful memories and the bitter cold.

Tomorrow.

Tomorrow he would once again pull himself right and focus on the task at hand—he'd keep his promise to his brother and visit his sister-in law. He'd find another broodmare for his stallion and take the necessary steps to set his life right. But tonight he would let the claret ease the pain, just as it had so many times before.

Tomorrow . . . he watched as the last tiny flame in the fireplace flickered and then went out, leaving only glowing embers.

He'd nearly fallen asleep, half frozen in his chair, when a rap sounded on a distant door.

William bolted out of his chair and looked to the pistol on a nearby table.

Rafertee.

But before he had time to react, footsteps echoed as they crossed the stone floor of the vestibule. He recognized the shuffle. It was Cecil, his butler. William relaxed when he heard the voice of his neighbor, Jonathan Riley.

Riley was the one friend who would still visit even though he knew the extent of William's downfall. William quickly stoked the fire to breathe life back into it, sending sparks flying, but he wasn't fast enough.

The door to the library opened and Cecil stepped inside. "Mr. Riley, sir."

Before William could welcome him, Riley strode in as confidently and intently as if he were the master of Eastmore himself. "Egad, man, what are you doing in the dark?"

William knelt next to the fire and used its dying embers to light a candle, and then used that to light yet another.

William forced his voice to be as normal as possible. "Caught me sleeping, mate."

William turned, but his effort to hide his face was in vain.

"Sleeping, my eye." Riley whistled low. "They did a number on you, didn't they?"

"What do you mean?"

"Was in town at Griffin's End." Riley sought out and opened the decanter of claret and poured himself a goblet. "Talked to Miller, who said there was a rowdy bunch in the other night, bragging about drawing a man's cork on the moors. Said they'd been in a couple nights prior, and he figured out they must be talking about you. So I had to come out and see for myself. Sure enough, here you are. What happened?"

William gave up stoking the fire and sank back in his chair. No need for pretense with a friend as old as Riley. "I was at Griffin's End, trying to convince old Peter Symes to sell me his thoroughbred mare. I saw the men there. Should have gotten a room for the night, but like a fool I thought it would be a good idea to return to Eastmore Hall. They waylaid me."

"I can see that." Riley tilted his head and squinted, struggling to see in the dark. "How bad is it?"

"Split lip. Swollen eye. Gash on the forehead. Bruised ribs. Could have been worse."

"I'll say." Riley pointed a finger at William. "They could have done permanent damage to that dandy profile of yours, and then where would you be?"

William huffed.

Riley's energy filled the space. He whipped his head around. "Why is it so blasted cold in here? I know you're dished, but this borders on the ridiculous." He tossed a log on the fire, and the glowing embers popped and hissed in protest. He added some kindling and was rewarded with a small flame that licked at the log's edge. "There, that's more like it."

If there was one thing William knew about Riley, it was that the man hated silence as much as he did. Riley would fill hushed moments with chatter, whether the conversation proved worthwhile or not.

Riley adjusted the remaining wood in the pile. "I didn't just come here to check on your wounds. I have a few matters I need to discuss with you."

"Of course you do."

"I am starting a new business venture."

"You are, are you? Shocking." William pinched the bridge of his nose. When wasn't Riley investigating this or that, looking for a way to further line his pocketbook? "And what, pray tell, are you exploring this time?"

Riley rubbed his hands together as if enjoying the banter. "Textiles."

William snorted. Textiles. With an abundance of sheep in the area, textiles and weaving had long been a way of life in Darbury and the surrounding villages. It was only a matter of time before Riley set his sights to finding a way to exploit it. "And what do you know of textiles?"

Riley shrugged, his ever-present crooked grin flashing in the shadows. "At present, very little, save for the fact that with all the wool available right here, it would be a lucrative venture. If done properly, that is to say."

"Is that so?" William tapped his thumb on the arm of the chair. He had the distinct suspicion that Riley was leading him down a path of sorts, and William, with sore ribs and throbbing temples, was in no mood for games. "And how exactly would one go about doing it properly?"

"That is where my new colleague, Jeremiah Carlton, comes in." Riley's easy smile slid across his broad, square face.

William leaned his head back. "What happened to your colleague in timber—that chap from Devonshire?"

"Bloody dull fellow. I never could trust a man with a French name. Back to what I was saying. Carlton has experience in power looms. Seems he tried to open a factory up around Manchester, but rioters burned it to the ground in the dead of night. Rogues." Riley shifted his weight and licked his lips. "I have made the decision to align myself with Carlton financially in this venture, but we are lacking a major component."

William propped his boots up on an ottoman and stared at the square toes. Ah, so this was it. He asked the question, already knowing the answer. "And what does this have to do with me?"

Riley smirked. "You own something we need."

This wasn't the first time that Riley had approached him

about land, and one plot of land in particular: the spot of land that Rosemere was on.

"I'm not selling you Rosemere, Riley."

Riley looked hurt. "You haven't even heard my plan."

"Don't need to. That land is leased."

Riley pushed an ottoman out of the way with his foot and sat down on the chair facing William's. He leaned forward, resting his elbows on his knees. "We go back a long time. This property means a great deal to you. To your father. I don't mean to pry, but clearly you are in a situation. I'm not here to judge. I'm here as your friend. And I am offering you money that you clearly need. And you'd be doing me a tremendous favor. I will pay you more than what the house and land are worth. Let me deal with the legality. I'll even cut you in on the profits. At least think about it."

William jumped up from his chair, having momentarily forgotten about the ache in his ribs until the sudden movement gave him a jolting reminder. He recognized the truth in what Riley said. But if he lost his land, what did he have left to fight for? "I don't need to think about it. I'll not sell it."

"You are a stubborn fool. Always have been." Riley slumped back in his chair.

"I have tenants at Rosemere. I can't evict them."

"Why not? I'll pay more."

He stared at Riley, trying to ascertain if he was in jest. People live there. Work there. And have for decades. He couldn't evict them without notice. Without explanation. Was his friend really that self-serving?

Riley did not relent. "Not all your land is leased. What about Latham Hill?"

William adjusted his forearm on the chair's arm. Latham Hill was a small plot of land adjacent to the Rosemere property. The rocky soil, unfarmable, was used for grazing. But the land did possess one enticing attribute—access to River Thaughley. But if William's plan was to be successful, he would require every inch of land, every corner. For horseflesh. Not textiles.

Riley stood, crossed the room, and propped his elbow on the stone mantel. "The way I figure it, I have money to invest, but no land. You have . . . er, limited access to money, but you are sitting on land waiting for commerce. Am I right?"

William shifted uncomfortably at the directness of the question.

"I appreciate that you don't want to sell Latham Hill. But let it to me until we can establish something more permanent. Partner with us. Carlton will bring the knowledge, I will provide funds, you bring the land, and we will go from there. We shall build the mill, and if it should fail, what harm is done? We will dismantle and your land will be yours, hardly worse for the use. If it should be successful, then we will need to find a bigger location. At which time your land will still be yours."

William glanced up at the portrait of his father above the mantel with his focused eyes and the determined set of his mouth. His father would never approve.

But then again, when had his father ever approved of anything he had done?

William snorted. "I suppose the more pertinent question would be, what do I have to gain?"

A wild, eager light shone from Riley's black eyes, and he shifted his weight, as if the excitement of what he was about to say had begun flowing through his veins. "We shall become equal partners—you, Carlton, and me. If it fails, what have you to lose? Your land reverts back to you. If it succeeds, then, well, you will be plump in the pocket." He stared down at the fire, his tone shifting. "We've known each other a long time, you and I. It pains me to see you like this, it really does. I would not bring this to you unless I thought it had a chance to succeed."

William studied his longtime friend, his face showing what was likely genuine concern. He wanted to believe Riley. But Riley had proved to be as reckless and wild as he himself had been. Would this really be successful, or would this be yet another example of his misguided ventures?

"I would need to think about it."

"Well, we don't have long. Carlton's visiting Ambledale Court at week's end. Will you at least meet him?"

William shrugged. "I suppose there is no harm in that."

"Good. Ride out on Saturday. He'll be there." Riley rubbed his hands together and rocked on his heels. "Trust me, Sterling. You'll not regret this."

7

F IRE!"
The urgency in the word sliced the murky space between
dream and consciousness.

Patience bolted upright in bed, heart pounding, pulse racing.

Was she awake? Dreaming?

With her next breath, her nose burned and tears stung her eyes.
Smoke!

Through her bedchamber window, eerie shapes of amber and
black cast shadows against the painted walls. She ran to the pane
and yanked aside the thick curtains. Holding her sleeve up to her
mouth, she squinted, struggling to see through the smoke's misty
vapors. A crash echoed from the stable. A panicked cry followed.

Charlie! Charlie sleeps in the stable!

Plumes of fire reached into the night sky from the stable. Thick,
black smoke curled even higher, lapping nearby trees and blocking the
moon. Figures dashed around the glowing stable. A shout. Someone
threw a bucket of water. A small body was mounting a horse.

She reached for her robe and stuffed her stocking feet into slippers. Her legs, tangled in her linen nightdress, fought to obey her mind's order for urgency. Stumbling in the dark and struggling to maintain balance, Patience stuffed her arms through the robe's sleeve, then the other, and grabbed the doorknob. She had to get downstairs.

Patience ran down the hall, pausing only to fling open her mother's bedchamber door.

"Mother!" she shouted, squinting to adjust to the darkness. In the white moonlight she spotted her mother's form beneath a mound of blankets. Patience ran to her, grabbed her shoulder, and shook it. "Mother, there's a fire in the stable!"

Her mother stirred, mumbled, but did not sit up.

"Mother!" Patience pulled on her mother's arm until she finally turned. "A fire! Do you not smell the smoke?"

Patience did not wait for her mother's response. She ran back to the corridor. She needed to get down there. Down to the stable. *Down to Charlie.*

The fastest way to the stables was through the kitchen entrance and through the courtyard. She flew through the west wing, down a main staircase, and through a wide corridor to the kitchen. All was dark save for the eerie glow seeping through the paned windows. Patience ran out the back door and into the night. The combination of frosty air and choking smoke stole the breath from her lungs. The fire's strength was even more impressive, more intimidating at ground level than from the height of her room. Almost instantly she spied George's silhouette, his bulky frame, struggling to lead a spooked horse away from the fire.

She squinted to guard her eyes from the brightness of the blaze and grabbed George's shoulder. "Where's Charlie?"

The fire's erratic light reflected from the sweat on his brow. "Sent him to Eastmore for the water wagon," he managed between coughs. "Probably frozen through after this winter. Cow's inside. Take this one."

He shoved the lead rope into her hand and ran back inside the stable. The carriage horse at the end of the rope yanked and pulled, and Patience threw all of her weight into coercing the frightened animal away from the burning stable. Finally, the horse complied, and she trotted alongside him to the pasture gate and released the animal. But when she turned, a child-sized silhouette, dressed in a gauzy gown, was running toward the fire.

Patience darted to the child and grabbed her arm, nearly knocking the girl from her feet.

The fire's light shone on the tears on the cheeks of young Emma Simmons.

"What are you doing?" Patience shouted, determined to be heard above the roar of the fire. "Do you not see how dangerous this is?"

Sobs racked the child's body. "Delilah!" she screamed, gasping for breath and fighting to free herself. "Delilah!"

The goat!

Patience gripped Emma's arm and struggled to hold the child, who seemed to be made stronger by fear. "Stop! Emma, stop! I will not allow you to go any closer!"

The child pushed and squirmed until finally Patience wrapped her arms around the girl so she could not move. "George will get Delilah, I promise." She looked back toward the house at a group of girls, clad in nightgowns and wrapped in blankets, staring at the fire. "Go with the others. Immediately!"

Patience half-carried, half-dragged the sobbing child to a respectable distance and left her in the care of one of the older girls, then ran back to the fire.

Chaos surrounded her. George tugged on the cow. Mary ran past with a chicken in her arms. Patience took the second carriage horse to the same gate where she'd led the other animal and released her into the pasture.

In the flickering light, she spotted a wooden bucket on the ground and snatched it up. The watering trough was already empty, and the well was on the far side of the building. Thaughley River was just on the other side of a thicket of small trees. She bolted through the undergrowth toward the river, sinking ankle deep in the half-frozen mud and nearly falling to the ground more than once. She plunged the bucket into the rippling water and hurried back to the fire.

As she got closer, her eyes watered with ferocious intensity, nearly blinding her. A low-hanging branch tugged at her hair as she dipped under a tree limb, scratching her shoulder through the thin robe. Even from a great distance the fire's heat trumped the bitter cold, and she drew as close as she dared before throwing the water on the blaze.

George, Mary, and the teachers were doing the same. Bucket after bucket of water was thrown on the fire. Over and over they repeated the action. But their efforts were of little consequence. It seemed the more they tried to tame the fire, the angrier the blaze grew, rising higher and burning brighter.

She was about to dive back into the trees when a hand caught the crook of her arm. She whirled around. George stood close, perspiration gleaming on his wrinkled brow, soot darkening his white beard.

He coughed. "It's too far gone, Miss."

Her instinct screamed to ignore him. She turned to go back to the river, but his arm stopped her again, his grip tighter this time. "Miss Creighton. You must stop. Someone will get hurt."

Patience tried to breathe, but the smoke was so intense, each breath burned tighter than the last. The teachers and staff were standing in a group behind them. She watched as the giant orange and amber tentacles devoured the structure. The far side of the building had already collapsed in a charred and fiery heap.

She pressed her eyes shut. She could not watch the burning. Her thoughts turned to her father. He'd taken such pride in the school grounds. Would he have been able to prevent this? Would he have handled it differently?

Defeat was apparent. She looked back at Rosemere, grateful for the broad distance between the two buildings. For the time being, there was little danger of the fire spreading. The fire cast odd, long shapes on the school, and she looked to the second floor. There she could see the silhouette of someone watching from a window. Her mother.

She turned back to the stable and pressed the back of her hand to her forehead. A sob nearly choked her.

It might only be the stable, but it symbolized so much more to her. The school—her home—was dying . . . she was losing her father all over again. And regardless of her efforts, she was powerless to save it. She looked back at her mother's form. Powerless to save so many things.

Behind her, the girls had gathered in the courtyard. She knew them so well. She scanned their faces, then frowned.

Something was wrong.

She began to count.

She counted again.

Suddenly, with a jolt as jarring as first seeing the fire, panic bubbled up as sharply as if the blaze had scorched her skin.

Patience cried, "Where is Emma?"

8

Riley's departure had been as sudden as his arrival. But the visit had been the distraction William needed. Ready to give way to slumber, William stood and stretched the kinks from his still-sore muscles.

The sound of a horse's hooves echoed on the drive.

"Mr. Sterling!" The sudden shout of his name by a youthful voice rose above the thunder of pounding hooves.

Interest piqued, William hurried from the library, the heels of his top boots clicking on the vestibule's stone floor. Not waiting for Cecil, he unlatched the wooden front door and swung it open on iron hinges. The faint scent of smoke and burning wood struck him as odd. The hair on his arms and the back of his neck prickled.

"Mr. Sterling!" The boy slid from the horse's bare back and ran toward him, eyes wide. It was the boy from Rosemere. He wore no coat, no shoes. Black smeared his cheeks. His breath came in ragged huffs.

William grabbed the horse's bridle to steady the anxious animal. "What is it?"

The boy thrust his arm in the direction of Rosemere. "Stable is burning, sir. George sent me to fetch the water wagon."

It was at that moment the pungent odor of burning wood smacked him. William drew a sharp breath as every muscle in his back tensed. "Burning?"

"It's almost to the ground, sir."

"What about the house?"

"Not yet, but George said to get the water wagon right quick."

William sprang into action, the memory of the girls he had seen on the lawn earlier flooding his thoughts. Lewis, alerted by the commotion and the smoke, ran from his quarters inside the stables, pushing an arm through a woolen coat and jamming a hat on his head.

With sudden energy and purpose, William sprinted toward Lewis. "Fire at Rosemere! Go to the coach house and prepare the wagon and drive it over. I am going to ride out."

The scent of smoke chased him into Eastmore's stables. Inside, the animals shifted and moved, uneasy as the vapors entered their space. One kicked the side of a stall. Another whinnied. Guided by the light of one weak, flickering lantern, William hesitated as he passed Slaten's stall. The racehorse flared his nostrils and tossed his black head, as if eager for an adventure. But it was Angus, steady and sure, that William needed. He headed toward the chestnut. Angus blew air through his nostrils, his head high, anticipating the ride.

William tossed a saddle on the animal's back and secured the girth with an experienced hand.

The horse followed him into the increasingly thick night air, and within seconds William swung his leg over and settled himself in the saddle. With a sharp shout, William urged the horse into a trot, then a gallop, willing the pounding of the hooves on the icy ground to drown out fear's hammering chant.

Frost blanketed the earth in white diamonds that flashed by at an unreasonable speed, but William noticed little of it. Increasing alarm trumped rationality, blinding him to anything other than the task at hand: getting to Rosemere as soon as possible.

William urged the beast to race even faster. He ducked lower and cast a fleeting glance over his shoulder, fully expecting to see the outline of Eastmore's water wagon breaking through the tree line. But nothing followed.

With every hoofbeat the scent of burning wood intensified, quickly snuffing out the last of the clean air in his lungs. And then, as he crested Wainslow Peak, he saw it: billows of amber-hued smoke curling into the black sky, fiery embers replacing the space where the stars should have been.

He approached the stable from behind, plunging his horse into the forest's shadowed thickness. He guided Angus through the thicket and emerged on the other side, pulling his horse to a sharp halt as the view unfolded before him.

Intense heat rushed at him, and black shadows darted before him. He stopped behind the stable to figure out where to go when he heard a shrill cry, a scream. He strained to hear. Even above the fire's roar, he was sure he heard it.

There! There it was again!

Angus, already grown skittish by the fire, refused to move closer. Instead of fighting with the animal, William swung himself down. And listened. He walked toward the stable.

The cry was coming from within!

Holding his forearm to his face to block the intense heat, William ran to the back gate and flung it open. With a quick glance upward to watch for falling beams, he scanned the room of fire. "Anyone here?"

A child's scream. Then a whimper.

Amid the rubble and burning straw he found what he sought: a panicked child yanking furiously on a rope fixed firmly to a goat.

Without another thought William snatched the child up in his arms. She wailed in protest and tightened her grip on the rope.

"Let go!" He forced the words through gritted teeth and struggled to keep his hold on the hysterical child.

Her scream gave way to a choking cough, and her strength weakened. William pried the rope from the child's hand. His own lungs burned, and coughs racked his body. Through his watering eyes he saw that the goat was secured to the post by nothing more than a slip knot. With a quick flick of his wrist, he loosed the rope, and the goat darted past him.

All around him flames roared. Mocking him. Taunting him. From a distance, a shout. He clutched the child's small body tight against his own and leaned over to protect her. But as he stepped back toward the door, a beam crashed to the ground, spitting embers and sending chunks of burning wood flying. Immediately he turned away from the fire to protect the child and his face, but then he felt the searing weight of fire fall on his arm.

Pain and panic gripped him. Fiery chunks rained down. He dove for the door, the child held against his chest, and as soon as he was clear, he rolled to the ground to smother the fire burning his sleeve. He clutched the tiny body tightly and scrambled to a clearing.

Gasping for air, he staggered, then dropped to his knees and let her roll from his arms. Horror registered as he realized the child was unconscious. He spun her to her back. The firelight behind him cast eerie shapes on her still face.

Emma Simmons.

He could not tell if she was breathing. Coughs racked his own body, and he glanced over his shoulder. Above the flames and smoke, he could make out part of the outline of Rosemere's chimneys.

With all the strength he could muster, he pushed through the pain of his burned arm, lifted the child close to him, and ran as fast as he could around the collapsing building in the direction of the house.

From behind the burning building, Patience saw a man running—no, stumbling—toward her.

She squinted to see better through the veil of smoke.

In his arms, a flash of white.

A long braid dangled over the man's arm.

Emma!

Patience ran toward the man, ignoring the gravel pressing the soles of her feet and the sharp sleet that was stinging her face. "Emma!" she shrieked. "Emma!"

The fire's light made them seem more like a vapor than flesh and blood. She doubted her own senses. But as she drew closer, her hope was confirmed.

Soot and sweat covered Mr. Sterling's face. His breath came in shallow gasps. "She . . . she . . ."

Patience did not wait for any explanation. "Here, give her to me."

Patience snatched Emma from him and hugged the child's alarmingly limp body to her own. She ran awkwardly toward the back entrance and burst into the kitchen.

"Merciful heavens!" Mary's chin trembled as she looked up from a kettle, oblivious to the water dripping from the rag in her hand. "Is she, she . . ." Her words trailed off, and Patience laid Emma on the table, the nearest flat surface she could find.

Patience held her hand up for silence, leaned close to the child, searching for any sign of life. Bittersweet relief gushed as she detected the subtlest motion: Emma's chest rose and then fell.

"Quick, we must get her warm. Warm water, a compress. Hurry!"

Patience quickly examined the child, looking for burns. She refused to look at the child's face, for the unnerving serenity she found there racked her to the core. She chose, instead, to focus on the slight rise and fall of her chest.

Patience dipped the cloth into the warm water and, finally looking at the little face, wiped black soot away from the girl's cheeks. Her eyebrows. Her nose.

Guilt bubbled ferocious and hot within Patience, causing her hand to tremble and her eyes to blur with tears. The child had no doubt been trying to rescue the goat. She should have demanded the child return to the safety of Rosemere instead of allowing her to remain outside with the older girls. Why had she been so careless? She was supposed to protect the children.

She. And she alone.

Mary's voice was always steady. "We must get her to cleaner air. She can't breathe."

Patience sniffed. "The smoke should not be as severe in the east wing."

Suddenly the child took a deep breath, and for a moment, everyone froze. Then a fit of hoarse coughs racked her tiny body. A groan followed. Her eyes remained closed.

Patience grabbed the child's hand. "Emma! Emma!"

Emma's breath came in a wavering gasp.

Patience stared and bit her trembling lip. She didn't even allow herself to entertain the thought that the child might die. She could not die. She could not.

Mary nudged her aside and waved a vial under Emma's nose.

No response.

Patience struggled to get her hands beneath the child's body. "Help me carry her, Mary."

A man said, "Allow me."

Patience jerked her head up and noticed William Sterling had followed them into the kitchen from the courtyard. She did not reply but merely stepped aside so he could pick up Emma. "Mary, heat a bed warmer and bring it upstairs. And more blankets. Quickly."

With an eye on her charge, Patience grabbed a candlestick and lifted it high to light the way. Neither spoke as she led the way up the back staircase, pausing only to look out the narrow window at the burning remains of the stable.

The air seemed cooler here. Cleaner. She tried to breathe deeply to calm herself, but her own lungs burned. The stairway curved up, and when she looked up, a strange, dizzy sensation seized her. She grabbed the rough wood railing and closed her eyes, waiting for the spinning to stop.

"Miss Creighton?"

She ignored the voice.

"Miss Creighton, are you all right?"

This has to be a nightmare, she thought. When she opened her eyes, she was certain to see the brocade canopy covering her bed.

But when the whirling subsided and she opened her eyes, she saw William Sterling, limp Emma hugged to his chest with one arm, his other reaching out to steady her.

She pushed his arm away. "Yes. I am fine."

They continued in silence. Up the stairs to the top floor. Down the hall. Like she had done so many times before. On the floor below, girls were filtering back to their rooms, their reverent silence broken only by a haggard cough or a rough whisper. Each footfall of Mr. Sterling's boots that echoed from the close walls and low ceiling seemed overtly out of place, yet offered a little comfort.

Patience led the way to an empty chamber. She pushed aside a stack of dusty books on the bureau and placed the candle in their place. Its weak light reached to every corner. The modest room was cold, and with trembling hands she turned down the bedcovers.

"Lay her here," Patience said, stepping back to give Mr. Sterling room to lower the child onto the bed.

"Owww." Emma groaned and her eyes fluttered. "Delilah?"

Patience was grateful for the question as she tucked the blankets around the girl and smoothed Emma's hair from her face with the most tender touch she could manage. "Delilah's fine," Patience said, not knowing where the goat was or if she had even survived the fire. "Dearest, she is fine. Hush, please. You've been through quite the ordeal."

The child remained quiet. And unnaturally still.

Cassandra bustled in with tea and another blanket. Patience took the cup of tea and lifted the child's head to help her drink the warm liquid, but when the tea met the child's chapped lips, she sputtered. A fresh coughing fit ensued.

Feeling helpless, Patience stepped aside when Mary pushed past her with the bed warmer and extra blankets.

As she watched Mary work, every bad thing that had transpired since her father's death rushed at her and pressed down with an unrelenting fervor. She wanted to blame someone. Anyone. Her father's death. Her mother's inability to cope. Her brother's abandonment. And, as much as she loved her students, the responsibilities of being in charge of such an establishment. Grief, fear, and exhaustion all trampled on her determination to keep optimistic. Their weight seemed unbearable.

She trembled. She wanted help. She *needed* help. Cassandra and Mary were doing their best, but she needed more. And her thoughts turned to what her father would have done.

He would have prayed. *All things work together for good to them that love God. Wait upon the Lord.*

She could hear his voice, even as she looked at the child, who looked as if she were only sleeping.

Patience wanted to pray. But why would the words not form? Ever since her father's death, she found it difficult to pray.

How could God let this happen? How could He keep allowing such things not only in her life but that of her mother? Where was His comfort? His guidance? His support?

Yes, she should pray. But she pressed her lips into a hard line. God seemed to have vanished.

9

William stepped back as far as he could against the stark plaster wall in the narrow room. His presence was not needed, yet he could not make himself leave. He stared, unblinking, unbelieving, at the still child before him. It was a nightmare come to life. Her hair looked wild against the pillow, her lips appearing almost blue against her colorless skin.

The women fussed over the child, but it was Miss Creighton's voice he heard above the others'. "Mary, we need another bed warmer. Fetch it, will you? Quickly."

Mary abandoned her task of preparing the fire in the iron grate and hurried from the room. Spying his opportunity to be useful, William took her place and stoked the little flame she'd brought about, bringing it to a greater glow.

Every movement raked the charred fabric of his sleeve against the burn on his arm. He ignored the throbbing sting as he set about his task. The scent of scorched linen and skin was enough to gag him, and so he stoked the fire harder. He stole a quick glance at Miss Creighton. Her side was to him, her hand on the child's forehead.

He licked his dry lips. His injury was nothing compared to that of the little girl. "How is she?"

At first he wondered if Miss Creighton had heard him. But then she straightened, pressing her hands to the small of her back, her eyes never leaving the child. "It is hard to tell, but I think her color is improving. Her breathing seems a bit easier."

The words seemed shallow and meaningless when compared to the magnitude of the situation. He brushed his hair from his forehead with his good arm. "She needs the surgeon. I will ride into town."

"Miss Baden said George has already gone for him." Miss Creighton looked up at him as if just now realizing that he was in the room, and then her gaze landed on the blackened sleeve. She gasped. "You've been burned!"

William didn't look down at the wound. He did not need to see it. The pain was excruciating. For even in the bitter coolness of the closed-off room, fiery perspiration beaded on his forehead.

Miss Creighton rushed toward him and placed her hand on his arm, but looked back at Miss Baden. "Mr. Sterling was burned. I will tend to it. Be sure to notify me if there is any change."

He shook his head. "No, I do not need—"

But Miss Creighton picked up the candle and turned, ignoring his protest. "Follow me. We have salve and bandages."

With the child cared for and calm, and with the burn refusing to be ignored, William consented and followed her. A cough echoed from somewhere. The limp, damp fabric of Miss Creighton's muddied dressing gown trailed her, and the single black braid bounced against her back with each hurried step. He almost had to run a bit to keep pace with her.

He followed her back down the narrow, drafty staircase to the kitchen. The fire in the hearth was burning brightly, almost cheerfully, as if to mock the stable's demon fire.

Miss Creighton hesitated and then reached out her hand. "Here, let me help you."

It took him a moment to realize that she intended to help him with his coat. It was going to be a feat to remove it without inflicting even more pain, but the sleeve practically disintegrated, and her gentle touch was swift. Within moments the coat was off his body and on the chair next to him.

"Come sit by the light," she instructed, her tone raspy and matter-of-fact. She pulled the candle near and leaned close. "Rest your arm here."

He consented and positioned his arm so that the top of his forearm was facing her. "Really, Miss Creighton, there is no need—"

But she paid him no heed. With long, slender fingers she rolled the linen fabric of his shirtsleeve, and he winced as she pulled the scorched fabric away from the wound. "My apologies," she muttered, folding the fabric above his elbow and tucking it in place.

He should protest. The child needed tending. And yet, the young woman's feathery light touch intoxicated him. Soothed him. His breathing slowed. His shoulders relaxed. He eased his back against the chair.

She pulled the candle even closer, and the heat from the nearness of the flame seemed to hurl fresh fire on the wounded skin. She dipped a piece of linen in water and looked up at him. "This might be unpleasant."

Miss Creighton worked lightly, quickly, cleaning his arm, her manner as calm and cool as if she did this type of work daily. He fixed his gaze on the wall ahead of him, trying to think of anything else besides the discomfort . . . or the nearness of his nurse.

She carried the scent of smoke and snow, of mud and river water. She was so close he could feel the warmth of her breath on his arm. He stole a quick glance at her, for she was but inches away as she bent over his arm, but her eyes were focused solely on her task.

She looked up only to reach for a jar of white ointment. She removed the cloth covering and dipped a fresh linen inside. "This is Mary's liniment that she keeps on hand for burns. Linseed oil and lime water. 'Twill probably sting."

William jerked his head up and breathed sharply through his nose as the ointment met the wound, careful not to mutter a word unfit for feminine company. The word *hurt* was an understatement, for surely a branding iron must be pressed against his skin.

Miss Creighton winced at his evident pain. "I fear this is not your week, Mr. Sterling."

William wiped perspiration from his brow with his free arm and shifted. He managed a grunt through gritted teeth. "Oh?"

Satisfied that the ointment was properly applied, she pulled a strip of linen from the basket. "This is twice you have been in my kitchen during the dark of night with an injury." She looked up, and for the first time since he'd arrived, she looked him directly in the eye.

William drew as deep a breath as his parched throat would allow. "Yes, I thought of that. Most people would be in a hurry to be rid of such a burden."

But as quickly as she glanced up at him, her gaze returned to her work. "I would hardly call you a burden, Mr. Sterling. Anyone would do the same, for were you at fault for either? I'd say after your rescue of Emma tonight, you are quite a hero."

He would have laughed had his lungs not been damaged from breathing the smoke. A hero? Him?

She smoothed the strip, her tone as calm and steady as if they were discussing business affairs. "I'll wrap this around your arm. It will help keep it clean. I am afraid I am not skilled at this. I cannot recall ever having a burn like this here at Rosemere, not in recent years, anyway. But I suppose there are enough people at Eastmore who know more of what they are doing to properly tend it."

William stared at the top of her head as she bent over his arm, her hair damp and curling from the wild wind and sleet. Apparently she did not know of his recent change in circumstances, for he doubted anyone besides Martha might actually know what to do for such a burn. And why should Miss Creighton be aware of his situation? Her world began and ended with the school. Why should she pay heed to him?

She lifted his arm and held it in her free hand to begin to wrap the bandage around it. Warmth radiated from her, and her movements felt strong and sure. Her braid fell forward, grazing his folded sleeve and taking his mind where it probably had no business going.

"Can you tell me what happened with Emma?"

William tried to focus on her words, but between his pain and her nearness, his concentration, even on something as simple as a string of phrases, was blurry. He cleared his throat and focused his gaze over her shoulder at the wall. "Your boy came to alert us to the fire, and I took the path over Wainslow Peak. I heard her scream coming from the stable, so I went in and there she was."

"Wait." Miss Creighton held up a hand to stop him. "Emma was *inside* the stable?"

"Yes." William felt like his words would get the child in trouble. "She was after the goat, I believe."

Miss Creighton shook her head. "If I weren't so grateful that she is alive, I would be furious. That child is fearless. I told her to stay away from the fire."

William chose his words carefully. Yes, it was careless for her to be in the stable, but would he not do the same himself to rescue his horses? To rescue Slaten? Angus? Any one of the mares? "No, Miss Creighton. Brave."

"Brave?" She huffed a laugh low under her breath and returned her attention to dressing his arm. "Please do not let Emma hear you say such things. I already struggle to keep her focused on her tasks. I do not need her rescuing all of the wayward animals of Darbury."

He watched as her fingers made quick work of smoothing the linen strips. He didn't realize he was staring at her face until her eyes flicked upward, her face close to his own. She nearly jumped back when their eyes met at such close proximity and dropped his arm against the table. Crimson flushed her pale cheeks, almost matching the rims of her eyes, reddened, no doubt, by the smoke's effect. "I . . . I, uh, I mean, I did not mean to be so close."

Her innocence fascinated him, distracting him from the pain. She wiped her hands on her robe and brushed long locks of loose hair from her face. "That should be good for a couple of hours, Mr. Sterling."

She fastened the lid back on the ointment and rolled the linen strips with trembling fingers.

He was clearly having an effect on her.

Or was it presumptuous to think so?

But what he could not account for was how this quiet woman had such an effect on *him*.

He was used to flirtatious women, women who were interested in his funds. And at one point he had enjoyed their attentions. But Miss Creighton was of another sort . . . there was nothing flirtatious about her manner. In fact, her concern seemed genuine. She tended to him as one would to a friend, not as someone hoping to benefit.

Why was she being so kind? Did she feel obligated? Or was it merely in her character to do so?

For despite her benevolence toward him, William was uneasy, and he jerked as Rafertee's men barreled through his mind. They had attacked him on the moors, not far from this spot. Would they also attack his property, his tenants, to prove their point? He doubted Miss Creighton would be so kind if she knew that he could ultimately be the one to blame for the fire.

The idea quickly squelched the warmness he was beginning to feel from her. She was good. It was evident in her compassion. She was different from him, and that idea both fascinated him and frightened him. Miss Creighton was how he wished he could be, but it was too late for such ideas. For he saw something in her he wanted to protect, to shield from the outside world, but how could he do that if he himself was dangerous? Unpredictable? Impulsive? If she knew the real William Sterling, knew of his past and of the danger surrounding him, she would know better than to be so kind to a man like him.

Miss Creighton, with a sharp nod of satisfaction, stood up and stepped away. "I think you will be all right now."

"And you?" he blurted out, standing up from the chair.

She whirled to look at him. "Pardon me?"

"And you?" he repeated, his boldness surprising even him. "Will you be all right?"

Their gazes locked and her lovely eyes narrowed, as if assessing his sincerity.

He needed to speak quickly, otherwise he'd think twice about speaking to her so openly. "It has been a trying night. You have been through an ordeal."

He thought he noticed a tremor in her lip. "I'm fine." She looked away.

But, as if entranced, he could not look away.

She was so proper. So controlled. Or at least her words were. But the expression in her eyes conveyed a message far deeper, far different.

What he would give to know her thoughts. Her *real* thoughts.

He noticed her hand as she returned the jar to the shelf. He reached out to warn her. "Be careful, you're trembling."

But his warning was too late. The jar tipped and fell. William lunged forward and caught it before the glass container smashed on the stone floor, but in doing so he brushed against her robe.

She jumped back, as if she were the one who had encountered a burn. She masked her discomfort behind a wary laugh. "How clumsy of me. My hands . . . I suppose it is the cold. Or, I mean, the fire. Or—" Her words stopped short. "I'm fine."

He didn't believe her. Not for a minute. She wasn't fine. He held her gaze, not allowing her to look away. His stomach churned with an unfamiliar ache. For a story was hidden behind those red-rimmed eyes. Her chest rose and fell with shallow breaths. Her cheek twitched. The desire to comfort her, to protect her, welled up within him, reminiscent of feelings he thought long buried. He sensed the emotion radiating from her, and as strange as it seemed, he almost felt as if he could identify it. And at that moment he knew he'd not rest until he knew what it was.

He should keep his mouth shut. He was tired. Hurt. All the more reason why he should guard his tongue. He never had possessed the gift of saying exactly the right thing at the proper time, and in instances such as this, he had the unfortunate tendency to play the fool.

He looked down at the ointment jar, still in his hand. "Here."

She eyed him before allowing him to place the jar on her outstretched palm.

She swiped the back of her other hand across her cheek, and by doing so spread black soot over her flushed skin.

"You, uh . . ." His throat felt dry. Too dry to speak. He lifted his hand, hesitated, and smoothed some of the soot from her cheek with his thumb.

But at his touch, she recoiled. Alarm brightened her tired eyes, and she sucked in a deep breath.

A sharp reprimand sliced through his mind. What had he been thinking to touch her? They were not at a soiree in London. She was a headmistress in a country school who had shown him kindness.

Miss Creighton grabbed a linen from the table, turned her back to him, and wiped her cheek.

The spell between them popped. Was gone.

She looked back at him. "It is almost dawn. You must be weary. Can I offer you a room upstairs?"

"Thank you, no," he stammered, feigning to adjust the bandage around his arm. "My groom is outside waiting for me. I'll be by soon to assess the damage and see if any part of the stable can be saved. If not, we'll determine next steps."

He reached for his coat. This time she did not offer to assist. He managed to slide his good arm through the coat and left his injured arm out of the sleeve.

"Take these with you." She retrieved the ointment and extra bandages. "I am sure your housekeeper has what you will need, but you might as well have them. Mary can make more."

He glanced—quickly—at her eyes, making a memory of her before looking away. For whatever had transpired between them he was certain had affected him in a way that he would not soon forget.

10

William showed himself out of Rosemere. In the court-yard, smoke still twirled in the wind, clouding the night air and blotting out the moon's gray light. He stepped closer to the still-burning remnants and to Lewis and young Charlie. In front of them stood a goat.

William tilted his head and assessed the pudgy animal. "Delilah. We meet again."

The goat returned the stare, and William knelt down and looked her in the eye. "You caused quite the trouble for your young mistress, not to mention me."

The animal bleated a response before bolting away. Charlie shouted and took off after her.

William tapped an empty bucket with the toe of his boot, and it rolled across the path. With the heat of the fire, all the snow around the stable had melted, leaving everything a slushy mess. He looked at Lewis. "What are you doing?"

"Letting it burn out. Nothing here to save." Lewis nudged a

piece of burning debris that had rolled away from the fire. "I moved the water wagon back by the gate. They've lost their carriage and their cart, but the animals are sound. The housekeeper said she believes they lost a chicken or two." He nodded toward William's arm. "You all right?"

"A little burn. It will be fine."

"George told me what happened. How is the girl?"

"She is asleep." William glanced up at the windows. They were all dark. The house was settling back down, its occupants returning to sleep. "She will recover, although I fear she breathed in much more smoke than is healthy for one so young."

Lewis tossed a rope in his direction. "George went for the surgeon. He will know how to help her, certainly."

William stared as if entranced at the mess of glowing beams and flickering flames. The surreal night was coming to an end. Soon the sun would climb into the broad expanse of the sky, shedding light on the full extent of the damage to the Rosemere stable.

Now that the immediate danger had passed, he feared what was next.

He knew that other landlords would refuse to take responsibility for such an incident. But his father had set the precedent. Everyone in the county would no doubt recall how his father had rebuilt the Camdon cottage when it burned ten years ago. How would it look if he did not do the same, especially when the building in question was merely a stable?

William scratched his head, then scanned the burning heap. He tried to calculate what it would cost to rebuild the structure, but in his exhausted state he could not begin to factor. He vaguely recalled Mr. Livingstone speaking of repairs to tenant cottages or outbuildings, but he had never paid attention to the sums. All he knew was that whatever the cost, he did not have the funds for it.

And still pay Rafertee.

He'd check the lease in the morning. Surely when his father drew up the paperwork, he'd included terms to clarify responsibilities in such an incident. His father had been steadfast in financial interests and likely freed the Sterling family from any obligations.

But even if that were the case, William could not simply walk away.

How Miss Creighton's red-rimmed eyes haunted him. The sight of the limp child plagued his thoughts. And this tragedy could be a result of his own foolishness.

No, he could not—would not—walk away.

Lewis lifted the lantern. "Come here, I want to show you something."

William pushed himself from the post he'd been leaning on. "What is it?"

Lewis motioned for him to follow, and William stepped over some debris and followed the groom around the remains of the stable. Lewis led the way through the smoky mist to a clearing by the river. "Look."

William's eyes were still watering with such intensity that making out anything was difficult. "What are we looking at?"

"Here, take the lantern. Lean down."

William knelt down in the spongy mud, squinted, and then—he saw it. A mess of hoofprints and footprints, in no apparent order. At the sight, his heart pounded, each beat harder than the last. He stood and handed the lantern back to Lewis.

William whispered, "Does anyone else know about these?"

"Doubt it. George is the only one who would likely take notice, and I doubt he would come down this way."

William tried to rationalize it. "Could be Angus's hoofprints from a few days ago. My own boot prints. I believe I rode through this clearing."

"Perhaps, but look." Lewis leaned down and pointed at the

hoofprints. "Different sizes. Last I checked, all of Angus's shoes were the same size."

William felt as if he had swallowed rock after rock. "Are you thinking Rafertee's men?"

Lewis shrugged. "They were out here on the moors at night a few nights ago, and look what they did to you."

"But why would they be here? Why not Eastmore's stables?"

"Eastmore's stables are more exposed. Closer to the road. Maybe it would be too obvious of a message to outsiders." Lewis shrugged again. "I'm not sure."

Dread simmered, then bubbled into anger. William snapped a twig from a nearby tree and slammed it to the ground. He muttered, pressing the twig remnants into the soft, cold mud. "I've got to get the rest of that money, and soon."

"Well, we can't solve it tonight." Lewis headed back toward Rosemere. "Let's get the horses and take what animals we can back with us to Eastmore. We'll figure it out by the light of day."

L

When Patience awoke, sunlight flooded her room.

If it weren't for the scent of smoke teasing her nostrils, she could almost believe that the horrible night behind her was only a vaporous dream. But then, as she rolled over, her thick hair, which had slipped from her plait, smelled so strongly of smoke she almost gagged.

She rubbed the kinks from her neck and glanced over at the window. When she finally had come up to sleep after the fire, the sun was just below the horizon, the eastern sky a light purple and the rest of the sky still gray. She shivered and wrapped her blanket around herself before crossing to the window to assess the grounds below.

Bright morning light pained her eyes, and even when she pinched them closed, she had no relief from the burning. The fire was gone, but the smoke lingered, woven into the fabric of the air.

As her eyes adjusted to the light, she was met with the reality she had hoped was but a nightmare. The stable, or what had been the stable, was a charred heap of scorched timber. Smoke and fog still rose from the ashes and debris. The snow was absent around the remnants, a stark contrast to the rest of the white landscape. Patience arched her neck, looking to see if anyone was about. But the grounds were empty. She shivered and pulled the curtains tight. Even in her solitude, a flush rose to her cheeks when she realized what she had done.

She was not looking to see if *anyone* was about.

She was looking to see if *he* was about.

Patience tightened the blanket around her shoulders and turned away. The memory of the roughness of William Sterling's thumb on her cheek as he brushed soot away brought the oddest quiver to her stomach.

Shame on her. She should have been aware of how close she was. Of perhaps sending a message she had not intended to send. Such an intimate act to one who was practically a stranger was an impropriety.

Or was it?

Heaven help her, she did not understand the effect William Sterling had on her. Under normal circumstances, she was calm. Collected. Rational to a fault. Around him, she was unsure of herself, for his very presence made her question everything she thought she knew. Thought she wanted.

With his tawny hair and clear eyes, he was handsome, to be sure, but it was the memory of the corded muscles in his forearms that twitched as she cleaned his wound that refused to leave her. She turned to pull a clean robe from the wardrobe, and when she did, she caught her reflection in her small mirror. Her hair hung wild and tangled about her pale face, and sure enough, black soot was still smudged across her cheek.

She lifted her fingertips to the black residue.

So his touch had been intended to be helpful, not forward.

She tried to wipe it off. But it would not budge.

The last time a man had touched her had been many years ago. Ewan O'Connell.

Ewan had been the romance of her youth. She had been but nineteen, and he was her father's protégé and lived with them in Rosemere. Ewan made her an offer of marriage, but she, silly and young, refused him, waiting for someone more handsome. More exciting. More romantic.

But that someone never came.

She wiped her cheek harder, unshed tears itching her eyes. She could not allow such silly thoughts of William Sterling to permeate her mind.

Thoughts of his hair, which she could not quite decide if it was light brown or dark blond.

Or thoughts of his tone, which she could not quite discern if it was flirtatious or sincere.

For he was a wealthy landowner, used to fine things, fast horses, and fancy women. She was a mere spinster headmistress of a modest girls' school.

She called for Mary to come help her dress and did her best to bury her thoughts in the busyness of the day ahead. After donning a high-waisted, long-sleeved gown of charcoal muslin with black ribbon around the hem of her sleeves, she hurried to check on Emma.

At Emma's bedchamber, she slowly opened the door and poked her head inside. Sunlight filtered through the room's only narrow window onto Cassandra, who sat in a chair, leaning forward against the bed, her russet head cradled in the crook of her arm. Both slept.

Patience tiptoed over the planked floor, but as she stepped on an uneven floorboard, a creak echoed from the plastered walls. Cassandra jerked upright, sleep marks creasing her face. Her nose wrinkled in sleepy confusion, and her hair hung limp about her face.

Patience held her finger up to her lips and stepped closer to look down at the sleeping child. Emma's tangled hair spread out on the white pillow, the dark hue of each strand contrasting sharply with the stark linen fabric. Traces of soot still colored Emma's forehead, and her long black lashes fanned out on her olive skin. Her lips were parted in easy slumber.

Patience whispered, "How is she?"

Cassandra yawned, leaned forward, and smoothed the blanket. "She has not woken, although she had a few coughing fits and has moaned in her sleep."

Patience placed her hand on the child's forehead. "She does not feel feverish."

Her stomach churned at the thought of the pain the child had experienced. "I need to check on Mother, but then I'll be back to sit with her."

She squeezed Cassandra's shoulder and left the room as quietly as the uneven floor would allow. She trudged back to the west wing and then to her mother's room. She found Margaret Creighton sitting up in bed, graying hair in disarray and blankets strewn about.

"Mother, have you not slept?"

Her mother fussed with an embroidered handkerchief. "How could I after such tragedy has befallen Rosemere?" She pressed the fabric to her nose. "And where have you been?"

"Well"—Patience hesitated—"I just came from Emma's room. And before that, I was sleeping."

Her mother huffed. "I see you have tended to the needs of everyone else. Just like your father would have done." Her words seemed hurled as an accusation instead of offered as a compliment. "How quickly I am forgotten."

Patience ignored her mother's jab and for once let the chamber curtains remain closed.

"Let me call for tea. I am sure that after—"

But she stopped, silenced by the tears sliding down her mother's cheeks.

Patience had grown accustomed to her mother's emotional outbursts. Even though they were increasingly frequent, they were never easy. "Please calm yourself. I know this has been difficult, but I assure you, I—"

Her mother's nightcap slid to the side. "Difficult? Difficult? Your father devoted his entire life to this school. Poured every ounce of his soul into it. To say it is difficult is an understatement indeed."

Patience feared anything she would say would only further anger her mother. Yet remaining silent was not an option. "Of course he would have been upset, but I am certain he would realize that the stable is just that, a stable. It can easily be rebuilt."

"Do not preach at me, Patience. I am fully aware of how serious this could have been."

At the sharpness in Margaret Creighton's tone, Patience pressed her lips together and clasped her hands behind her. How was it possible to comfort someone who did not wish to be comforted?

Patience shifted the conversation. "Mr. Sterling said he would be by soon, and he will—"

"You know how I feel about William Sterling," her mother snapped. "I've told you so time and time again. Why, he didn't even attend your father's funeral. And he and his steward have neglected us. I don't trust that man."

Patience bit her lip to prevent the retort that would surely spill forth if she did not. Why did she feel the need to defend William Sterling? To tell her mother that it was he who saved Emma? Was it that she herself believed him to be a kind man, in his heart a decent man, or was it to spite her mother's negativity?

But after her mother's outburst, Patience could not help but wonder why Mr. Sterling's visits had suddenly started now. Was it because of what she knew about his injury on the moors? He indicated that he wanted to keep it quiet. Did he think that if he helped her she would keep his secret?

Her mother's rant continued. "How could a stable, in the middle of the night, simply burst into flames?" She wagged a finger in Patience's direction. "Something is amiss."

Patience had barely allowed her thoughts to go to the possibility of foul play. It seemed unlikely that one of the girls had been involved, and who would want to harm a girls' school?

Patience took her mother's hand. "You are upset." She drew a sharp breath before forcing herself to voice the words she knew her mother wanted to hear. "I will write to Rawdon again. He will be here. He will sort this out."

Patience had been correct in her assumption. Her mother relaxed at the mention of Rawdon's name.

"You are right. He will know the best course. He's always been such a clever man. So like his father. He will be able to help us through these dark times."

Patience winced, almost as if she had been struck. How her mother's words pierced her and lingered like a bitter aftertaste. How hard Patience had worked in the months following her father's death to keep the school afloat. How many nights had she stayed awake, tending to sick children, planning meals with the housekeeper, and planning lessons? Her mother noticed none of it. Instead, she seemed to place all of her hope, her security, in

Rawdon, who had been conveniently absent from any workings of the school since the day he departed for London after their father's burial.

Patience turned away from her mother to hide the pain she was sure must show on her face. She sniffed. "I'll send Mary up with some hot chocolate. I'm going to wake the girls. There is much work to be done."

11

A flurry of activity swirled in the recovering Rosemere. After leaving her mother's bedchamber and another visit to sit with the sleeping Emma, Patience stole away to the quiet of her father's study.

The somber room's paneled walls and heavy mahogany furniture always seemed a fortress. As a child she had snuck beneath this desk, inhaling the scent of her father's tobacco, listening to the sound of his quill scratching paper as he worked.

But now, this room was not a place of escape, but one of responsibility. Letters needed to be written. She reached for her father's weathered teak writing box, pausing to wipe a smudge from the polished surface.

How she missed him. His determined strength. His self-assuredness that acted as a shield for them all.

In all her years she had never known him to seem rattled. Frightened. Dismayed. His demeanor was always strong and steady.

And she felt weak and small.

Before grief could get a fresh grip on her, she snatched a piece of paper and penned a quick, curt letter informing her brother of the fire and sealed it with little confidence it would actually reach his hand.

She pulled another sheet of paper from the box, and her thoughts turned to Emma. There was still another letter to write. Emma's guardian, whoever that person might be, needed to be notified of the child's injury.

As far as Patience was aware, Emma had no family. The details of the child's past were shrouded in mystery. The local vicar, Thomas Hammond, brought the child to the school several years past, indicating that the guardian wished to remain anonymous.

The notion of an unidentified guardian was not uncommon—the tuition for two other pupils at Rosemere was also paid anonymously. But mystery lurked behind the child's pale blue eyes and olive complexion. Her exotic appearance fed the fire for fantastic stories surrounding her history. Patience's father had encouraged Patience and the other teachers to treat Emma as any other student, and the mystery of her past had faded in the sameness of routine and structure. The arrangement had been longstanding and unquestioned. But in light of the circumstances, Patience needed to learn more about the child.

She went to an old armoire that held information on students, past and present. Rarely had she felt the necessity to look inside, much less look through the contents for any student.

She swung open the ornately carved door and, with the motion, dust swirled in the air, the filtered sunlight illuminating each mote. Her nose, still burning and sore from the effects of smoke, twitched. With a careful eye she skimmed the names scrawled on the outside of a variety of boxes and small crates. Frances Ashbrooke. Dorothea Hey. Susannah Bright.

She found Emma's name and pulled the oddly shaped hat box

from the armoire and brushed the dust from the top. She frowned at the box's light weight, doubting that such a light carton could hold the answers she sought.

Patience lifted the lid. As the afternoon light fell on the contents, Patience sighed. She lifted out a prayer book and thumbed through it, a pair of gloves, a copy of Shakespeare's *Romeo and Juliet*, and a small velvet pouch containing an amethyst brooch. Nothing of significance. But then her hope mounted as she noticed a letter at the bottom of the box. Eagerly, she grabbed it. Someone had already broken the seal, and she unfolded it. Money fell to the desk, and the words scrawled on the page indicated the money was intended to be given to Emma when she became of age. Patience clenched her jaw. Whoever was responsible for the care of the girl seemed intent on having nothing to do with her.

That simply would not do.

She spread the items before her on her father's desk, studying each one as if it held the secret of Emma's veiled past. She'd ask George and Mary to see what they could remember, but doubted they had any other information. She sighed, folded the letter, tucked the money inside, and leaned back in the chair. She would check the books yet again for any record of the paying party—after all, someone was responsible for her tuition—and if that did not satisfy her curiosity, she would have to pay a visit to the vicar. He was the one who brought Emma to them. Surely he would have the information.

Later that afternoon, when the sun was beginning to settle over the bleak, desolate moors, Patience grabbed her cape and bonnet and hurried from the kitchen door, determined to go unnoticed. The day had been chaotic, and with most of the girls in quiet study time and Emma resting, she'd take advantage of the rare solitary minutes.

The weather had shifted quickly, as it did often on the moors, and a light freezing rain had fallen earlier in the afternoon, further dampening the still-smoking debris. She lifted the hem of her gray cape and hurried to Rosemere's front gate. Once on the main road, she sidestepped to avoid the deep ruts, which, for the most part, were shrouded with a layer of ice and snow. Fortunately, the road was passable. For the past several weeks, the excessive rain and snow often kept the roads dangerously soggy or icy. But today the road was a little firmer.

The wind carried a damp chill. Even as she distanced herself from Rosemere and the rubble of the stable, the phantom smoke seemed to follow her.

The walk to the vicarage was but a short one. Her will to fight for Emma had surged and energized her. She didn't even stop to think about what she would say before she tapped her gloved knuckles against the door. As she waited, she jutted her chin out in confidence.

The door was opened by a young maid.

Patience forced a smile. "May I speak with Mrs. Hammond?"

The girl ushered her in, took her outside things, and showed her to a sitting room. Patience sat nervously, noting that this was the first time since her father passed that she was visiting these family friends. At one point, she and her mother would visit Mrs. Hammond at least once a week. But those days were gone.

In a flurry of periwinkle sarcenet, Mrs. Hammond rounded the corner, arms outstretched, her eyebrows drawn together in apparent concern. "Miss Creighton! Oh, how are you, my dear? I have been so worried about you and all the young ladies."

Patience stood, accepted her outstretched hands, and allowed herself to be folded into a brief hug. She was grateful it was Mrs. Hammond, and Mrs. Hammond alone, who greeted her. Even now that she was quite grown, the austere presence of Mr. Thomas Hammond intimidated her. Frightened her, even. "We are managing quite well, thank you."

With a wave of her outstretched hand, Mrs. Hammond directed her back to the sofa and then sat next to her. "I was shocked, absolutely shocked, when I heard the news of the fire. I can smell the smoke from here! And poor Miss Simmons. How is she faring? I wanted to come see her straightaway as soon as I heard of it, but Mr. Hammond insisted she needed her rest."

Patience folded her hands, feeling the warmth that comes with the concern of an old friend. "Emma's breathing is steadily improving. I am hopeful that a day or two in bed should be all that she needs."

"I was so afraid. It could have been worse. I am fond of the girl."

Patience nodded, for it was true. On more than one occasion the Hammonds had opened their home to Emma while the other girls were away on holiday. "Actually, Emma is the reason I am here."

"Oh?"

"Yes. You see, I wish to notify her guardian—or family, if she has any—of her injury, but I have searched my father's records and have not been able to discover her guardian's name. I even checked the payment records, and while everything is paid regularly, there is no name accompanying them. I am certain you will agree with me that in the instance of such an injury, the family must, of course, be notified. I am hoping that you or Mr. Hammond might be able to offer guidance."

Mrs. Hammond frowned and tapped a finger to her lips in thoughtful contemplation. "Let me think. I do recall the day that Mr. Hammond brought Miss Simmons to Darbury. Indeed, I recall it in great detail. But you know Mr. Hammond. In light of his position, he often keeps details of such things private. But I am sure he would hear your questions. I will fetch him."

Patience tried to hide her disappointment that Mrs. Hammond did not possess the information she sought. "I've no wish to trouble him."

"No trouble at all. I will return shortly."

The time seemed to stretch to eternity. The odd events of the past several days had affected her perception of time. Nothing seemed real. Everything seemed independent of reason or sense. The maid reappeared with tea, and Patience poured herself a cup. She sipped it, allowing the steaming liquid to serve as a balm. She closed her eyes and drew a deep breath, as if by doing so she could open them again and everything would be different from what it was when she closed them. But when she did open her eyes, she beheld the same glowing embers flickering in the confines of the stone hearth, the same long afternoon shadows playing on the faded, floral-papered walls and low, beamed ceiling.

A nervous quiver danced in her stomach as hushed whispers and heavier footsteps sounded from within the house. She recalled as a child fearfully watching Mr. Hammond in the pulpit as he spoke of hell's fire and God's wrath. She'd known him all her life, yet she regarded him with timid reserve. Childish qualms would not suit her. She no longer had that luxury. Emma depended on her.

The vicar entered the room, dressed in a severely cut black tailcoat and gray breeches, followed by his wife. Patience stood and forced her eyes to meet his.

"What a pleasure it is to see you in our home, Miss Creighton." His voice was as rich and deep as it was each Sunday.

"I hope my visit does not take you away from your work, sir."

"Indeed, no. It has been far too long since you have been a guest at the vicarage. Please, be seated."

Patience sat primly on her chair. "I will not keep you long. I am here on behalf of Emma Simmons."

Mr. Hammond pushed his spectacles farther up on his nose

before casting a glance at his wife. "Precious child. We heard about what happened. I hope she is recovering."

"She is. She is strong. I am hoping, however, that you can help shed light on something for me. I would like to notify Emma's guardian of her situation, but I cannot find any information in my father's office. She came to Rosemere through you, and I was hoping you could assist me. Do you recall the name of her guardian, her mother or father perhaps?"

Mr. Hammond tented his fingers and licked his thin lips. His manner was hesitant. Reserved. "I do recall, Miss Creighton. But I am sad to say that the child's mother is no longer living."

Disappointment surged through her. She had suspected as much but still had hoped for happier news. "That I am saddened to hear. Her father, then?"

Mr. Hammond pushed himself up from the chair, and with hands clasped behind his back, he moved to the window and looked out over the white lawn. The gray light fell on his head and shoulders, making his hair appear much grayer than she recalled. "I admire what you are doing, Miss Creighton. Indeed, I do. But I gave my word, many years ago. I must ask you to respect the necessity to keep the child's family's identity private."

Patience scooted to the edge of her seat. "But certainly you cannot agree with that. You must understand my dilemma. What father, regardless of how estranged, would not want to be informed of his child's injuries? A child needs her family at a time such as this."

Awkward silence hovered between them. Then, with his voice low and controlled, the old vicar turned and said, "I agree with you, Miss Creighton, but you must accept that my position often makes me privy to information that I cannot reveal. I must insist that you refrain from asking further questions on this matter."

Patience was almost offended at the request. But she had to

continue to try. For Emma. "Well then, if you cannot share this man's identity, perhaps you can see to it that the father is notified."

His words were resolute. "I am afraid I cannot do that, Miss Creighton."

What was wrong with Mr. Hammond? Could he not see that she was trying to help a child? Patience pressed her lips together but in the end was unable to keep a sharp insult from flying forth. For after all, if she did not fight on Emma's behalf, who would? "Well, if that is indeed the case, then I think it is a sorry state." She jumped up and snatched her gloves from the table.

As if aware of her frustration, the vicar extended his hands, as one would to pacify an agitated animal. His words softened. "Perhaps Mrs. Hammond and I can help. Miss Emma is welcome to stay at the vicarage while she recovers, or perhaps I could go read to her."

"No, no, that will not be necessary." Patience tilted her chin in the air, not allowing her eyes to meet his. The idea that this man knew the name of the man who could potentially ease the pain and loneliness of a child, yet refused to reveal the identity . . . despite his offer of hospitality, she could think of no other explanation. He was selfish.

But then again, perhaps he was wise. Perhaps he knew something about this man that she—and Emma—would not want to know. "If you have a change of mind about contacting Emma's father, please inform me and I will be happy to pen a missive."

Mrs. Hammond placed her hand on her husband's shoulder. "What are your plans, Miss Creighton? I would imagine things are in quite an uproar at the school."

"On the contrary, the girls are handling the situation quite well."

"Will your brother be returning to Darbury?"

Patience drew a sharp breath, finding that with each passing minute she was growing more tense. Why did *everyone* inquire about Rawdon? Did they all really believe her to be incapable of handling the school's affairs?

But instead of verbalizing the stinging retort that simmered, she kept her voice steady. "I wrote to him this morning to notify him of the fire."

But Mr. Hammond would not allow the subject to pass. "I am sure his return will bring great comfort, not only to you, but to your dear mother."

And with that, Patience took her leave.

12

William paused in his brushing of Angus. He rubbed his
eyes, still raw from the smoke. The idea that Rafertee's
men might have been behind the blaze angered him. It
was one thing to physically threaten him. It was another entirely
if they extended their threats to his land. His tenants. To women
and children.

William brushed the currycomb in circles, sending up a flurry
of dust and hair. He was operating under the assumption that the
hoofprints in the clearing by the river belonged to Rafertee's men.
He could be wrong. But who else would be in such a remote area,
so off the path?

Urgency was setting in. His time to make things right was
short. He needed to take some drastic measures. The obvious
answer was to sell his land. But that was only as a last resort. And
since he had yet to hear from Bley, perhaps the proposed arrangement with Riley was the best course.

He heard footsteps outside the stable door, and Lewis, who
was cleaning the stall next to William, lifted his head.

"Ho, there!"

Using the pitchfork as a cane, Lewis stepped to the half door and peered out. "It's George. Appears the last of the Creighton animals are here."

William and Lewis walked out to the courtyard.

"Where would you like them?" George called. Charlie and George had already been by once to deliver a cow and a horse, and they were back again with more Rosemere animals.

Lewis chuckled and swept his arm in the direction of the open door. "As you can see, we have more than a few empty stalls. Take your pick."

The old man slid from the horse's back. "Miss Creighton wishes me to thank you for opening your stable."

William waved his hand in dismissal. "Think nothing of it."

Behind George, a boy was riding a plump pony.

Charlie and Violet.

William resisted the urge to pepper the boy with questions about the start of the fire—what he saw, what he might have heard. But there would be time for that, and the expression on the boy's face suggested he was tired and overwhelmed. Frightened, even. Instead, William said, "It was good of you to ride out to tell us of the fire, young man."

A grin spread across the boy's freckled face, and with a jerk of his head he flipped his hair from his eyes. "Just doin' what Mr. George tells me to do."

George headed into the stable with the horse, then turned and waved a finger toward the pony. "Bring 'er over here, boy."

Charlie nodded and led the compliant, pudgy pony into a stall.

William watched the boy stroke the pony's back and pull a carrot stump from the pocket of his coarse linen coat. He stroked the pony's muzzle, then closed the stall door and left the stable.

"Where's he going?" William asked.

But before George could respond, the boy appeared, leading a goat.

"Ah, Delilah." William snorted. "I forgot she would be joining us. Hey, Lewis, do you recall when last there was a goat at Eastmore?"

Lewis shook his head and leaned on the pitchfork, his lips twitching in amusement. "No, sir, can't say I do."

Once inside the stable, the goat planted her hooves on the dirt floor and refused to move. She bleated and jerked her head backward, nearly pulling the lead rope from Charlie's hand.

The boy yanked back and eventually claimed victory. He led the animal to a smaller pen and closed the door.

Amused, William leaned back on the stall door.

"The little ones are fond of that goat," George said, pointing his thumb in the animal's direction. "Charlie here is no different." He waited until Charlie untied the animal and walked out of the stall, carefully again closing the stall door. "You'll probably have a handful of visitors coming by to visit the goat, if I know them students."

William cocked an eyebrow. Children? At Eastmore? There hadn't been children on the grounds since he had himself been a child. Even his own niece, Graham's daughter, Lucy, had been to visit only once or twice.

George adjusted his hat. "'Course, it'll be hard on Charlie to go back home and be away from the horses . . . Tends to 'em day 'n night, he does, 'specially since that groom of ours left."

Lewis hooked his arms over the stall wall. "Yes, we heard Temdon left a few months back. Heard he took a post over at Ambledale Court, if I'm not mistaken."

George shook his gray head. "Yes, sir. Left like a thief in the middle of the night, he did." He clicked his tongue and ruffled Charlie's hair. "But we manage all right, don't we, lad? This one here's got the makin's of a fine horseman."

The boy grinned at the compliment.

William leaned with his elbow on a fence and nodded toward the stable. "You might be interested in the fact that we have three in foal, one of them due in a couple of weeks."

Interest flashed in the boy's eyes, but it was George who kept them on task. "Just so we are clear, we'll be earning these horses' keep. Charlie'll be by to tend to our animals. No need for Mr. Lewis to do it. Charlie's fast too. If you have any tasks for him, I am sure he would oblige."

Lewis pushed himself away from the stall wall. "He needn't come back and forth every day, 'specially with no place to board a mount at Rosemere. There are quarters in the back of the stable. I sleep in one, Charlie is welcome to the other."

The boy looked up at George, as if looking for permission. George simply nodded.

"It's settled, then," William said. "Welcome to Eastmore Hall, Charlie."

It was snowing again.

That was fine with Patience, for the sullen gray sky and nipping wind suited her mood.

Oh, how her soul longed for warm, carefree days with azure skies and puffy clouds, with purple heather dotting the moors and the lure of the nightingale's song whispering through the tall grasses.

But those days seemed so long ago . . . so far away.

Her half boot sank in the mud. She muttered under her breath and held out her hand for balance. This winter had been one of the darkest, coldest, snowiest winters she could recall. And the thickening clouds confirmed that they were not done with it yet, even though spring should be appearing any day.

But at least here on the broad expanse of the moors, despite the falling snow, the air felt fresh. She could breathe without effort. It was the evening snow that obscured her vision, not a threatening curtain of smoke.

She quickened her pace, determined to visit Charlie at Eastmore by nightfall. As a child she had always been a little frightened of Eastmore Hall, with its stone embattlements, formidable gates, and the fortress of trees reaching their black limbs toward the heavens. She rarely had cause to visit, but occasionally her father would take her to call on old Mr. Sterling. And when Mrs. Sterling had been alive, she had permitted Rosemere's students to visit her garden to study the flowers and vegetation.

But that had been many years ago. After she crested Wainslow Peak and headed down toward the gothic house, she found the structure slightly intimidating, but not frightening. If anything, the unkempt ivy clinging to the facade gave it a dejected appearance, and the overgrown shrubbery made it look lost. Forgotten. Forlorn.

Patience walked past the main house toward the massive stable. The half door was open, and yellow light spilled out on the snow marred with boot and hoofprints. Welcome warmth radiated from the structure's confines, and the earthy smell of hay mixed with the undeniable scent of horses seemed to beckon her to draw nearer. Winking lanterns hung from iron hooks down a long, wide corridor, illuminating two rows of wooden stalls. Horses' ears pricked at her arrival, and she heard voices. She stepped inside, let her cloak's hood fall to her shoulders, and tapped her gloved knuckles against a wooden beam. "Is anyone here?"

A heavy wooden door creaked open, and as her eyes adjusted to the light behind him, she recognized the man as the one who had accompanied Mr. Sterling to the fire. He wiped his hands on his pants and smoothed his wool coat. "Can I help you, Miss Creighton?"

"Yes, thank you. I am looking for—"

She did not need to finish her sentence, for young Charlie came rushing from the room with the enthusiasm of youth. "Miss Creighton!"

After the days of injury and soot, disappointment and cold, Charlie's freckled cheeks warmed her heart, and his happy smile made the cold walk worthwhile. She hurried to him and pulled him close, pressing a kiss atop his sandy head. "Charlie! How I have missed your smiling face. How are you finding things at Eastmore Hall?"

Boundless energy radiated from the boy. "Just fine, Miss Creighton. And look! I will show you. I have taken good care of the horses, like Mr. George told me to do."

He tucked his hand in hers and led her to a section of stalls where the two Creighton horses stood. King and Queen. Patience smiled and rubbed her hand across the elderly mare's velvet muzzle.

"And see, I've taken care of Delilah too."

Patience turned and peeked over the stone stable wall down into a straw-padded stall. In the middle of it stood Delilah, who raised her head at the commotion and bleated.

Patience regarded the animal with reserved familiarity. "There you are, you cheeky animal." The goat bleated. "You caused quite a commotion."

The goat bleated again.

Charlie motioned for Patience to come closer. "Is Emma all right?"

Patience could not help but smile at his concern. "She will be. You are kind to ask."

He shifted nervously, his eyes darting from the goat to the horses. "Will you tell her that I will take good care of Delilah for her? Do you promise?"

"Of course I will." Patience hesitated, trying to decode the emotion playing on the boy's stoic expression. She remembered the basket on her arm and held it out to him. "Look, I brought you something."

Brightness returned to Charlie's eyes, and he peered meekly at the basket.

Patience bit her lip and leaned forward as if to whisper a secret. "Do you want to see what it is?" She led him to a stool and sat down, balancing the long basket on her lap. She pulled back the cloth and revealed jam tarts and rolls and a jar of honey. "Mary and the girls packed it for you. They were worried that you would go hungry."

He grinned, and she pulled the cloth back farther. "Jane sent you this scarf she made, fearing you would be cold"—she pulled the cloth off the rest of the way—"and I brought you a book."

His brow creased at the sight of the bound volume.

"You do not think I would let your studies suffer simply because you are not on Rosemere grounds, did you?"

"No, ma'am."

She smiled and deposited the book in his hands. "I think you will like it."

"Yes, Miss Creighton."

The boy leaned in to her. Her heart swelled with affection for the child, who, even though he was a stable boy, was like a student to her.

"At least the horses and cow are safe." Charlie sniffed. "And Delilah and Violet."

Without warning, there was a commotion out in the court-yard, and the stable door flew open and banged against the wall. A tall cloaked man leading a bay horse walked in and stomped snow from his boots. "Blasted cold," the man murmured, tossing the reins in Lewis's direction.

The groom cleared his throat. "Mr. Sterling, we have a visitor."

"Huh?" Mr. Sterling whirled around and paused in the middle

of pulling off his gloves. The intensity by which his startling blue eyes locked with hers slowed Patience's breathing. She suddenly felt self-conscious of the manner in which the wind must have tugged at her hair.

"Uh, Miss Creighton." She had caught him off guard. He swept his hat from his head and pushed his hand through disheveled hair. "My apologies. I did not see you there." He offered a stiff bow.

Perhaps it was the effect of the wind's bite, but Patience thought she noticed Mr. Sterling's face redden.

Finding her voice, she set the basket down and stood up. "No, please, do not apologize. I was only visiting Charlie. How is your arm?"

He lifted the wounded arm and cocked his head to the side, the hint of a smile dimpling his cheek in the subtlest manner. "I am managing fine. Thank you."

She hesitated and placed her hand on Charlie's shoulder. "Again, Mr. Sterling, I cannot thank you enough for your generosity in allowing the animals to stay here. And, of course, Charlie. I am sure he is as comfortable here as he ever was at Rosemere."

Mr. Sterling patted his horse's rump as Lewis led the animal away. "Think nothing of it, Miss Creighton. I am happy to be of service." He nodded toward the empty stalls. "As you can see, we have plenty of room. My horses could use the company."

Patience looked down the row of empty stalls. She'd always heard that William Sterling was rumored to be an expert horseman. But now that she took the time to look, she wondered where all the horses were that were said to be housed here.

She turned back to Mr. Sterling, trying to stay focused as he drew nearer. In the hustle of the fire, she had failed to notice that the bruising around his eye had faded and the cut on his lip was barely noticeable with the slight stubble on his chin. The light brown hair falling over his forehead hid the spot where the gash had been. His eyes appeared piercing and intense under the lantern's glow, and a flush crept up from her neck.

What a silly schoolgirl inclination. She was here for Charlie. "I see that your eye appears to be much improved."

"It is, thank you. How is the little girl?"

Patience relaxed at the sincerity in his voice. "Emma grows stronger by the hour. She will no doubt be back to her mischief in no time."

The sound of Charlie rustling in the basket brought her back to her senses. She needed to be on her way if she didn't want to cross the moors in the black of night. She knelt next to Charlie, giving him her best reassuring smile. "It will soon be dark. I must go, but I will return in a few days to see how you are. George said he'll be here in the morning. Are you sure you are all right?"

Charlie nodded and wiped his hand on his trousers. "Yes, ma'am. I am sure. Thank you for the basket."

"Of course, Charlie. You were so brave yesterday. I am proud of you."

He beamed at the praise and then cast a sheepish glance at the men. Patience felt reluctant to leave him. Yes, he was their stable boy, but he held a special place in her heart. She squeezed his shoulder, turned, and walked down the corridor. Mr. Sterling was waiting at the entrance.

She smiled and nodded. "Good evening, Mr. Sterling. And thank you again."

Mr. Sterling followed her from the stable and looked around. "Where is your horse? I will fetch him for you."

"That is not necessary, Mr. Sterling." Patience adjusted her cape. "I walked."

Her answer brought a frown to his face. "You walked? But surely you cannot walk home. It is getting far too dark. Here, I will have Lewis ready the carriage."

Patience lifted her hand in protest as he started to step past her. "You needn't bother, sir. 'Tis but a short walk. I should be home before the sun sets."

"At least allow me to saddle one of our horses for you. We have a sidesaddle, I am sure."

"Oh no, we have no stable in which to give your horse shelter tonight. And in any instance, I do not ride."

He blinked, shocked, as if she had told him that she didn't believe the sky to be blue. "You do not ride?"

"No."

"Why ever not?"

"Darbury is a small town. I can walk anywhere I need to go. I never had the need to learn."

"Miss Creighton, everyone has need to learn to ride a horse."

His enthusiastic certainty brought a smile to her lips. She shrugged. "My father forbade it."

"But your pupils ride, do they not? I assumed the students would ride the pony."

"Violet belongs to one of our former students who took a position as a governess in Somerset and could no longer care for the animal. The pony has been with us ever since."

"Did your father never ride? Your brother?"

"Perhaps you recall my father walked with a limp. As a boy he was thrown from a horse and broke his leg. He never rode again, and I was not allowed to learn."

"A true shame, Miss Creighton." He looked in the direction of Rosemere, his straight nose and fine profile a black silhouette against the unstable clouds. "Well then, you must at least allow me to escort you back to Rosemere."

The lighthearted banter she had been enjoying with him suddenly fell flat. Surely he was in jest. Patience looked at the ground, unable to meet his gaze. For what sort of man—what sort of gentleman—would ask to escort her home alone? It was preposterous!

"Thank you for your concern, but that is not necessary."

He pressed his lips together. His confident composure had slipped, and he pushed his fingers through his hair. "I know how that must seem, Miss Creighton, but allow me to explain." He lowered his voice as if he were someone with a great secret to tell. "I suspect you are aware that I was not thrown from my horse the other night. I do not mean to frighten you, but all is not as it seems. And with the fire . . ." His voice trailed off and he lifted his eyes to the moors. "I ask you to trust me when I say this. I insist upon seeing you home. For your safety."

Her eyes locked with his. No trace of a smile warmed his expression. His relaxed countenance had sobered.

So her suspicion was now confirmed. It made sense. The split of his lip. The swelling of his eye. He'd been attacked. And was he suggesting that the fire might not have been an accident?

A little shudder traveled her spine, and she looked back to the moors, where blackness was already swallowing Sterling Wood whole. She'd never been frightened of the moors, but then again, she'd never been issued such a warning.

He continued, "I will bring my horse for the return ride." She swallowed and nodded, propriety trumped by caution. He disappeared back into the stable, and she tightened her shawl.

As she waited, her thoughts jumbled in chaotic disarray. Yes, she knew what was proper. She should stop him. The impropriety! Walking alone with a man—on the moors—and in the shadow of twilight, no less! And not just any man, but a man of Mr. Sterling's situation. His reputation. She tried to think of any excuse. But it was hard to argue with the visible manifestations that had marred his face. If vagabonds would do so much to a man, what would they do to a woman?

But another sensation, stronger and more prevailing than fear, refused to leave. The unmistakable flutter within her when he touched her cheek last night, in the silence of Rosemere's kitchen. After the fire. When he asked if she would be all right. When, if ever, had anybody, with the exception of Cassandra and perhaps Mary, cared to ask? The idea that he might care, sincerely care, moved her and pushed away her sense of propriety.

He returned from the stable leading a large horse, his beaver hat atop his head, his caped coat billowing around him in the failing light. His face was shadowed, and yet she noticed he was smiling at her.

"Are you sure you will not ride?" he said as he approached. "I can teach you and make a fine horsewoman of you yet."

The humor in his voice had returned but did little to set her at ease. "No, I am certain. I am sorry for you to have to saddle your horse again after you have just taken it off."

"Think nothing of it. Angus here fancies a walk." He nodded toward the path leading to Wainslow Peak. "Shall we?"

At first they walked in silence, their feet crunching the snow and ice the only sound. She was rarely at a loss for words. But he made her . . . nervous.

She could scarcely recall being nervous in the company of others. Not even Ewan O'Connell all those years ago. And yet a new thought fluttered within her, and her palms were clammy. The mystery of William Sterling intimidated her as much as it intrigued her. She tried to think of something clever to say, something to fill the silence. And yet, she was distracted. Distracted by the directness of his gaze when he looked her way. Distracted by the slightest hint of a cleft in his chin. The rich timbre of his voice when he said her name.

Fortunately, it was he who spoke first. "Thank you, Miss Creighton, for tending to my arm last night."

The memory of his closeness renewed her shyness. "My pleasure."

"I, uh"—he looked at the ground as he walked—"I apologize if I made you feel uncomfortable. I did not mean to overstep my bounds. Forgive me."

Patience knew immediately what he was speaking of and was grateful for the darkness, for no doubt her cheeks were flaming pink. "No need for apology, Mr. Sterling."

"I was impressed with the manner in which you handled the children and managed to keep them calm. I would imagine that can be quite a difficult undertaking."

At his questions, she felt her tensions ease, for his interest seemed genuine. "I have been around the school and the children my entire life. Experience has taught me that the best way to keep the children calm is to stay calm myself."

She felt his gaze on her. It warmed her.

His voice was strong and sure. "That school seems to be a great deal of responsibility for one person."

The weight of his praise at first made her uncomfortable, but then a smile tugged at her lips. He had noticed her. Noticed the work she was doing. It felt . . . good. "My father was an excellent teacher. He prepared me well. And my mother is there, of course."

"And what of your brother? Does he not assist?"

Was he yet another person who would believe her brother to be the only one who could tend to the school effectively? And yet, no judgment weighed in his words. She relaxed her shoulders. It was merely a question. "If the truth be told, Mr. Sterling, I do not know where my brother is. In fact, we have not heard from him in months."

She regretted the words as soon as they were free from her mouth. How carefully she'd tried to give the impression that all was well within the walls of Rosemere. But the admission of her brother's betrayal, in a small way, made her feel more free than she had felt in a very long time.

Mr. Sterling looked over at her, his expression sincere. "I'm sorry to hear it."

"We are managing quite fine, my little staff and the girls." She decided to change the subject. "Are you fond of children, Mr. Sterling?"

"Me? Fond of children?"

She cast a sideways glance at him, almost finding amusement in the difficulty he was having answering such a simple question.

He cleared his throat. "Well, with the exception of my niece, I've never been around any."

She'd hoped to hear more about his family, but when he offered no more information on the subject, she said, "Emma seemed quite taken with you."

"Well, she wasn't too pleased with me in the stable during the fire, I can tell you that."

His tone was so light, so seemingly carefree, that she felt her shame of walking alone with a man on the moors dissipate.

They continued down the snow-blanketed path. Patience felt no fear. In fact, the cold silence of the moors calmed the anxiety that had been battling in her mind. She allowed the wind to wash over her. She looked up at the clouds. No stars shone down on her.

The ground beneath her half boots was rocky and uneven, and under the shadow of twilight it would be easy to misstep. Twice she had to sidestep the path, where the mud had turned to slush and snow had blown over the path. She did not wish to seem awkward, yet at the same time, her half boots were no match for the terrain.

She tried to hide her effort, but he noticed. He noticed everything. He extended his arm toward her. She looked ahead toward Rosemere. The walk was still a distance, and with the darkening night and the insufficient support of her shoes, she hesitated. Not only walking alone with a man, but on his arm?

"I only mean to be of assistance."

She allowed her eyes to meet his for a moment, and her heart fluttered.

She stepped as close as she dared, kept her eyes low, and tucked her gloved hand in the crook of his arm. Fire seemed to reach up from the touch, and yet, at the same time, it felt natural. Emotions battled within her as she could feel the muscles in his arm twitch, even beneath the thick wool of his coat. She felt safe. Protected. What surprised her the most was the emotion tightening her throat. How long had she missed this? How long had she longed for support, for someone to share her load, even something as simple as offering her their arm?

She stole a sideways glance at him as he pulled the horse into movement with his other hand. Her heart ached at the beauty of him—handsome out of a fairy tale. Quickly her brief romance with Ewan flashed before her. Could it be William Sterling she had been dreaming of? Waiting for ever since that day that Ewan quitted Rosemere?

But she needed to remember he was beyond her reach. She would be a fool to assume otherwise. He was doing her a kindness. Perhaps out of responsibility. Out of pity. She could not know. For did he not have the name of another woman on his lips just days ago? Were she not careful, her heart would pay a price for her folly.

"I remember you, Miss Creighton."

"Oh?"

"From when we were children. You came with your father to Eastmore. You were sitting in the foyer, waiting."

She did not recall the incident, but the fact that he did brought a smile to her lips.

"You had a doll with you," he added, "and you were showing it to my mother."

"That would have been a very long time ago, indeed."

"Amazing how quickly the years slip by."

He sidestepped to lead his horse around a rock in the path, and by doing so he moved closer to her.

"I heard that you spent a great deal of time in London." She felt brave for bringing up what she had heard of him, but at her words, his lips formed a tight line.

"That is another world away, Miss Creighton. One best left in the past."

"But do you not miss it?" she asked, suddenly hungry to learn as much as she could about him. "Darbury is so small."

His steps slowed until finally he stopped walking altogether. He hesitated and then turned to face her. Night's shadow blurred his features, but his voice was sure. "Have you ever been to London?"

"I have not."

He looked off to the distance, as if carefully choosing his words. "London is brilliant, but it also has a dark side. Do not doubt it, Miss Creighton. For a number of reasons, London is no longer my home."

She searched for the meaning behind every word. "So you will be staying at Eastmore, then?"

A smile warmed his expression in the twilight's bitter cold. "Right now I can think of no reason to leave."

There could be no mistaking his meaning, for at the words, with lead rope in hand, he covered her hand in the crook of his arm with his other hand. At the simple movement, the blood raced through her ears with unprecedented fervor.

"Miss Creighton, I hope I do not overstep my bounds when I tell you that I admire the work you are doing. I do not question your abilities. I only wish to say that if you are ever in need of assistance, I am at your service."

"I thank you for that." Whether it was the darkness of the night or the honest nature of the conversation, she felt emboldened. "I might accept your kind offer. For as much as I love the school, there always is so much to be done."

"And your mother? Does she help?"

She wondered if she would regret sharing her thoughts, her fears. But as the words started to slip from her lips, her confidence grew. She shared snippets of her struggle, and he listened with earnest interest.

They finally stopped outside the courtyard wall's wooden gate. Despite the impropriety of the situation, her heart felt light, her soul, free. Her hand slipped from his arm.

Now that they were back at Rosemere, reality pricked her. She suddenly felt anxious about being discovered, painfully aware of how it would appear for her to be discovered alone with him under the shadows of the birch branches. Her eyes flicked nervously to the top of the house, the only part visible over the courtyard wall. "I must go."

He nodded, but the look in his eyes, the affection in his expression, fixed her to her spot, unwilling to let her go.

Her feet did not seem to obey her command. She tightened her cape around her shoulders, hoping her words did not sound as hopeful as the thoughts running through her mind. "Will we see you at Rosemere soon, Mr. Sterling?"

He looked toward the house and then back at her. A grin dimpled his cheek in the night's dark shadow. "Nothing could keep me away."

13

He should not be so eager to see the woman.

Yet William could think of little else.

How was it possible that in such a brief time, memories of her infused themselves into his mind? Miss Creighton's soft touch when she tended his arm. Her gentle voice as she soothed Emma. The innocence in her expression and the feel of her hand on his arm during their twilight walk on the moors. And those magnificent green eyes.

Ever since the fire he'd been able to entertain no other thought. He had searched for any excuse to visit.

And rebuilding the stable was the perfect reason. Hardly romantic, yet practical. He guessed she would fly away if he should express romantic interest, but the stable and the school were important to her. And with each passing day, they were becoming important to him too.

William knocked sharply on Rosemere's door.

While he waited for an answer, he reminded himself of

one important fact: their lives were different. At one point, the mere fact that he was master of Eastmore Estate and she was the headmistress's daughter would have been enough to keep them apart, but recent events were closing that gap. But if he wanted to rebuild his life and restore Eastmore Hall to its former glory, he needed to stay focused on the prize. Any diversion could prove disastrous—or deadly, if Captain Rafertee's men had anything to do with it.

But one more visit could hardly hurt.

The door opened.

"Ah, George."

"Good day, Mr. Sterling." The burly man opened the door wider and stepped back, out of the way.

William walked in and removed his hat and coat and handed them to the servant. "I've just been out to see Hugh Strong. He will be by tomorrow with plans to begin work on the new stable."

George draped William's coat over his arm. "Good. I'll be expecting him then."

"I've come to speak with Miss Creighton about it. Is she available?"

George ushered him through Rosemere's oblong foyer and down a narrow hall to the study.

Last time he was in the building, William had little interest in his surroundings, but as his attraction to Miss Creighton grew stronger, he found himself wanting to know everything about her—even the little details of the home she grew up in and the school she was so devoted to. But today he noticed the wainscoting. The long string of portraits lining the hall. Everything looked so orderly. So tidy. At least in these front rooms, there was no indication that twenty-nine children lived within these walls. In fact, the silence indicated that the children were either amazingly well behaved or still in shock from the fire.

George opened the door to the study and stepped aside. Miss Creighton looked up and smiled when William entered. She was seated next to the fire with a little girl on her lap, who was wrapped in a blanket, book in hand.

"You'll have to forgive me if I do not rise, Mr. Sterling." Miss Creighton's smile was pretty, her expression relaxed. "We have been reading. You remember Miss Simmons, of course."

Emma stared up at him. Her color was brighter. She looked . . . better. And she clearly recognized him. But the expression of shock that had been on her face when he first saw her was gone. Instead, a sweet smile dimpled her cheeks. "Good day, Mr. Sterling."

He knelt down to look at her at eye level. "And how are you, Miss Simmons?"

Emma's light eyes flicked toward Miss Creighton before refocusing back on him. Her voice was still raspy. "Very well, thank you."

He smiled. "You gave me quite a fright in the stable."

She cut her eyes back to Miss Creighton. Miss Creighton nodded, and the little girl climbed down from her lap. Her small boots tapped as they hit the wood floor, and she shook the folds out of her gown. Primly, she folded her hands in front of her. "Thank you for saving me, Mr. Sterling." Her little chin began to tremble, and she looked again toward her headmistress, then back to him. "I am sorry I disobeyed you."

Taken aback by her sudden apology after such a strong fight, he did not know what he should say. What he should do.

Still down at her eye level, he said, "It is quite all right, young lady. I am happy you are well."

"Miss Creighton said you hurt your arm." Her little eyebrows drew together. "Was it my fault?"

It was his turn to look up to Miss Creighton for guidance. He cleared his throat. "Of course not, Miss Simmons. It was an accident. And besides, it is all better now."

Her thin shoulders seemed to relax, and her words flowed more freely. "And thank you for saving Delilah. She is not really as naughty as everyone says she is. Miss Creighton says maybe when I am all the way better I may go visit her at your house."

"You are welcome to visit her anytime."

He stood, expecting their conversation to be over. But the child stepped even closer. "Did you bring your horse?"

Slightly confused, he asked, "My horse?"

"Yes, the big one."

William had never thought of Angus as a particularly large animal, but he supposed that to someone Emma's size, the horse would seem massive. "Of course. He is out front."

She ran to the window, enthusiasm restored, dark hair swinging at her waist. "He is handsome."

William stood behind her and looked at his mount tied outside. "Yes, I suppose he is."

"Is he the one that hurt you?"

Miss Creighton rose from her seat and stepped toward the child. "Emma!" She placed her hands on the child's shoulders and turned her from the window. "Remember your manners."

Emma pinned him with her gaze. "But he threw you?"

Suddenly, William remembered the conversation he had with the child before the fire. "It was not his fault. It was mine."

"But he threw you."

Miss Creighton caught his eye and then nudged the child backward. "I think that's enough for today."

"But Mr. Sterling said—"

"You can ask him your question later. Mr. Sterling is a busy man. Why don't you find Miss Baden?"

A pout formed on the little girl's lips. "Yes, ma'am." With her shoulders slouched, she dropped a reluctant curtsy. "Good-bye, Mr. Sterling."

He bowed formally, surprised to realize that he was smiling. "Good day, Miss Simmons."

Miss Creighton waited for the door to close behind Emma. "You will have to forgive Emma, Mr. Sterling. The past few days have been upsetting for her. She is still not quite herself."

"No need to apologize, Miss Creighton."

"And do you have news of Charlie?"

"He is well. He helped Lewis shoe one of the horses this morning, and he seems quite natural with such tasks."

An expression of genuine happiness crossed Miss Creighton's face. "Oh, I am so glad to hear it. Won't you be seated?"

"I've no wish to keep you from your duties. I merely stopped by to inform you that there should be men by tomorrow to begin work on the stable."

She clasped her hands in front of her. "Oh, that is excellent news! I was so afraid we would have to wait because of the weather."

"Weather permitting, they should be done relatively quickly. Although the sky is growing dark, I am afraid. Not a good sign."

Wheels suddenly clamored outside. William leaned over to look out the narrow window overlooking the drive below. A black coach drawn by four matching bays lurched to a stop on the circular drive, leaving behind hoofprints and wheel tracks in the snow.

"It appears you have visitors, Miss Creighton."

The young headmistress stood and joined William at the window, bringing with her the scent of rosewater. She looked out, and had he not been looking directly at her, he would have missed how her eyes glazed with tears and her color paled.

Unsure of what to make of the sudden change of demeanor, he said, "Who is it?"

Miss Creighton wrung her hands, then looked out the window once again. "It is my brother. It is Rawdon."

14

A strange mixture of relief and apprehension swirled within Patience as she hastened from her father's study, her guest forgotten, and hurried to the entrance of Rosemere. She could scarcely prevent the quickening of her steps as she flung open the door and stepped into the bitterly cold afternoon.

With Rawdon here, the burden would be shared. Her mother might finally smile. No longer would she have to sort through the daily struggles on her own—a most welcome relief. She no longer cared to know the reason for his absence. What mattered was that he was *here*.

Once outside, her steps slowed at the sight of him, her smile faded. Rawdon stood next to the carriage, his rigid stance suggesting irritation, from his fists bunched on his hips to the firm set of his jaw. His eyes were fixed firmly on the stable's charred remains. The shock of the scene had almost worn off of her, but he was seeing it for the first time.

Patience stepped next to him and placed her hand on his arm.

He flinched at her touch but did not look at her. "How did this happen?" The brusqueness in his question cut deep.

His question was rhetorical, she knew. And she was glad. For how could she begin to explain what she did not understand herself? But the sharpness of his tone chilled her more than the churning air.

His nostrils flared, and his eyes did not waver from the charred heap. "Stables do not simply catch fire, Patience. Something must have happened."

Rawdon's words sounded more like an accusation than a statement. He muttered under his breath and swiped his hat from his head.

Six months had passed since Patience last saw him, but in that time he had not changed. Hair as black as her own curled over his collar, and green eyes, paler and more narrow than hers, were watchful.

He finally looked at her, as if resolving to change the subject, but his question seemed void of sincerity. "Are you well?"

Patience had hoped to find comfort in his expression, but his curtness offered little reassurance. She nodded and rubbed her arm.

"And Mother?"

Patience froze. Had she been a better sister, she would have prepared him in her letters. She should have given him some notice of their mother's altered state, of her depressed mind. But the few letters she had sent him focused on the needs of the school. What good would it have done to burden him with the information before this point? "You will find her much altered."

"How?"

The inflection made her defenses rise. A clever retort toyed on her tongue, but she pressed her lips closed. Arguing with her brother, especially this early after his arrival, could only bring about trouble. "Father's death has been difficult for her."

"As it has been on all of us."

Undoubtedly, her brother had been hurt by their father's death. But to deal with his grief, he had left Darbury—escaped to London, where every object and task did not hold memories. Patience had been left alone to deal not only with the grief of losing her father but the added grief of losing her mother to melancholy thoughts.

She forced a smile, and even though she was angry with him, she harbored an empathetic happiness for her friend, Cassandra, who would be so pleased to see her beau. "Come inside. Mary has kept your room ready for your return. We've been expecting you ever since the fire, and I am sure that Cassandra—"

"Wait."

A hint of light that she remembered touched his pale eyes, and a smile twitched at his lips. "Before we go inside, there is something I must tell you."

Taken aback by his sudden change in demeanor, Patience frowned. "What is it?"

Sudden enthusiasm lit his face. "Well, perhaps I should say there is someone I would like to introduce."

With a small jump in his step, Rawdon stepped toward the carriage and unlatched the black door. Face beaming, he reached inside. Patience sucked in her breath in shock as a dainty pink glove settled in his outstretched hand. Seconds ticked by as a petite blond woman stepped from the carriage, dressed immaculately in a pelisse of rose wool trimmed in rabbit fur. A jaunty cap sat atop smooth blond hair. The woman curled her arm possessively around Rawdon's.

Patience struggled to comprehend what she was seeing and knew her mouth had dropped open at the display, but she had little desire to close it. The woman giggled and turned brilliant blue eyes on Patience.

Patience snapped her mouth shut and looked to her brother, awaiting an explanation. She did not have to wait long.

Rawdon placed his hand on the small of the woman's back. "Patience, I would like to introduce my wife, Mrs. Lydia Creighton."

Patience almost laughed.

Surely he was in jest. She stared, eyebrows raised, while her brother continued the introduction.

"And, my dear, this is my sister, Miss Patience Creighton."

The young woman—who could really not be more than a child of eighteen or nineteen—rushed to Patience, grabbed her hand, and squeezed. Her eyes gleamed from behind long lashes, and her cheeks flushed pink in the cold.

Dread washed over her as she realized that Rawdon was quite serious.

Lydia's words came in such a rush that Patience barely had a chance to comprehend them. "Oh, how I have longed to meet you! I have been asking Rawdon for weeks to come and pay a visit, but you know men. So slow about such things."

Patience drew her hand away and settled it back by her side, ignoring the hurt look on her new sister-in-law's face. She narrowed her gaze on Rawdon. "For weeks? How long have you been married?"

Lydia stepped back next to her husband like a fragile kitten that had been scolded, as if sensing she had spoken too much too quickly.

Rawdon wrapped his arm around Lydia's shoulders and answered on her behalf. "Three months."

No wonder he had been too busy to respond to her pleas for help.

Rawdon lowered his voice, his expression serious, his words thick with innuendo. "I knew you of all people would be pleased."

"Pleased?" Patience wanted to give him every piece of her mind, but the tiny woman next to him looked as if she would burst into tears at any moment. "How did this happen?"

"It happened rather quickly." He turned away from her and tucked his new wife's hand in the crook of his arm. "I will fill you in on the details at another time, but for now I would appreciate it if you would welcome Lydia into our home as a sister."

Our home?

Patience pressed her lips together. This had not been his home for months. Six months, to be exact.

But then the reality of the situation settled in. With her father gone, this school, including the name that bore responsibility for the lease, belonged to him. Even though she was the one who'd assumed the role as headmistress, Rawdon would likely expect to be in charge. She looked at the woman next to him, whose eyes, now brimming with tears, suggested that her reception from her sister-in-law had not been what she had expected.

Patience barely noticed that George had approached to carry in their trunks. Hurt slowly replaced shock. Had he thought her not important enough to share such important news? Did an entire childhood of sharing dreams and goals not warrant a simple letter to inform her of his nuptials? True, they had not been as close in recent years, but what of their mother? Why would he not tell her?

Patience found her voice, and with the servants coming to take the trunks, she did not want to cause a scene. "How long will you be staying?"

Rawdon glanced at his wife. "As long as necessary. And if my Lydia here takes a liking to it, we will make this our home."

Patience swallowed and looked again at his wife, trying to recall her manners through the foggy haze in her mind. "I apologize for my reception, Mrs. Creighton. You must imagine, this is sudden news." Employing every ounce of discipline, Patience tried to smile and extended her hand toward her sister-in-law. "Welcome to Rosemere."

Lydia seemed to relax at the words, and Patience froze as a thought commandeered her mind.

Cassandra.

⚜

Alone in Miss Creighton's study, William sat down.

Then stood.

Then sat again.

The fire crackled, and from somewhere in the school he heard the melodic cadence of children reciting a verse. Then the pings of a pianoforte.

He stood and crossed to the window to look out at the curved drive below. A black carriage with four matching bays filled the drive. One of the horses pawed the earth and whinnied, and the driver was tossing trunks down from the top.

Next to it stood Miss Creighton, the wind whipping long strands of black hair about her face as she talked to a tall man. It had been years since he last saw Rawdon Creighton, but there could be no mistaking the man's identity. Hair every bit as black as Miss Creighton's, he was the spitting image of his father, with a long, narrow face and a tall, lanky form. He failed to recognize the blond woman on his arm, however. Miss Creighton had not mentioned that her brother had taken a wife, but he could hardly doubt that role with the possessive hold she had on Rawdon Creighton's arm.

William made up his mind to leave, to politely excuse himself, but as he turned away from the window and passed by the desk, something caught his eye.

In a shallow box on the desk's corner was a small velvet pouch drawn tight with a silver cord. The item gave him reason to pause. It looked so familiar.

He hesitated.

Could it be the same one that had been in his possession so many years ago?

Rational thought denied the idea that an item, so long ago parted with, would make an appearance on the desk of a headmistress. William studied it again. It couldn't possibly be the same pouch . . . or could it?

He reprimanded himself for the foolish inclination and took several determined steps toward the door. But then he stopped and turned. The silver cord of the pouch gleamed in the late-afternoon light.

It couldn't be. Could it?

Temptation called too loudly. William cast a glance toward the open door to make sure he was alone and then stepped back toward the desk. As soon as the soft fabric touched his fingers, a million ghostly memories were released from their confines. He opened the pouch and tipped it upside down, and was not surprised when an amethyst brooch slid into his palm.

His mother's brooch.

He flipped it over. There, engraved in the setting, were his mother's initials—EAS. He ran his thumb over the scalloped edge.

But how did it get here?

Blood pounded in his ears, making it difficult to decipher his own thoughts. Yes, the piece had been his mother's, but after her death he had given it to Isabelle—on the day he proposed, the last day he saw her.

He'd forgotten about the brooch. But here it was in a box atop a headmistress's desk.

His tailcoat felt too tight, his cravat, like a noose.

As the fog of frustration cleared around him, questions

bombarded him. He curved his fingers around the trinket. The gold grew warm in his hand. He could demand answers of Miss Creighton. But he had the burning suspicion that she was not the person with whom he needed to speak.

He knew full well who—the man he had avoided since the day that man refused to tell him where Isabelle had gone. That man was Isabelle's uncle, the vicar, Mr. Thomas Hammond.

William looked back out to the front drive. Miss Creighton, her brother, and the mystery woman were headed toward the door. He hesitated and then returned the brooch to the pouch and stuffed it in his pocket.

He hurried from the room and met Miss Creighton as she reentered the school. He mumbled a good-bye, murmured a greeting to Creighton, and did not wait for an introduction to the woman. For whatever link this school had to Isabelle's disappearance, he needed to think, and he needed to be far from here.

Far, far from Rosemere.

15

Patience drew a steadying breath. Two tasks lay head of her, neither of which would be pleasant.

First, she needed to talk to her mother, who would either be pleased at her prodigal son's return or angry at him for marrying without any word.

Second, she would speak with Cassandra. This task was even more harrowing than the first, for how could she begin to tell her dearest friend that her beloved had married another?

Patience drew yet another deep breath before opening her mother's door. She forced brightness to her expression and lightness to her voice. "Mother, I have a surprise for you!"

"Close that door at once," her mother scolded. "You will let the chill in, and goodness knows, there is enough draft as it is."

Patience ignored the sharp tone. "I have news. A visitor has arrived."

"I have no wish to see anyone."

Patience retrieved her mother's shawl. "This is a pleasant surprise, I assure you."

"My head aches, Patience. Please, let me be."

"Nonsense. A walk is what you need, then."

Refusing to allow her mother to waste the rest of the day in the confines of her bedchamber, Patience waited as her mother wrapped the shawl around her shoulders and adjusted the cap on her head.

She led the way to the drawing room where she had left Rawdon, trying her best to ignore her mother's complaints on the way down the stairs. Patience half feared and half anticipated her mother's reaction to seeing Rawdon. Perhaps seeing her son would help her escape the dark cloud that had hounded her. But then, the shock of his unannounced marriage might cause her to retreat further.

In the drawing room, when her mother saw her son standing next to the blazing fireplace, a cry escaped her lips and tears flooded her eyes. "Rawdon! My Rawdon!" she cried and ran to embrace him, oblivious of the young blond woman in the corner.

"For shame!" Her mother managed to scold him between sobs. "What took you so long to arrive? We have needed you here. And where have you been? Have you not received our letters?"

Rawdon pulled a handkerchief from his pocket and gave it to his mother. "I did, but I had business to attend to."

"Business?" She pressed the cloth to her eyes. "But what business would pull you away from your family in such a fashion?"

Patience held her breath and watched as her brother's expression beamed and he extended his hand to Lydia.

Margaret Creighton gawked as the woman stepped forward.

"Mother, no excuse can erase my bad behavior, but I do have news that I think may bring you pleasure." Rawdon's chest puffed with unmasked pride, and his face beamed with pleasure. "I'd like for you to meet my wife, Mrs. Lydia Creighton."

Her mother's face went from white to red in the blink of an eye, her graying hair trembling about her face. She then, just as quickly, went quite pale.

Patience could only stare, fearful of her mother's response.

Lydia's sweet expression could not have been warmer or more sincere. She rushed forward. "Mrs. Creighton, it is my greatest pleasure to make your acquaintance."

Patience was quickly realizing that her new sister-in-law's charms would soothe even the most ruffled countenance. Even Patience found herself softening to her presence. Rawdon's wife possessed a natural softness to her voice and a gentleness to her nature that at least on the surface was attractive.

Part of her wanted her mother to throw the outsider from their home. But then she looked at her mother. Was that a smile?

Her mother reached for Lydia. Lydia smiled and took her mother's hand. Her mother embraced Lydia.

This was too much. Too quick. Patience needed air. And quickly.

As soon as a natural break in the conversation presented itself, Patience excused herself from the drawing room's stuffy confines. Sharp pain pulsed through her head, brought on, no doubt, by the sudden shock of her brother's news. Her mother seemed to be welcoming of her new daughter-in-law. But Patience could not make peace with it.

Patience wanted to understand her brother. She wanted to understand why he had stayed away for so long and left her and her mother to deal with the burdens of the school.

But she could not.

And what baffled her even more was how he could do this to Cassandra. Without a word.

Dear, sweet Cassandra. Rawdon had loved her. 'Twas no secret.

For years Rawdon had wooed her. Pursued her. By the light of an early spring moon, Patience had even once spied her friend in her brother's embrace. In her heart of hearts, Patience believed them to have a secret understanding. But Rawdon's announcement of his bride, Mrs. *Lydia* Creighton, dashed that thought.

Patience turned down the hall and moved with slow steps to the east wing. With dinner within the hour, Cassandra would likely be in her bedchamber. The thought of sharing such news with her friend pained her, but it would pain her even more to have her friend find out—or worse yet, encounter the newlyweds—without so much as a warning.

Patience knocked on the door. "Cassandra? Are you in there?"

The door unlatched and swung open. A lighthearted smile lit Cassandra's face. "Patience! Come in. I thought you were in the study."

Patience walked past her friend, gripping and ungripping her hands. "I . . . I was."

"Dearest, what is it?" Cassandra frowned. "Is it Emma? Your mother?"

"No." Then the words rushed from her mouth. "It's Rawdon."

Eager enthusiasm played on Cassandra's soft features. "Rawdon? Have you received news at last?"

The anticipation in Cassandra's tone was like a knife to her own heart. "Yes. Well, that is to say, no."

Cassandra looked confused. "Well, which is it?" Her nervous laugh betrayed her calm expression. "Hopefully it is good news. Perhaps he is returning to Rosemere?"

Patience could not bear the hope in her friend's voice. She squeezed her eyes shut and blurted the words. "He is here but—"

Cassandra flinched, and her mouth fell open in disbelief. Color rushed to her cheeks. "Here? Now?"

Patience nodded.

"Well, I must go to him. I must—"

Patience held up her hands. "Wait."

With every second that passed, Cassandra's smile slowly faded. "Why? What has happened?"

"I must tell you something."

A hesitant laugh slid from Cassandra's lips. "Patience, you are worrying me."

"Rawdon has taken a wife."

Cassandra's face blanched to an unearthly shade of white. "A wife? No . . . no, no. You mean he's . . . he's—"

Patience's stomach churned as she watched her friend try to understand the news. "I am so sorry. It pains me to—"

"You are mistaken, surely." Cassandra spun around, shaking her head in emphatic disagreement, and dropped onto the bed. "I do not believe you."

"You must. He is here, Cassandra." Patience winced with each word, aware each syllable stabbed at an already tender wound. "*She* is here."

Cassandra's dark eyes glazed with tears. "But I don't understand. He's only been away for six months. He told me that I . . . that we—" She wiped the tears from her eyes and drew a steadying breath. "Who is she?"

"I've never met her before. Upon my honor, Cassandra, I have no idea what has happened."

The intensity with which Cassandra shook her head increased, and she repeated her question with sharp enunciation. "Who . . . is she?"

Patience swallowed against the lump of emotion forming in her throat. "Her name is Lydia."

"And she is here." Cassandra made it a statement, not a question.

Patience nodded, her throat tightening.

"Then I must leave." Her friend burst into a flurry of activity and knelt to pull a traveling case from under the bed.

"Leave? No! Why should you leave?"

"I cannot see him. What would I say?" Cassandra's tears now fell freely.

"You have done nothing wrong. You have nothing to be ashamed of."

"How can I stay? How can I face him? Face *her*. Everyone will know. I could not bear it." Cassandra whirled with sudden speed to her wardrobe, pulling clothes and stuffing them in the case. "I will not be here to face him."

"I know how this hurts you. Believe me, I do."

"How could you?" Cassandra shot back. "How could you possibly know? I do not mean to be harsh, Patience, but you have never loved another as I love your brother. Do not fool yourself into thinking that my feelings are like those you had for Ewan. I loved your brother. I *love* your brother. I refuse to be here. Refuse to stay."

"But where will you go?" Patience would not let her protest die. "Rosemere is your home. You are not alone in this, I—"

"How can it be my home?" Her shoulders shook with sobs, each more violent than the last. "This is *his* world, not mine."

"You are wrong. You have lived here most of your life! Plus, it is your livelihood." Patience could not bear the thought of living day after day without her friend. "Do not leave me alone here. I need you."

The reality of her words hit her. How could she survive without the strength of her friend . . . the person who had been her support and confidante since her father's death?

"I am sorry, Patience, but you must understand." Cassandra's chin trembled. "I must go."

16

Patience returned her fork to the table and looked around the small dining room. Evidence of lack of use was all around her. Dust had gathered on the sideboard on the south wall, and the chimney smoked from having been ignored.

This room had once been the room where she, her mother, her father, and her brother escaped from the busy happenings of the school and enjoyed family dinners. Often Cassandra, being Patience's closest friend, would join them. In the years that Ewan O'Connell had lived at Rosemere, he used to take every meal with them in this room. In fact, Lydia occupied the chair that had belonged to him. But in the months following her father's death, the dining room had become a sad space, cold and uninviting.

George had done his best to get a fire sputtering in the grate and bring warmth to the room, but despite his best efforts, a chill blanketed the room. Nevertheless, her mother had insisted that the dinner be held here. Her mother's interest on such matters had become so rare that Patience could hardly deny her.

Patience had a headache. And the mutton on her plate turned her stomach. She wished she could blame her lingering discomfort on the weather or the smoke from the fire, but in truth, she could think of little else besides Cassandra and how Rawdon had hurt her.

Never had she seen Cassandra in such a state. Never had she seen such pain and anguish. Patience had managed to convince Cassandra to not leave in the dark of night, to at least remain until the sun's first light. She hoped that her friend might change her mind before the sun again rose over the moors.

Patience could hardly blame her if she did not.

And this she did know: this was Rawdon's fault.

Patience watched him across the table. Despite the grief he'd displayed at their father's funeral, he seemed to have recovered his charm. Cleanly shaven, he beamed at his wife. He then turned his smile to their mother, who seemed all too jubilant at her son's return.

Patience became aware that her brother had asked her a question, a question she had not heard, so wrapped up was she in her own thoughts. "Pardon?"

"Egad, Patience," he exclaimed, the corners of his mouth turning up in his customary good-natured smile, "you look like you just ate a sour apple."

She wiped a corner of her mouth. Her gaze traveled from Rawdon to Lydia. "You will have to excuse my demeanor, Mrs. Creighton. I've received upsetting news, and I am afraid it has come as quite a shock."

Lydia's round face showed concern, but it was Rawdon who spoke, a twinkle still gleaming in his eyes. "Is it such a surprise that I would find a lady as lovely as Lydia to marry me?"

Was he making light of her? Patience adjusted her napkin in her lap. "It is Miss Baden. Surely you remember Miss Baden,

Rawdon?" She pinned him with a look. If she had not been looking square in his face, she would have missed the twitch of his eye. "She has decided to leave Rosemere."

Patience heard her mother gasp, but she refused to let her brother look away. She did not feel as much satisfaction as she had expected to when she noticed the tremor in his square jaw. She purposely remained silent to let the full effect of her words sink into his conscience. Whatever had befallen him, he had to know the consequences of his actions.

Her mother placed her napkin beside her plate. "What's this? Has she found another position?"

Patience was surprised at how genuine her mother's surprise seemed, for she was fully aware of the relationship between her son and her former pupil. "No, she has not."

Lydia, her voice gentle, said, "Forgive me, but may I ask who Miss Baden is?"

Patience wanted to hear her brother's account of Miss Baden, but when he remained silent, she responded, "Miss Baden is, or was, a teacher here at Rosemere and a great friend. She has lived here since she was a student here herself."

"Oh, I am sorry to hear that she will be leaving."

The sincerity of Lydia's expression took her aback, and Patience felt a little guilty about bringing up such a topic in front of the young woman who could not possibly know the history.

Rawdon cocked an eyebrow, and the look he gave her sent a clear message.

Patience felt a bitter resentment but turned to Rawdon's wife. "Tell me, Mrs. Creighton, where are you from?"

The young woman gave a giddy little shrug. "Oh, please, call me Lydia."

Patience hesitated. To be so casual with one she barely knew felt strange. "Very well, then, Lydia."

"I was raised in London."

"Do you have a large family?"

She pressed her napkin to her lips. "Yes. I have four brothers and two sisters. Plus, I have fourteen cousins, all of whom live, that is to say, *lived* within walking distance."

"A large family, indeed. Well, our family is quite small, as you see, but fortunately there are always people about to keep one from getting lonely. I would imagine that Darbury is quite different from London."

"It is, but from what I have seen, it is lovely. Very quiet. And the air is clean."

Her brother leaned his elbow on the table. "Lydia's father is Mr. Archibald Daring. You remember Mr. Daring, do you not?"

At the mention of the name, recognition burned bright. "Of course. Mr. Daring." Patience remembered the man well. Her father's business partner. He'd visited on several occasions, especially when she was younger, and provided funds more than once to the school.

This was not a conversation for the dinner table. Patience cast a glance at her mother and could only assume by her relatively jovial demeanor that she was pleased with Rawdon's return and the introduction of his wife. "Mother, is Lydia's gown not lovely? I don't know when I have seen fabric in such a lovely shade of blue."

Lydia nodded. "It is lutestring. I adore it. I had hoped that upon arriving here in Darbury I might find a seamstress. I would like to have one or two new dresses made, now that we are settling down."

Patience cocked an eyebrow and turned to her brother. "You will be staying for a long while, then?"

He obviously took offense at the question. Irritation flashed in his eyes. "This is my home, is it not?"

In his will their father had been specific that the responsibilities and business of the school should pass to her brother. It had

been Rawdon whom their father had named to see to the future
of the school. Rawdon whom their father named the headmaster.
And as the man in the family, he was the one to continue the lease
for the land, not her.

Patience had been hurt by this provision, more than she cared
to admit. At one point in the past, every member of the family had
been heavily involved with the running of the school, so much so
that it seemed impossible to separate the family members from the
school itself. She had embraced it. But since their father's death,
Rawdon had done his best to reject the school and the responsibilities accompanying it.

She had always imagined that the school would continue on
as it always had. But now that her brother was the one their father
had specified to be in charge, would it? His lack of participation
since their father's death gave her reason to wonder. In light of his
changed circumstances, did he have other plans?

"I only meant to inquire about how long you would be here,
Rawdon. No need to get in a tizzy." She returned her attention to
Lydia, and with the gown having been discussed, she noticed that
the sleeves did seem too tight. "Well, if you need something done
quickly, our Mary can let out or take up a gown. As quickly as these
girls grow, she has had much practice. There is a seamstress in the
village of whom we are quite fond. Of course, her work does not
equal that of what can be found in London, but she has always done
good work for us."

For the first time, Lydia seemed to relax. "Thank you. I should
like to visit her."

"No need to visit her. I will send for her. I am certain she would
be more than happy to visit us here at the school. In fact, a few of
the girls' dresses are in need of alteration."

Patience watched her brother the rest of the evening. She hoped
to find time to speak with him alone, but no opportunity presented

itself. She decided one thing: Cassandra would not leave because of Rawdon's actions. She made it her mission to make sure Cassandra would stay at Rosemere, where she belonged.

William slowed Angus from a canter and trotted into a clearing at Ambledale Court, Jonathan Riley's estate. A dusting of snow swirled around him.

He should have come earlier. Night fell early across the moors, especially this time of year. But then as quickly as the thought entered his head, he chided himself for feeling anxious. Never before had he allowed fear to rule his actions. Now was not the time for timidity or to second-guess a decision.

Riley's butler had the door open before he even handed Angus's reins to the stable boy. The observant servants scurried about their tasks with pinpoint precision—prime examples of how a house *should* function.

He thought of his own Eastmore Hall, a mere shell of its former glory, with most of the rooms closed and a skeleton crew of servants. He chose not to dwell on that fact and, instead, reminded himself that agreeing to the proposal from Riley could take a step toward regaining his life.

He needed to learn everything he could.

William followed Ambledale Court's poker-straight butler to the billiard room, where he heard—and recognized—Riley's voice. Another voice, which was much lower and possessed the slightest bit of a Scottish lilt, he could not place. Once he entered the smoke-filled room, Riley was immediately at William's side, cue in one hand, goblet in the other. "Ah, finally! See, Carlton, I knew he would not let us down."

William watched as the heavy-set, middle-aged man came

toward him. He'd expected the man to be younger. More agile. His greasy hair was tied in a queue at the base of his neck. Unkempt sideburns did their best to hide pockmarks on his cheeks.

The man's mouth seemed too large for his face, his spectacles, too small. "Sterling, I presume. Been waiting to meet you. Heard you have a bonny bit of land, ripe for commerce."

William nodded, not ready yet to respond. He'd never been one to judge a character too quickly. Perhaps a characteristic he should reconsider.

The man said, "Your estate is near here, am I correct?"

William nodded. "You are, sir. Eastmore Hall. Due east."

"Ah."

Riley propped his foot on an ottoman and rested his elbow on his knee. "Got himself some pretty ponies on that estate, at that. Too bad you're not a horseman."

"Do you?" Carlton lowered himself back down into his chair. "Don't mind if I sit a spell, do you, Sterling? Blasted gout." Carlton rubbed his leg before settling back against the chair. "So, you are interested in joining us on this venture, so I hear?"

"Considering it." William moved to the fire to warm himself after the ride. "Riley here tells me you have had quite a bit of success in the textile business."

"Wool. That's where the money is, lad. If I can only keep the bloody heathens and riots away from my looms. Rowdy lot."

William glanced over at Riley, whose expression suggested he was eager to squelch any chatter that might lead to misgivings related to their venture.

Riley leaned in. "Well, you won't have to worry about them here in Darbury. Quiet town, am I right?"

William shrugged.

Carlton's raspy laugh filled the space. "That's what I like to hear." The hours passed by and William's tension eased, whether from the comfort of being introduced to new company or the effect of the port. After he decided to call it an evening, William showed himself to the room where he always stayed when a guest at Riley's estate . . . the Blue Room.

With naught but a lighted tallow candle in a pewter holder, William settled in for the night. A fire had been lit in the room in anticipation of his arrival, and it had died down, the embers in the grate glowing orange and red. No moonlight filtered through the windows. The fire's shadows danced on the walls that had been painted such a dark blue that they looked black in night's darkness.

He sat on a chair next to the fire to remove his boots, but the smoldering embers distracted him. He could not help but be reminded of the blaze at Rosemere.

And, by association, the expression of strength on Miss Creighton's face.

He removed his coat and, at the movement, felt the weight of the brooch still in the welt pocket of his waistcoat.

How he hoped that when he reached his fingers in the pocket the brooch would not be there—that the entire ordeal was but a strange misgiving. But his fingers grasped the object, still secure in the fabric pouch.

As he held the jewelry, he thought about the proposed business alliance with Riley and Carlton. What would his father have done? But throughout the evening, he could not help another thought: What would his mother have done? As much as his father had poured every ounce of energy into his land and his work, his mother had poured every ounce of her being into her faith. How she had tried to instill in him a faith. But his will had been too strong. How he wished he could recall the verses she used to recite to him as a boy. He had thought them meaningless at the time. As he struggled with his feelings of abandonment and the sting of his failures, he tried to remember—he wanted to remember.

His mother had prayed daily. He had thought it a ridiculous waste of time. But she had been at peace. Even when trials littered her path, she was never riled.

Maybe she had been on the right path after all, and he had been the ridiculous one.

17

The next morning Patience sat at the desk in the study, intent on clearing the mess away. The fact that her brother returned the day her office was in shambles embarrassed her. She moved several boxes to the armoire, pausing once again to sift through the contents of Emma's box, hoping to stumble upon something she had missed.

After placing Emma's things in the armoire, she stood at the window and watched the men working on the stable, just as Mr. Sterling had promised. One man raked up debris. Another man in a dusty coat and floppy hat guided a mule pulling a cart, and yet another stacked lumber off to the side. The new stable clearing looked larger. Mr. Sterling seemed to have not held back on the expense. She wondered at the necessity of it, seeing as they only had one carriage, two horses, a pony, a cow, a goat, and a smattering of fowl. But he had been insistent on the details.

Now Patience wondered about him. Were the stories she had heard about him true? Was he as reckless as they had said? And why had he left Darbury all those years ago? And now he was back. She had heard rumors of financial troubles, of servants being dismissed. If the rumors were true, what would account for the fine stable he was having built at Rosemere?

"I hope I am not interrupting."

Patience turned to see Lydia peeking around the door. Surprised that her sister-in-law was even up at this early hour, Patience motioned for her to enter. Lydia's blond hair was perfectly curled and swept away from her face, and even though her jonquil silk gown was a bit ornate this early in the day, Patience could not help but compare its fine detail to her own drab frock. "I trust you slept well."

"Oh, I did." Lydia smiled and blew out a shaky breath. "Traveling always exhausts me. I feel I could sleep for days!"

Patience returned the smile but could hardly relate. She'd had little opportunity to travel outside of Darbury, except for the summer when her father took her to Manchester to pick up a student.

Lydia opened a book on the corner of the desk and turned a few pages before looking at Patience. "I want to assist."

"Assist?"

"Yes. With the school. Both my father and Rawdon have told me of the work you do here, and I am eager to be a part of it."

Patience drew a sharp breath, feeling almost sorry for the girl. Lydia was but a child, hardly a woman. Could she be any older than the oldest pupils, still preparing to make their way in the world? "Here, sit here. What is it you would like to help with?"

"Teaching."

Patience swallowed, unsure how to handle the feeling that the new Mrs. Creighton was treading too far into her world. "Do you like children, Mrs. Creigh—I mean, Lydia?"

Her eyes brightened. "Oh yes. Quite. I even helped teach my young cousins to read."

Not knowing what else to say, Patience muttered, "You must miss your family."

Lydia nodded and looked at the floor. "Indeed. But God is good, is He not? He has given me a husband and a new sister in you. I miss my family, but I shall see them again."

The words of God spoken so freely took Patience aback. "Well then, what is it that you would like to teach? Have you a special area of interest?"

"I play the pianoforte. And I sing. Rawdon says that both of those are taught here."

"Indeed, they are." Patience felt a twinge of guilt for not being more welcoming to this young woman who was far from home. She offered a smile. "I will speak to the other teachers. I am sure they will be grateful for the assistance."

Patience was about to say more, but the study door flew open, as it did nearly every day, and there, in the doorway, stood Cassandra.

Cassandra's flushed expression changed when she beheld Lydia.

Patience jumped to her feet, fearing that Cassandra would disappear as quickly as she had come or, worse yet, would say something she might regret.

Patience rushed to Cassandra and took her by the arm. Her friend was trembling. Clearly, Cassandra had figured out Lydia's identity. Patience wanted to soothe the pain that she knew must ache, but at some point, the women needed to meet. As long as Cassandra was at Rosemere, it was inevitable.

"Lydia, allow me to introduce Cassandra Baden, a teacher here and a great friend."

Lydia stood and smiled, seemingly oblivious to any discomfort, and clasped her hands before her. "How lovely to meet you, Miss Baden."

Patience winced at Lydia's unchecked enthusiasm. Her pretty brightness. She cast a quick glance, taking note of the subtle gathering of moisture in Cassandra's brown eyes and the slight reddening of her nose. The words felt dry in her mouth, yet Patience continued, "And Miss Baden, my sister-in-law, Lydia Creighton."

She marveled how Cassandra managed a smile, a proper greeting, and a nod, all before politely dismissing herself.

Lydia gave a little giggle as Cassandra closed the door behind her. "I think I shall be happy at Rosemere, Miss Creighton."

Patience eyed the empty space where her friend had been standing. Time was changing. Everyone around her was changing, moving in their own rhythms. Could it be that she was changing too?

18

A few hours later Patience sat across from Lydia in the drawing room while they worked on their embroidery. Her
mother had even joined them, and little Louisa, who was
feeling poorly, slept on a sofa just across from Patience, her head
on Lydia's lap. As she stole another glance at Lydia, Patience was
reminded of the Shakespearean tragedy she had read with the girls
so many times—Brutus betraying Julius Caesar.

Cassandra was in an upstairs room, weak from crying and sorrow, and here she sat with the woman who was at the source of her
dearest friend's heartache. Patience had managed, after the awkward interchange between Lydia and Cassandra in the study, to
convince Cassandra to remain at Rosemere until she at least found
another position. In the light of this new day, Cassandra seemed
more rational, but even with this small victory, Patience feared losing her friend forever.

Patience shifted uncomfortably and looked at her mother,
enveloped in a wingback chair. She was clad in modest black

bombazine with a widow's cap atop her graying head. For the first time in months, the older woman's pudgy fingers worked an embroidery needle. The lines on her face seemed softer today, and her color was decidedly improved. Patience looked down at her own embroidery. Red roses intertwined with ivy with a most intricate backstitch. She had embroidered a verse her father had often quoted:

> *Trust in the Lord with all thine heart; and lean not unto thine own understanding. In all thy ways acknowledge him, and he shall direct thy paths.*

The words, which she had worked with such love, seemed vacant, hollow.

At any other time Patience would have been pleased that her mother was resuming one of the tasks she had enjoyed. But instead, the step forward was bittersweet. Patience remembered how for months she had been unable to rouse her mother from despair. With Rawdon's return, her mother had joined them for dinner last night and seemed to enjoy Lydia's company. Patience should be grateful, but her heart would not allow it.

As Patience pulled out an incorrect stitch, she stole several glances at her new sister-in-law. Earlier that morning Lydia had looked pale, fragile. By early afternoon, she seemed much improved. Pinkness colored her cheeks a becoming hue, and her eyes, bright blue, were fixed firmly on her needlework.

"Your work is quite lovely," Patience said.

Lydia looked up and smiled. "Why, thank you. I fear my governess spent many hours trying to teach me the art. You would think for all of her teaching my skill would be greater than it is."

Patience lowered her work. "You were educated by a governess?"

"Indeed." Lydia looked wistfully to the ceiling before turning back to Patience. "Miss Wimple. She first taught my older sisters. She has been with my family for as long as I can remember."

Lydia appeared barely old enough to be out of her governess's care. Even with her hair swept high above her head, her fair skin and fresh expression made her seem so young. "Forgive me for asking, Lydia, but what is your age?"

"Eighteen." A playful smile curved her lips. "And I can guess what you are thinking."

Patience bit her tongue. There is no way Lydia could possibly guess what was in her mind.

"I am young to marry, to be sure, but my father was pleased. Rawdon is an impressive young man, and my father has long admired him and found the match most agreeable."

"And why would he not?" Patience's mother beamed proudly. "Rawdon is the kindest man. So like his father."

Patience saw—and seized—the opportunity to learn more. "How did you become acquainted with Rawdon?"

"It was just under six months ago at a ball my parents were hosting, and my father introduced me to him. The first time I danced with him, I knew my heart had been captured."

Patience drew a steadying breath. Her brother at a ball? So soon after their father's death? She swallowed her misgivings and looked down at her needlework. "Your courtship was quick, indeed."

"Yes." Lydia sighed, and a flush rushed to her cheeks. "However, I fear I am quite a romantic. Some things are meant to be."

The talk continued until the late-afternoon sun created long shadows across the drawing room's modest rug. Despite her reservations when she sat down, Patience was surprised to find herself actually becoming fond of her new sister-in-law. The young woman possessed an easiness, an openness. And it was nice to finally hear her mother laugh.

Eventually a comfortable silence settled over the room. Patience allowed herself to enjoy this free time, the diversion of her needlework. But it wasn't long before a carriage sounded on the drive. She heard a man shout.

Patience looked up. They'd been expecting a new student—a young girl from Manchester.

"That must be the new Sutter girl, although I wasn't expecting her for another day or two." Concerned, Patience put down her needlework and went to the window.

On the drive, the carriage rocked to a stop, and a tall, thin man with a tall beaver hat and caped greatcoat stepped down. Patience frowned and squinted, trying to get a better view, but the man's hat brim blocked his face.

No child exited the carriage. Something about the man's gait seemed familiar and gave Patience reason to pause. His arms swung in a recognizable manner when he walked.

Unable to contain her curiosity, Patience hurried down to the entrance in time to be present when George opened the front door.

"Can I help you, s—" Her words dissolved into silence as she beheld the man. He was far from a stranger. In fact, no man could be less of one. For before her stood none other than Ewan O'Connell. She could not have been more surprised if the Prince Regent himself stood outside her doorway.

"Ewan," she stammered, barely able to hear her own words over the violent beating of her heart. Then, realizing she had addressed him by his Christian name, she quickly corrected herself. "I mean, Mr. O'Connell."

She could not think of an appropriate welcome. Her disciplined etiquette fled. Her wit slowed.

He returned her stare, his light brown eyes fixed on her, as if he were as shocked to see her as she was to see him. He snatched his hat from his head clumsily and held it in midair. Then an easy smile crept over his lips, crinkling the corners of his eyes. "Patience Creighton. I trust you are well."

Patience remembered to breathe. Such formality from the person who had shared her schoolroom. Shared her family's table. Even proposed marriage to her!

Memories of the day she refused him flashed before her. His red-rimmed eyes. The hurt. Today, quite another man stood before her. A much more confident man who now did not seem the least bit affected by seeing her again.

"Indeed, I am." She suddenly felt dizzy, as if she had seen a ghost. But Mr. O'Connell was no ghost.

Patience grew uncomfortable under the weight of his gaze, and she finally managed to find her voice. "What brings you to Rosemere, Mr. O'Connell?"

He stepped closer, his smile never leaving. He seemed to tower over her. Indeed, he was much taller than she remembered. "Your brother asked for my assistance."

Rawdon? Rawdon knew about this? If Rawdon knew Ewan was coming, why did he not say as much?

The grin on Ewan's face faded. "I see Rawdon did not mention I was coming."

"I am sorry, he did not." Patience forced a pleasant expression to her face. She had navigated through difficult situations several times this month alone, and she would manage through this one. "But you are always welcome at Rosemere, Mr. O'Connell."

She must have looked quite the simpleton, standing dumb-struck, staring at the man as if he were a court jester.

"Dare I presume that my room is still available?" His Scottish lilt was much less pronounced than it had been those many years ago.

His room? She thought of the small chamber on the third floor he had stayed in, the room directly above where she slept. Did he still think of that as his own after he abandoned them in the middle of the night?

A wave of guilt swept over her. Or, in truth, did he feel pushed out of their family by her refusal?

"Of . . . of course," she stammered, absently smoothing her hair from her face. "George will take your things up and will see that a fire is started."

"Thank you." Ewan adjusted his satchel over his narrow shoulders and turned away as if to follow George, but then stopped and turned back. His eyes locked on her in a manner that was far too intimate. Far too possessive. "It is good to see you again, Miss Creighton."

Miss Creighton. Never before had he ever called her that. Always Patience. "Let me call for my brother, Ew—Mr. O'Connell. He will be—"

Before her lips could form the rest of the words, Rawdon burst through the front entrance. "O'Connell! I thought I heard a carriage! Good man," he exclaimed, clasping the man on the shoulder.

"Creighton."

"I see you have already been reacquainted with Patience."

"Yes." Ewan looked at her with those eyes again. The eyes that, even when they had been children, felt as if they could see to her soul. "It has been too long."

She shifted uncomfortably, wishing that any interruption would come. A girl running in the hall. A pupil needing assistance. But for once, the hall was quiet.

Desperate to end the suffocating silence, she blurted out, "How long will you be staying?"

A flash of confusion darkened his features, then a smile appeared. "Well, that remains to be seen."

Patience tried to resume her normal day—or as close to normal as she could manage.

She led the older girls in their arithmetic exercises, checking sums on slates and nodding in confirmation or pointing out errors. But her attention was diverted.

She tried to focus on addition, but thoughts of her brother and Ewan dominated. How could Rawdon ask him to return, knowing their history? And furthermore, not even make mention of it?

She needed to speak with Rawdon privately to ask him what she could not ask in the presence of an audience. She'd not had a moment alone with her brother since his return. She wanted to hear from him why Ewan was here and what his intentions for the school were. And she needed to hear why he had betrayed Cassandra. She had tried to remain calm, tried to give her brother space to readjust, but that was before he brought back a ghost from her past. Without even so much as a warning.

When she finally finished with lessons, Patience sent her young charges off for quiet study and hurried upstairs. She flew into her room and closed the door.

Her bedchamber, even though small, was peaceful. She used to imagine that the floral wallpaper was a garden and she was hiding there amid the fairies and pixies. Her furniture, although dark and old, was like a cherished friend. The bed had comforted her when she was ill. The chair next to the window had wrapped its arms around her when she cried. It bore witness to her secret dreams. Her ambitions. Her regrets.

But all peace vanished when she heard the click of boot heels on the wooden floor above her—a sound she had not heard since Ewan left Rosemere six years ago.

Surely her heart should feel a sensation besides this unrest. Ewan O'Connell had been her one romance—if such a fickle inclination could be called such.

She walked to her window and looked down at the spot where Ewan had proposed those many years ago. On that fine August afternoon, the school was hosting a picnic, and she and Ewan had been sitting on a quilt beneath the large elm. She'd been but nineteen. She recalled how the sun filtered through the rustling leaves, dappling his chestnut hair. The conversation was as vivid in her mind as if it were again the day it occurred. He'd been dressed in a tailcoat of light brown linen and speaking of his plans to attend the university. He had always been a dreamer, with ambitions limited only by the constraints of his own mind. As her father's pupil, he shared many of their beliefs. He was easy to talk to. Familiar. Safe.

She had never doubted his affection for her. And over time, as his brotherly affection deepened to romantic regard, she relished in his attention. His infatuation had been obvious, and she, a silly young woman, encouraged him. She had not realized the extent of his feelings, however, until that day. She recalled the pain in his eyes when she refused him. And on the yard that day was the last time she saw him. Until today.

Why had Ewan returned after all these years? Was it really to help her brother? She did not dare to think that he would return for her. The thought of a second chance to have a family stirred her. At one time she had loved him as a brother. Never did she love him as a woman loves a man. But marriage would provide security. It would provide an opportunity for a family. Love might come later. Or it might not come at all. But at least she would not be alone.

Whatever Ewan's intentions, he would not have returned without the invitation from her brother. There must be a reason why Rawdon wanted Ewan to return, more than the excuse of needing help running the school.

It was silly to waste time wondering. She would simply ask Rawdon outright.

19

She didn't bother to rehearse what she would say. Patience stomped down to the main floor, nodded at two students as she passed them in the corridor, and did not slow her pace until she reached the study.

The paneled door stood ajar, and through the opening, she spied her brother sitting at the desk, quill in hand.

How much he looked like their father, with his black hair, white cravat, and dark coat, sitting at the desk where their father had so often sat. Haunting memories of the two of them as young children rushed at her. It had been such a different time. Such a happy time. Full of broad dreams and hopeful promise.

Rawdon did not look up from the letter he was writing when she walked in. "I was wondering how long it would take for you to come here."

"What do you mean?"

He lowered his quill and leaned back. The chair creaked beneath his weight. "O'Connell."

She folded her arms across her chest, determined to stay

rational and controlled. "Why is he here? I do not know what you are doing." Although her intent was to remain calm, once she opened her mouth, the words flew as if they had wings. "First you abandon Mother and me when we needed you, then you betray Cassandra. How can you be so unfeeling? To Cassandra? And Ewan? How do you expect me to react? Just to stand idly by and—"

"Stop."

"No, I won't, Rawdon. You need to hear what—"

"I said stop!"

Stunned, she snapped her mouth shut. Never before had she heard him shout. Never.

He yanked at his cravat. "What's done is done. I'll not apologize for the decisions I have made, nor do I need to explain them. As for Cassandra, I will not speak of her. And neither will you. Not to me. Not to Lydia. Am I clear?"

The blood began to pound in Patience's ears, and suddenly the lazy fire in the hearth seemed much too warm. A million retorts tumbled in her head. But the harshness in his eyes silenced her. She did not like the direction this conversation was taking.

His cheek twitched. He examined the quill, then threw it down on the desk. "I did not abandon you. I did what I needed to do to keep my promise to Father."

At this, she could not remain silent. "I don't see how."

His eyes narrowed. "Do not fool yourself. You knew the extent of Father's debt. I told you. I went to London to speak with one of Father's financiers."

"And while you were there you just happened to get married."

"That is not a crime."

Tension intensified, making the air even thicker than when the stable fire's smoke wove its way through the rooms. Rawdon was a good man. An intelligent one. And a lifetime with him had taught her that if she chose to engage him in a debate, she'd likely lose.

There was time enough to get all of her questions answered. She needed to focus on why Ewan was here.

"All that does not explain why Ewan is here."

"Neither one of us knows how to run this school."

Patience sucked in a deep breath at the insulting blow. "And what do you think I have been doing these many months?"

"Will you hear what I have to say before you become defensive? Ewan was the one who learned how to be an educator from Father. Not me. Even though Ewan has been gone for many years, I knew he would know what to do. And I was right. He's been headmaster of a boys' school in London for the past three years."

Patience pursed her lips and looked over at the fire. Angry as she was, she could not look her brother in the eye as he stepped out from behind the desk and walked toward her.

"You are aware of the financial situation of this school. Things cannot continue as they are. Besides, you are not a headmistress."

She winced at the offense and met his gaze with her own unwavering one. "What do you mean, not a headmistress? What else have I been doing?"

"Nurse? Governess?" His voice oozed with condescension. "I don't know what you have been up to, Patience, but do not fool yourself. You might as well be aware of my intentions. I am opening a boys' school in addition to the girls' school to make money, and I need O'Connell's help."

Patience felt as if she'd been struck in the chest. "A boys' school? You cannot be serious."

"If this school is to be profitable, we need more students."

"Then we will take on more girls." Frustration propelled her to the window, where the cool air seeping in around the casings cooled her. "Father would never have approved."

"Do you not remember? It was Father's plan. If—when—he ever turned a profit."

"We have done well as a girls' school for over thirty years. This was Father's vision."

"Well, Father's vision is going to bankrupt us all. He may have been able to survive and thrive on his ideals, but I have a different future in mind for my family."

"But we don't know the first thing about educating boys."

"O'Connell does."

His words smacked as sharply as a slap across the face. There was his argument. This is why he brought Ewan back.

"We don't have the funds to invest in expanding. You said so yourself that the school's financial situation is less than stable."

"I have Lydia's dowry, which is substantial enough to apply toward such a venture." Patience shot him an incredulous look, and he quickly added, "And Lydia knows full well my intentions."

"So you married that poor girl for her fortune? Rawdon, how could you—"

"Of course I did not marry her solely for her fortune," he hissed. "But I did also need to consider my future. And Mother's. And yours."

Patience winced at the reference to herself. He thought her a burden. His spinster sister whom he was obligated to provide for.

Rawdon walked to the fireplace and turned to face her. "Neither of us is fit to do the work that Father did. He and O'Connell are of the same school of thought. I have decided we need O'Connell, and I have hired him to run things. And that is final."

Patience felt again as if she had been struck. The past few months had been hard, but she had poured her everything into them. Her heart. Her soul. And he was not even going to give her a chance to prove herself. "The situation is not as dire as you think. I have been overseeing the books. After all, someone had to." Patience could not prevent the biting retort from slipping her lips. "Perhaps if you had stayed instead of leaving right after Father's death, you would understand how things are."

His face reddened. "Do not speak of things you do not understand. I was the one Father named to run the school, not you. And I have taken the necessary steps to secure our futures. The school's future. And since I have returned and seen things with my own eyes, I am even more certain of the path that must be taken."

Patience was not about to give in without speaking her mind. "And where do you propose that you will house these boys?"

"In the west wing."

"The west wing? But that is where we live. How do you—"

"We will build a cottage. On the grounds. You and Mother will live there. With Lydia and me."

Patience crossed her arms. "Have you spoken with Mother about this?"

"No."

"She will not leave Rosemere."

"Are you so sure? She is miserable here."

"She is miserable only because she is still grieving. She would grieve anywhere she was. This is her home."

"Her home, yes. But there are too many memories here for her. I can see that, and I have been home only one day." His voice lowered. "You may not believe me, but I am thinking of you too."

Patience sniffed. "There is no need to concern yourself with me."

For the first time since his return, Rawdon's words softened. "This is no life for you, Patience, cooped up here. Working day in and out. You need to be married, you—"

At the word, heat rushed to her face. "I do not need to be married. I am doing fine on my own."

"Do you not wish for a family?"

She needed to make him understand. "This is my calling,

Rawdon. This is why God put me on this earth. I've no desire to marry."

"Every woman desires to marry."

"What a presumptuous thing to say." She tapped her index finger on the desk. "My place is here. I am happy here." As soon as the words were out of her mouth, things started to make sense. "So this is why you had Ewan return. Did you think of him as a suitor for me?"

Rawdon shrugged. "He's a good man. And after all these years, he remains unmarried. I never understood why you refused him."

Her chin trembled. "How dare you meddle with matters of the heart. *My* heart. I already made my decision on that point quite clear, and it has not changed. Really, Rawdon. I will not have this conversation with you." She stomped from the room and slammed the door, her face flaming with embarrassment and anger.

Did he think she was not capable of knowing her own heart?

ℒ

"So here it is," muttered William as he dismounted Angus, planting his feet firmly on the iced grass. "Latham Hill."

He heard Carlton dismount behind him, his boots crunching the unmarked snow.

"Yes." Carlton groaned, his breath heavy from the exertion and puffing white in the frigid air. "Very nice, indeed."

Riley walked in front. The raw wind swept from the bare birch branches and caught his great coat, billowing it behind him. "See, Carlton, just as I told you. The river is down past those trees. See there? The trees will need to be removed, but there is a shortcut that runs along the river to town square. Even a bridge. Nothing extravagant. Ideal location."

Carlton pivoted on his heel, surveying the land along Sterling Wood, a greedy gleam in his eyes. "Yes. And what's that over there?"

William followed the direction of his nod. Rosemere's stone chimneys rose above the barren tree line, and the new stable was visible through the black branches.

William said, "That's Rosemere."

Carlton raised an eyebrow. "Tenants of yours, I presume?"

William nodded. "Yes, sir. It's a school run by the Creighton family."

Riley folded his arms across his chest and looked toward the school. "That bit of land is the jewel in the Eastmore property crown, is it not, Sterling?" A smile spread across Riley's broad face, but his voice held a hint of . . . something. Contempt? Annoyance? Riley turned back to Carlton. "But he'll not sell it. No, sir. Won't sell this land either. Believe me, I've tried to buy it myself a time or two."

William gritted his teeth, then relaxed his jaw. "Like I've said before, the land is not for sale. Besides, Rosemere is leased. If you want to buy a horse, I can help you, but the land is off limits."

The older man shifted his weight and looked out to the moors. "Everything has a price, lad."

A sickening feeling swept over William. If he would sell even a portion of his land, his problems with Rafertee would be over. Like that. But the fullness of unfulfilled expectation weighed on him. If he had any pride, any dignity left, he needed to keep his birthright intact. Or at least have a better reason for parting with it than covering his gambling debt.

William studied Carlton, watching the portly man's every movement. He walked over to the edge of a large boulder and rested an arm on top of it. "We are discussing a partnership, not a land sale. If I am mistaken, make your intentions clear, for I have other matters to attend to."

Riley stepped between them, holding his hands out as one would to a horse. "Gentlemen. Sterling's right. Nobody is going to buy or sell any land. We just need a location. And this one should suit nicely."

Carlton seemed to let his argument go. He knelt down, brushed the snow away, and dug a clump of loose, frozen dirt and rocks out with his stocky fingers. "It would take awhile to get supplies up here to build, but once we did, shouldn't take too long. Weather depending, of course. Might have to wait a bit more toward spring, after it warms up. Must be fireproof. Getting the iron here will take the longest."

William tried to concentrate on the man's plans, but his gaze kept flitting to Rosemere. The mist hung heavy, shrouding the building in filmy drapes. What would Miss Creighton think of having a mill so close to the school? It would be visible. Traffic would increase. The path leading from Darbury to Eastmore and running behind Rosemere would likely become a road, just on the other side of the stable fence.

Why should he care? This was his property, was it not?

But he *did* care.

He did want to please her. To know she was happy.

Riley laughed at something Carlton said, jolting William back to the task at hand. But his thoughts were far from the conversation occurring on Latham Hill and far more intrigued with what was going on inside the walls of Rosemere.

"So let's forget about this selling land business and get down to mill business." Riley rubbed his hands together. "Do we start building, gentlemen?"

Both pairs of eyes were on him. William drew a deep breath and then nodded slowly.

A short laugh burst from Riley, and he slapped William on the back. "You won't regret this, mark my words."

20

As William rode down the narrow path from Latham Hill, heading to the shortcut to Eastmore Hall, he mulled over his conversation with Riley and Carlton. The answer seemed so obvious. They would build the mill. He would share in the profits. It sounded good, too good.

And that was what worried him.

He recalled seeing a mill in Manchester similar to the one that Riley had described. It was big. Dirty. Carlton had promised that the mill he proposed would be relatively small. But what if it was indeed successful and expanded? Was he prepared to evict tenants to free more land? And what of the local weavers? He knew of at least two men, one of whom was a tenant, who made his livelihood by selling wool.

As he wound his way toward Wainslow Peak, he sat up straighter in the saddle and arched his neck. Through the branches of the trees, he could see the stone walls of Rosemere. The setting sun painted pink ribbons against a darkening sky, the shadows making the snow appear almost blue in the fading light. All was quiet on the school's grounds. Light poured from several windows, and a shadow could be seen passing a window on the second floor.

So full of life.

So different from Eastmore Hall.

William and Angus moved farther down the path, and through the trees, he saw two men walking around the new stable. He recognized Rawdon Creighton. After the shock of discovering his mother's brooch the previous day and not wanting to intrude on their reunion, his words to Creighton had been short. Instead of continuing on his way home, he turned toward Rosemere. In the still hours of evening, he found a gate in the stone wall and rode up to the new stable.

"Ah, Sterling," Creighton exclaimed as he drew closer. "Come to check on the progress?"

William stopped his horse by the men. "I was riding to Eastmore and saw you out here." He looked at the building in progress, squinting to see in the fading light. "It appears they are moving quickly."

"Indeed." Rawdon studied the stone foundation before turning toward the man next to him. "Allow me to introduce my colleague, Mr. O'Connell."

William nodded. "Good day."

"You may remember O'Connell. He studied under my father for several years. I have persuaded him to come back to Rosemere as headmaster."

The words struck William as strange. Miss Creighton had not mentioned anything about anyone coming to help. In fact, it appeared that she had everything under control. "Well then, welcome back to Darbury, Mr. O'Connell."

Creighton patted his hand down Angus's neck. "We were about to return to the house for dinner. Won't you join us?"

William shook his head. "I could not intrude."

"I'll take no refusal. We are celebrating. And you have yet to meet my wife. Besides, I have a business matter to discuss with you."

William's pulse quickened at the invitation. He would spend time with Miss Creighton, and that would be reason enough. Perhaps he could learn more about how the brooch he'd given Isabelle came to be in her possession. "If you are certain it is not an imposition, I will be most happy to join you."

"Excellent. We will get George to tend your horse until it is time to depart."

William followed the men inside. Indeed, he was glad for the diversion of dinner at Rosemere. He was growing weary of dining alone, with only Lewis for company occasionally. Yes, this diversion was exactly what he needed.

Patience opened the door to her wardrobe and studied her modest selection of gowns.

Ewan O'Connell would be joining them for the evening meal. She felt more like one of her schoolgirls, selecting a gown for a first dance rather than for a simple dinner with family. She closed her eyes. Long-suppressed memories of her brief romance with Ewan flooded her. She slammed the wardrobe door shut. She would not let her mind go to that place. She had made her decision many years ago. She would abide by it and think of it no more.

Realizing she had forgotten to select a gown, she opened the door wide enough to pull out a modest long-sleeved garment of black crepe trimmed with black velvet.

Cassandra, who was helping Patience dress for dinner, took the gown from Patience's hand.

"Mr. O'Connell's return must be a shock, but everything will be fine." Cassandra smoothed the ruffles on the sleeve. "You will see. Time, I am sure, has healed all wounds."

Patience wasn't sure if Cassandra was referring to Ewan's wounds or her own, but she had Cassandra help her pull the dress over her petticoat and then turned around so she could fasten the tiny buttons down the back.

Cassandra patted Patience's shoulder when she was done and smoothed the folds of the gown. "Think of this as dinner with an old friend. That is all, nothing more. I am sure that he will not stay in Darbury too long, and all will be as it was before."

If only those words could be a comfort, but Patience knew better. For had Rawdon not said that he wanted Ewan to stay on as headmaster? To run the school? How she wanted to tell her closest friend everything that Rawdon had told her about the plans for the future. But such an act would be a selfish one, for how could Patience tell Cassandra news of Rawdon without causing further injury?

Cassandra nudged Patience toward the dressing table. "Sit. I will dress your hair."

Patience tried to remain still as Cassandra adorned her hair, just as she had so many times before. Her gaze followed Cassandra's silver brush as it slipped through her own black tresses.

Pretty, sweet Cassandra, with her kind smile, her warm eyes. Long, dark lashes. But instead of her usual ruddy cheeks, she looked pale. Ashen. All of these recent developments must have been unimaginably hard on Cassandra.

Patience winced as the brush caught a tangle in her hair.

She looked at her own reflection. The candle sitting on the dressing table cast a warm glow on her complexion. She pressed her lips together, watching her cheek dimple as she did so.

Ewan had been the only man to call her beautiful. But that was so many years ago. How foolish she had been, delighting in his praise. In her naivety, she did not realize where the compliments were leading.

And since his return, what did he think of her?

At twenty-five, she was a spinster. That fact had never embarrassed her before, but now, facing a man she had once refused, she could not deny the sting. She had always expected a handsome and dashing man to sweep her away. But he never came.

Once her skin had been bright and smooth. Was it still? And her eyes had shone with brightness. Ewan had said they were like the sea . . . like green glass. She'd never seen the sea, but she sincerely doubted her eyes still shone with the vibrancy of unaffected youth. Responsibility weighed heavy on her. How she would love to go back to the innocence of those days.

Patience tapped her toes against the floor as Cassandra swept her black hair up off her neck and pinned it away from her face in a style that still allowed tendrils to cascade down her neck. The sight seemed odd after months of wearing her hair up in a simple twist.

After a knock, the door swung open, and Mary, round and flushed, hurried into the room. "We are to have another guest tonight for dinner."

Patience whirled around. "Another guest? Who?"

Mary placed a tea service on the table. "Mr. Sterling, Miss. Mr. Sterling has arrived. He called on Mr. Creighton, he did, and of course he was invited for dinner. I declare, I hope there is enough food. First he invites the Hammonds, then Mr. O'Connell arrives. I hadn't planned for all of this company."

Patience heard nothing after "Mr. Sterling." "You say Mr. Sterling is here?"

"Yes. Been down with the men nigh a quarter hour. You know how your brother fancies a large gathering. Always been the social one of the family. And him and his missus being so used to London, he must miss all the people."

Suddenly the thoughts of Ewan faded like the wisps of morning fog as the memory of her time alone with William Sterling on the moor replaced them.

Mary left the room, and Cassandra leaned down and spoke low, a teasing smile toying on her lips. "My, my. Mr. Sterling."

Patience looked down and twisted a ribbon around her finger. "What do you mean?"

"Nothing." Cassandra shrugged and tucked an ivory comb in Patience's hair. "That is to say, Mr. Sterling is an interesting man."

Her throat felt dry. She'd told no one of their walk together on the moor and doubted anyone would have seen her, and yet Cassandra seemed to know something. "He is our landlord, nothing more."

Cassandra smoothed one last lock of hair into place and then touched the pleated shoulder of Patience's gown. "I know you just dressed, but in light of our new guest, I think you should wear something different tonight."

Patience looked down at the lightweight fabric. "But this is my best mourning gown."

"It has been six months, Patience." Cassandra shook her head with a *tsk*. "I am not suggesting that you wear pink or yellow, but consider." She scurried to the wardrobe. "Here, this lavender . . . or this dark blue would be appropriate."

"Mother would never approve."

"Well, the choice is yours, not hers, and you cannot wear black forever."

Patience tilted her head to the side and studied the fabric. It shimmered in the candle's light, and as much as she tried to deny it, the idea of wearing a gown made of a color other than dark mourning colors appealed to her vanity. "I suppose it would not hurt. Mother will likely be too preoccupied with the guests to notice."

"Good. Then that is settled." Cassandra selected the gown of midnight blue. "What of this one?"

Patience reached out and ran her hand down the fabric. It was a simple gown of sarcenet with a lace overlay on the bodice and long sleeves. A wide ivory ribbon circled the gown's high waist. It had been her favorite last winter, and she had not touched it yet this season.

"Here, we can cover the light ribbon with a black one, and no one will be the wiser," Cassandra said.

Patience removed her gown. Cassandra helped her adjust her petticoat and slip into the gown. Then she fastened the back. They turned to look in the mirror.

Patience had to admit the change of color, while still dark, was enough to make her appear not so pale. Even though the neckline was lower and the bodice more fitted, it was still a simple gown. Nothing, she imagined, that William Sterling was used to seeing on the ladies in London. But she was far from the type she imagined he was used to associating with. And they were far from London.

And yet, perhaps it was these differences that intrigued her so.

"I have just the thing. You stay here." Cassandra hurried from the room as Mary reentered.

Mary's eyes opened wide as she assessed Patience's gown. "Look at that! So nice to see you out of all that black, Miss Creighton. Pretty young woman like you should not be in mourning for so long. Not with so many attractive men dining here. Imagine, two young and available men at Rosemere!"

"Mary!" The scold was out of Patience's mouth before she could prevent it. "The idea!"

Mary raised her shoulders in an innocent shrug. "What? Do I not speak the truth? Just what a man needs, a little competition."

Patience could feel the blush rising to her cheeks. Surely Mary remembered the circumstances that surrounded Mr. O'Connell and her those many years ago. Why would she bring it up? "I assure you, Mary, that that is the furthest thing from my mind."

"If I were a young lady, it would certainly not be far from my mind." Mary's face reddened and she looked down. "My apologies. I did not mean to offend." Mary slipped out the door and closed it quietly.

Patience immediately regretted the sharpness of her tongue. Mary may be the housekeeper, but she had been a part of the Creighton family for so long that topics that would usually be improper for mistress and servant to address were often openly and easily discussed. Normally, Patience would take Mary's light-hearted teasing in jest. But tonight every muscle in her body felt ready to snap, and her nerves felt as raw as the wind over the moors.

Alone in the room, she drew a deep breath and pressed her eyes shut. She could almost hear her father's voice. He'd had an uncanny way of saying verses from the Bible instead of offering his own advice. He believed that God's Word could solve problems and soothe pains. At this particular moment, she was wishing she had listened more closely. What wouldn't she give to hear his rich baritone voice tell her the verse she needed to hear.

Cassandra returned, eyes bright. She extended a necklace with a small sapphire pendant. She held it up to the light. "See, this will be perfect! Turn around."

Patience turned and stood still while Cassandra fastened the jewelry. She tried to feel happy, tried to feel pretty, but her concern for her friend pressed on her. Would the heaviness in her heart, the quiver in her stomach, ever subside?

Once Cassandra was finished with the clasp, Patience pivoted and assessed her appearance one last time. Her life was changing, shifting before her. For the first time in months, she breathed a prayer.

21

Once settled inside the parlor at Rosemere, William tried to relax. Creighton and O'Connell did not know of his struggles—or at least they gave no indication of such.

He looked down at the crystal goblet in his hand, the fire's light catching on the intricate angles and sending out slivers of light. The dark liquid swirled in the glass. In the chair opposite his, Ewan O'Connell took a long swig. William searched his memory, but nothing about this man looked familiar. O'Connell was not a tall man, and with dark hair and pale brown eyes, his person was quite plain. And yet he moved about the room with an air of authority, a fact that William found interesting.

William set the glass down on a side table next to him. "I have not had the opportunity to congratulate you on your recent marriage, Creighton."

"Thank you. I am a lucky man, indeed."

"I hope I will get the opportunity to get to know both of you. Do you intend to stay in Darbury?"

"Yes, if Mrs. Creighton takes a fancy to it. If the past few days are any indication, I would say we plan to stay for quite some time. My wife is very fond of my sister and mother."

William nodded. "Do you intend to teach?"

Creighton huffed, as if amused with the idea. "No. I was not blessed with the patience it takes to teach, as my father was and my sister is."

"I see." William cast a glance toward O'Connell. "With your sister in charge, I am sure you feel quite comfortable with her running things. She has greatly impressed me with her ability to stay calm in the midst of trial."

"My sister is a capable woman, indeed, but I fear she has been burdened with the responsibility for long enough. She should pursue more feminine pursuits. And that is why I have persuaded O'Connell here to stay on as headmaster."

William shifted his attention from Creighton to O'Connell. He could not put his finger on it, but something did not feel right. The man appeared too comfortable. Too relaxed. He looked back to Creighton. "So what is it you plan to do?"

"I have plans to expand the school."

William shifted his position, his interest piqued. "Do you?"

"Yes, and in fact, that is the business matter I wanted to discuss with you. It is my intention to open a boys' school."

William rested his elbow on the chair's padded arm. "That is ambitious."

"Yes, and I believe we have the capacity to make this more profitable. But in order to do that, we will need to expand. It will be imperative that we keep the boys and girls completely separate, with separate living quarters."

"Sounds reasonable."

"We will, obviously, be making modifications. With your approval, of course, I intend to have a cottage built on the grounds for my family so we can move out of Rosemere and use the west wing for the living quarters and the school rooms for the boys. There is plenty of room for such an undertaking. It will only take time."

William considered the plan. The idea seemed sound in theory, but the logistics were another matter. "The grounds here are not that extensive. Where is your proposed location to build a cottage?"

"I was considering the space of flat land west of our front gate, where the main road breaks to the right of the river, next to Latham Hill."

William raised an eyebrow. *Latham Hill.*

He decided to keep his plans for Latham Hill silent at present and turned to O'Connell. "And you? Do you intend to reside at the school? Or let a place in town?"

O'Connell's smile seemed overly eager. "Here at the school, of course. I intend to run the school exactly as Mr. Creighton would have seen fit. 'Tis no secret that I owe my every success to Mr. Creighton. He became like a father to me. His family became like my family."

"How is it that you were fortunate enough to end up under his tutelage? I was under the impression that Rosemere has always been a school for young ladies."

"My father, who was a great friend of Mr. Creighton's, died when I was but twelve. Mr. Creighton was kind enough to take me in and educate me alongside his own children. I left for London many years ago for personal reasons, yet I confess, I've long wished to return."

William was about to open his mouth to speak when he heard the door creak open behind him and recognized George's gravelly voice.

"The Hammonds have arrived, sir."

William froze. Of all the names that could have possibly passed the servant's lips, this was the last name he would have expected.

The room suddenly seemed cold. Unwelcoming.

No, hot. And suffocating.

William licked his lips and glanced behind him, calculating exactly how many steps it would take to escape. Ever since Isabelle left, Hammond was the man William had vowed to avoid. Vowed to never speak with again. And he had been successful at it. But at the sound of boot heels on the bare wooden floor, he knew it was too late.

William diverted his eyes as the Hammonds embraced first Rawdon Creighton and then Ewan O'Connell. The obvious friendship immediately irked him.

It had been a mistake to come here. A mistake to believe that he could fit into any other world than the one he had been a part of for so many years. He waited in near agony for the man to notice his presence and watched as he walked around the room.

Thomas Hammond's eyes, even though they were now behind spectacles, were much softer than he remembered. For after Isabelle's sudden departure, William remembered Mr. Hammond's eyes were dark and mere slits, his face red with anger. Today he appeared relaxed. Calm.

William blew out a breath. He was in the situation now, there was no escaping it. "Mr. Hammond."

The older man's smile was irritating. "William Sterling. My, but it has been a long time. How many years? Ah, but it does not matter. How you do look like your father." William grew even more uncomfortable under the man's obvious assessment. "It's been too long, Sterling. Far too long for two men who live in such close proximity."

How could the man act as if nothing had transpired between them? Act as casual as if they had met in town at the inn or passing on the street? William decided to remind him. "Eight years."

Hammond did not seem fazed by the intentional hardness in William's tone. "That's a long time, to be sure." William stiffened as the older man patted him on the shoulder before taking a seat on the opposite settee.

He was about to sit again himself and reassess his situation when another door opened. He almost didn't recognize Miss Creighton when she stepped into the room. But at the sight of her, his breathing slowed. The angry pounding in his chest calmed. He forgot about Hammond. She smiled, and even though her smile was not directed at him, it was like a soothing balm that pacified his mounting anxiety.

She spoke to her brother. There was something different about her, and it took William a few moments to realize what it was: she wasn't wearing black. Or gray. With the exception of the fire when she was wrapped in a blanket over her robe, she'd been dressed in black or dark gray, right down to a black shawl. But tonight a gown of deep blue hugged her slender form. The change of hue was becoming. Her complexion seemed brighter, rosier. The rich color enhanced the green shimmer of her eyes, and the dark blue made her hair, which now hung in soft ringlets to her shoulders, appear even blacker. The candlelight bathed the smooth skin of her chest and neck.

And then she looked at him. Gone was the careful reserve that had kept her at a distance in their previous interactions. For now her smile held warmth, her eyes held their secret. She looked at him boldly, almost expectantly. Energy surged through him, infusing him with courage and optimism.

He stood, remembering his manners, and managed a bow. A greeting.

"Mr. Sterling." She gave a little curtsy.

She said something to O'Connell, who had approached when she entered, yet William could not take his attention from her smile. He wanted to recapture the Patience from the moors with the light touch of her hand on his arm and the hushed tone of her voice. How he wished everyone else in the room would disappear so he could have these moments alone with her.

"I hope you brought your appetite, Mr. Sterling."

She was speaking to him again. "Indeed, I did."

"Mary enjoyed cooking for Rawdon and Mr. O'Connell. She always said that the girls ate like birds, and she much preferred feeding souls with a healthy appetite."

O'Connell laughed. "I requested Mary's pea soup and mutton collops. I do hope that is agreeable. I am sure that is nothing like what you are used to at Eastmore Hall, Sterling, but I have to admit, she asked me what I desired, and that, to me, is Rosemere."

If William had been dining at Eastmore Hall this evening, the cook would have a hard time scrounging up a dish half as appealing. "After being out in the open air all day, it sounds like every bit of heaven."

Surprise struck William when Mr. O'Connell stepped close to Miss Creighton and offered her an arm. "Allow me to escort you, Miss Creighton." When she hesitated, a cheeky smile curled his lip.

Miss Creighton cast a nervous glance around before she gave him a short smile and accepted his outstretched arm. She flashed her eyes in William's direction, but then, just as quickly, looked back to O'Connell.

A twinge seared through William's gut. What was that? A bit of jealousy? Surely not. He had too much on his mind to wonder about the romantic entanglements of a headmistress.

Didn't he?

Patience wished she had worn gloves.

Yes, she should have worn gloves. But this was a simple family dinner, was it not?

As she walked toward the dining room, the sleeve of Ewan O'Connell's coat felt rough beneath her fingertips. She kept her eyes straight ahead, refusing to look over at the man who was escorting her on the short walk from the parlor to the dining room.

She felt ridiculous.

The overly formal act was foolish for such an informal gathering of family and friends. But the addition of Mr. Sterling to their party turned the dinner into more of an affair. It was one thing for a man of his circumstances to oversee the building of the stable on his own property. But to dine with them? The memory of their moment alone on the moors brought a flush to her cheeks. Panic tickled her stomach, and her heart beat in wild anticipation. For what if he were to misinterpret Ewan's presence here?

The wool of Ewan's coat seemed to burn her hand. She wanted to rip her hand away and put a good few feet between her and Mr. O'Connell, as if by doing so she could also distance herself from the memories he brought with him. But instead she focused on the dining room door straight ahead of her.

Only a few more feet.

"Just like when we were children, isn't that right, Miss Creighton?"

Patience forced a smile, but even in her attempt at confidence, she could feel it tremble. "Indeed."

That had been long ago. When they were children. They had been different people then, and pretending that anything was the same was ludicrous. But the last time they had walked in such a manner she had overstepped her bounds. Offered too much encouragement. Strange how the simple act of walking from one room to another could transport her back to that different time. Except she was no longer a girl of nineteen. She was twenty-five. A spinster.

In the candlelit dining room, she withdrew her hand and turned her face away quickly, grateful that Jane Hammond happened to be close behind her. She dared not look in Mr. Sterling's direction. Her head was beginning to throb from the complexities of the day, and she was grateful for a familiar face.

"Dear Mrs. Hammond, I am so glad you could join us this evening."

Mrs. Hammond waited for Mr. O'Connell to rejoin the men. "And where is Miss Baden? I declare I've seen naught of her since I arrived."

Patience cut her eyes toward her brother, who was in the process of introducing his wife to Mr. Hammond. Mrs. Hammond was correct. Normally Cassandra would join them at a party such as this. "She has been unwell."

Mrs. Hammond showed genuine concern. "I do hope it is not serious."

"She should be well soon enough." Patience managed a smile, although she wished that Cassandra's ailment were as simple as that. A sore throat or broken limb would soon heal, but a broken heart is another matter entirely.

"Well then, is she up for company? Perhaps I could pay her a quick visit after we dine?"

"She was asleep when I checked in on her a bit ago," Patience lied.

Mrs. Hammond leaned in close, her nose wrinkling in unmasked disdain. "What is Mr. Sterling doing here?"

Patience's heart skipped a beat at the mere mention of his name. "He's been most helpful during and ever since the fire. Apparently he called on Rawdon today, who invited him to stay for dinner."

Mrs. Hammond tilted her head. "Most odd." Mrs. Hammond watched him for several seconds before turning back around. "If I were you, dear Patience, I would advise your brother to be wary in his dealings with Mr. Sterling. He's a most unscrupulous man."

The words took Patience by surprise. A harsh judgment, and

from the vicar's wife, no less. Patience thought it wise to forgo mentioning the fact that he had shown up on their property, bloodied and unconscious, mere weeks ago. Or that they had spent a quiet moment together, walking at twilight on the moors. "I have heard he has quite the reputation, but he has been nothing but kind to help us ever since the fire. He even assisted us the night of the fire."

The click of the door resounded above the chatter, and the door swung open. Mrs. Margaret Creighton, dressed in a black mourning gown with a black fichu and thick charcoal shawl, stood in the doorway. Surprised, Patience rushed to her. "Mother! I am so glad you are joining us!"

Her mother's eyes appeared bright, and for the first time in weeks, color warmed her cheeks. "Well, with such a party brewing in my home, how could I miss it?"

Patience pressed her lips closed, quickly scanning the rest of the party. Was anyone else surprised by her sudden recovery? But everyone milled about, as if nothing unusual had just happened. Her mother brushed past her and took Rawdon's arm, smiling and laughing as they moved about the room. Even as Patience caught a glimpse of the mother she remembered, a sinking feeling took hold. For months she had been trying to help her mother smile. Trying to help her find a spark of life. She'd succeeded but a handful of times to get her mother to join her at dinner. With Rawdon home, suddenly she recovered? Suddenly she felt like interacting with friends and family?

It didn't make sense.

"Miss Creighton, are you well?"

Patience snapped from her shock and managed a little laugh to cover her thoughts. "Of course. I am pleased to see her up and about at last."

Mrs. Hammond leaned closer, her scent of lavender nearly overwhelming. "There is nothing like fine company to bring one from a dark place, Miss Creighton. I believe your brother's return may be just what your mother needs."

Patience employed every discipline to ensure that her expression remained stoic. Over the last six months she had tried—and failed—to do what her brother and his new wife appeared to have done in days: bring her mother joy.

Once seated at the table, she found herself settled between Ewan and Mrs. Hammond. But it was not who was next to her that caught her attention.

Directly across from her sat Mr. Sterling. He was talking with Lydia, who was seated to his left.

She stole another glance. Sandy hair fell over his forehead and curled over his high collar. Sideburns hid wind-kissed cheeks, and clear blue eyes shone beneath dark lashes. He was achingly handsome. How she wished he would look in her direction.

She thought back to that first night, when she touched a cloth to his cheek and wiped dirt from his brow. Then to when she folded back his shirt sleeve to tend to his arm wound. The touch—the innocent touch—when he brushed the soot away from her face.

Someone was staring at her. She felt it. She lifted her eyes to see Ewan's pale brown ones looking at her. He did not look away but grinned, as if caught in a guilty pleasure.

She quickly glanced around the table to see if anyone had noticed his brazen look, which certainly was not in keeping with the professional demeanor of a headmaster. Exactly *why* had he returned to Rosemere?

22

William lifted a spoon of pea soup to his lips. O'Connell had been right. The soup was delicious. The steam curling from the hot meal heated his face and hands. He'd still not completely warmed from his ride on the moors with Riley and Carlton. He moved his toes within his boots and slacked his posture slightly. He could have relaxed and truly enjoyed the dinner—if it weren't for the Hammonds.

The words that Mr. Hammond had issued that awful day still rang as true and as loud as if he had said them yesterday. "Isabelle is not for you. She has made her choice. To contact her would only bring about her ruination. Do her a favor and let her be."

William's lips formed a hard line, and he could not resist a glance at the man who had stood in the way of everything he had ever wanted. Or thought he had wanted.

He let his gaze drift slightly to the left to land on Mrs. Hammond, who had been equally vocal about her disapproval of the union. He'd barely been able to stomach her triumphant expression that fateful day. How vividly it had burned itself to his memory. He'd reconciled his feelings for Isabelle. He'd made peace with them. Accepted that she was gone. But his anger toward the Hammonds was different. He did not *want* to forgive them, as Lewis had prompted on more than one occasion. How much easier it was to blame another than take any ownership of his own missteps.

He took another spoonful of soup and looked across the table at Miss Creighton. She was a much more pleasant subject to linger on. After Isabelle, he swore he would never love again—a vow he'd had little trouble keeping. Or so he had thought. But the lightness of Miss Creighton's touch he could not forget. And the sincere expression in her eyes captivated him. Left him longing to know more about her. Nay, he wanted to know everything about her.

Of course, while at the parties in London, he'd flirted and even kindled a brief romance, but his intentions had never been on anything other than enjoying himself. With discreet glances, he studied Miss Creighton. He strained to hear her voice above all others present. She was so unlike any of the women he had known in London. She wasn't silly. Frivolous women who targeted him as a wealthy husband could be amusing, but in the end proved shallow and disappointing. There was something about Miss Creighton. Her passion for those around her intrigued him.

She glanced up at him, almost startling him with the intensity of her eyes in the candlelit room.

He smiled and nodded.

She smiled and nodded.

And in that moment, William forgot all about the Hammonds.

William was far from an expert on women, and certainly no expert on the likes of Miss Creighton, but something about her was not quite right this evening. Her expression, which normally exuded confidence and control, seemed almost sad.

He should look away. He was staring.

O'Connell, who was seated next to Miss Creighton, leaned in close to her. Too close. He watched for her reaction. He wanted to see her pull away from him. But instead, she gave a smile and said a few words. O'Connell seemed pleased with whatever she had said, for a beaming smile lit his face.

Like a lightning strike, a sensation jolted William. His nostrils flared.

And then his thought from earlier was confirmed: he was jealous.

Mrs. Hammond, who seemed equally as fervent in her fondness for the odd Mr. O'Connell as she was in her dislike for William, leaned forward and turned her head toward O'Connell. "Tell us, Mr. O'Connell, how was your time in London? We've so much to catch up on."

"Very educational, ma'am." O'Connell leaned back in his chair. "Such a different world in a town the size of London."

"And tell us of your post there."

"I taught Latin and French at a boarding school for young men."

Mr. Hammond chimed in, "Did not leave the realm of education, I see."

"No, for I fear it is in my blood. My profession chose me instead of I it."

Mrs. Hammond put down her fork. "And how long will you stay in Darbury?"

"As long as my services are required at Rosemere. I owe a great deal to the Creighton family and am honored to be of service."

Every word was perfect. What must it be like? William felt more out of place than ever. He was an impulsive gambler in the midst of men who valued education and religion. He glanced up at Miss Creighton. That, no doubt, was the type of man she would be drawn to as well. One with high moral ideals and principles. Miss Creighton would naturally prefer a suitor whose occupation was closely aligned with her own interests. For what occupation did he have to offer? Gentleman turned gambler turned horse breeder? Turned mill owner? Such inconsistent and less than noble pursuits darkened his credibility. He was trying, but breeding horses and being a pinchpenny would never dig him out from the mess he had made for himself.

And then someone said his name. It was O'Connell. "And you, Mr. Sterling. I must tell you, your reputation precedes you."

William settled his napkin next to his plate and chuckled. "I do not like the sounds of that."

"Never fear, Mr. Sterling, for I am speaking of your reputation as a horseman. I heard you were dealt a shocking blow at Newmarket."

William studied O'Connell, wondering if the fact that he brought up his dealings at the track was merely conversational or if he meant to imply more. "Yes. My horse suffered a tendon injury."

Mrs. Hammond, her words containing a thinly veiled accusation, said, "Why, Mr. O'Connell, I never suspected you to be one to follow horse racing."

O'Connell nodded and cast a quick glance over at Miss Creighton. "My employer took a fancy to the sport. I was privy to many of his conversations and recognized your name when I heard it."

"Yes, that horse's racing days are over. As are mine." The less said about his racing ventures, especially in front of the vicar and his wife, the better.

Miss Creighton leaned forward. "I saw the horse when I was out at the Eastmore stables to visit dear Charlie, our stable boy who has been staying there since the fire. A beautiful animal the color of coal. And he's to be a papa soon, is he not?"

William stared at her and opened his mouth to speak, but nothing came out. Had she, in a way, defended him?

Her words infused him with confidence, but before he could

verbalize his thought, the door opened, and a woman dressed in a dark dress curtsied and hurried over to Miss Creighton. She whispered to her, and Miss Creighton stood. "Please excuse me."

All eyes were on her, and a rush of whispers circled the table.

But William kept his focus straight ahead, acutely aware of how O'Connell's eyes followed her form from the room. The man was clearly more intimately connected with the Creighton family than he. Was he her beau? Did they have an understanding?

And if so, why did the thought irk him so?

Lydia Creighton lowered her fork. "Where is she going?"

"No doubt to tend to the girls," Margaret Creighton said. "They quite depend upon her. She has such a way with the children."

It was the first time William had heard her speak since she arrived in the dining room.

Rawdon wiped his mouth and put his napkin next to his plate. "That is the benefit of having her so committed to the school. A male headmaster could never understand the workings of a female mind, regardless of their age."

A chuckle circled the table—the type that seemed to have much meaning to everyone at the table except for William.

He felt a need to defend Miss Creighton. Even as an outsider, he was aware of how much she had done for the school. How could they not see it? Her strength. Her selflessness. He repeated his sentiment from earlier. "You would have been impressed with your sister's presence of mind during the fire."

The other conversations stopped. All eyes turned toward him. As usual, he spoke before he thought. He shrugged. "No man could have handled the situation better."

"Be that as it may, she has played her part," Rawdon said. "No doubt she will be grateful for O'Connell to take over the bulk of the responsibility."

William interpreted Creighton's words as a challenge.

L

The emergency with Emma kept Patience away from dinner longer than she had anticipated. The girls had been asleep for quite some time when Emma awoke with a nightmare and could not be quieted, just as she had every night since the fire. Patience held the child and stroked her hair until she once again slumbered. She pressed a kiss to Emma's forehead and then left the sleeping girls, pulling the door closed behind her. In the corridor, there was silence, a calm.

At least dinner had to be over. She hated to see Emma in such a state, but the escape from the dreadful discomfort of being so close to Ewan had been a relief.

She would do her best to avoid the amorous Mr. O'Connell. He sat too close to her. Leaned in too close when he spoke with her with far too much familiarity. At one time in the past, they had been close, but time had distanced them. She wished he would respect that change.

She paused at a small landing atop the east-wing stairs. A small mirror hung at the end, and she paused to check her reflection.

A strand had pulled loose from her intricately twisted hair, and she tried to smooth it back and then sighed. She could not help but compare herself to her sister-in-law, whose personal maid had woven satin ribbon into her hair. Dressed in a gown of pale green satin trimmed in dark green velvet, Lydia looked as if she were attending a ball instead of a simple neighborhood gathering. Compared to the lovely Lydia, Patience was certain she was hardly noticed in her sensible gown of somber blue.

She thought of William Sterling, whose blue eyes challenged her practicality. How her heart jumped at the recollection. The marks on his face were gone. Their interactions were growing less awkward. Less like a relationship between a tenant and landlord and almost more like that of friends. He'd looked at her as if he had something to say to her, his eyes communicative and his countenance cheery. But that, in itself, was odd. Why did the master of such an estate humble himself to attend their family gathering? Did he, too, share her feelings? How her heart raced at the idea.

She pinched her cheeks for color and hurried down the stairs. Voices came from the parlor, and as she drew closer, she recognized her brother's voice.

"On that matter you will have to ask my sister, Sterling."

Patience reentered the room. "Ask me what?"

The gentlemen all stood. Rawdon and Ewan flanked the fireplace, the warm light playing off their faces and dark coats. Mr. Sterling stood next to the window in the darkness of a corner. Patience cast a quick glance to the rest of the party. Across the room, her mother, Lydia, and the Hammonds were gathered around a silhouette screen, and Lydia was creating a silhouette of Mrs. Hammond. She turned back to the men.

Rawdon leaned forward. "He was asking about the school."

"Oh." Patience sat in a chair and pivoted a bit in order to see Mr. Sterling. "And what would you like to know?"

Rawdon folded his arms across his chest. "Mr. Sterling was asking about how the studies in a girls' school differ from that for young men."

"Well"—she turned to Mr. Sterling and smiled, pleased with his interest in her work—"our girls study many of the same subjects that one would find in a boys' academic establishment. Sums, literature, science. And of course they are instructed in the proper use of the English language, Latin, and French."

Mr. Sterling nodded in her direction, his eyes locked on hers. "Impressive."

"Impressive? Why?" She was enjoying the banter. She noted the directness of his gaze, the sincerity in his expression, as if they were the only two in the room.

He shrugged. "Not the typical subjects I imagined in a girls' school."

Patience smoothed a wrinkle from her skirt. She felt giddy speaking with him, like a schoolgirl herself. And yet she also felt brave around him, encouraged by his interest in her and the observations he had shared with her on the moors. "Why should their minds be suppressed, just because they are the fairer sex? My father believed that a woman's mind was every bit as valuable as a man's and should be exercised as such. I, for one, am grateful for his vision."

Ewan grinned, perhaps a bit too smugly, a bit too possessively. "Well put, Miss Creighton. It is refreshing to see that you take your responsibilities with such steadfastness."

"Of course I do. These girls have been entrusted to us. How could we do any less by them?"

The room fell silent after her passionate speech, and she silently reprimanded herself for not having been more guarded, wondering if she had overstepped her bounds. She pressed her lips together and looked down at her hands. But what surprised her most was how much she cared about what Mr. Sterling thought of what she had said. She stole a glimpse up at him and was unsettled seeing his eyes so directly focused on her. His expression was warm, his eyes, kind.

And he was smiling at her.

ℒℒ

"And where was your education, Mr. Sterling?" Mr. O'Connell asked.

William was forced to tear his attentions away from Miss Creighton. Her passion for those around her was contagious. But then, when O'Connell repeated his name, he shifted his weight, growing increasingly annoyed with anything that came out of the man's mouth. William sensed where he was going with his line of questioning—and he didn't like it. "I had a tutor. A man by the name of Mr. Grange."

"A tutor. Ah, so you were educated at home, then?"

He felt all eyes on him, including those of Miss Creighton. "Yes."

O'Connell seemed almost amused, an air of superiority in his tone. "And do you find that being educated at home is best?"

William narrowed his eyes. He knew what this man was doing. Even though their stations, their ranks, were beneath his, he was in a room of highly educated men. If O'Connell could not be superior with status, he was trying to do it on intellect. "My father was of the opinion that I could learn more about running an estate like Eastmore Hall by staying on the premises. I'm afraid I gave Mr. Grange a devil of a time. I preferred being out of doors. Mr. Grange would have preferred I stay in the schoolroom. But I am well prepared for my life's work."

A smirk touched O'Connell's face. "And, out of curiosity, what is your life's work?"

William tensed. His life's work? He'd opened himself up to that question with his last statement, and now he was not sure how to respond. What work had he really done in his life? A more accurate depiction would be to say that all the man had taught him had prepared him for the life he was reaching for. But he would save such details for another time. "Horse breeding."

"Yes," muttered Rawdon. "Patience mentioned one of your horses was to be a papa."

William ignored Rawdon's much lighter tone, still dealing with the condescension in O'Connell's. This man did not care for him, and he was making it abundantly clear. He cast a glance toward

Miss Creighton, who appeared to be following the line of questioning with great interest.

"Actually, O'Connell, I have been meaning to speak with Mr. Creighton here about another venture."

Creighton looked up. "Oh really? Interesting. And what is it?"

William turned to look at Creighton. "I wanted to inform you of improvements coming to Latham Hill."

"Latham Hill?"

"Yes. Construction will be beginning within the next couple of days on a mill there."

Rawdon's eyes flashed to his sister and then back at William. "A mill, you say?"

"Yes. A textile mill."

William waited for a smart reply from O'Connell, but none came. "I doubt it will have much effect on you or the school, but the traffic will likely increase along the path that runs alongside the property up to Wainslow Peak. What with the new building you were proposing on the property and the new structure coming to the hill, this area should look different in the coming months."

"But so close to the school." Miss Creighton's words were more of a statement than a question, and he turned to look at her.

"I assure you, Miss Creighton, this will not have the least effect on you or your young charges." He ignored the twinge in his gut and forced his attention back to her brother. "You undoubtedly know Jonathan Riley from Ambledale. He is my partner in this venture. What with the property so close to the river and in such close proximity to town, it was a logical choice."

"Yes, very logical." Rawdon cut his eyes again toward his sister, then looked back at William. "We wish you the best of luck in your new endeavor and wish it every success."

"Thank you."

Guilt sliced at William, and he could not bring himself to look at Miss Creighton, for he had no desire to see what emotion might be in her expression. He'd hoped to share the news of the mill with Rawdon Creighton in a more professional and private manner, but he'd allowed his defenses to be tweaked by the intruder who had made so much of his lack of a formal education.

When would he learn?

23

The next afternoon Patience looped her arm through Cassandra's as they headed back to Rosemere. "Thank you for walking with me."

"The weather suits me today," Cassandra said, lifting her face to the pewter sky.

Patience was silent as her footsteps fell in time with her friend's. Ever since the dinner the evening before, melancholy thoughts weighed on her mind, leaving her jumpy and discontented, and now she needed the lullaby of the wind through the bare branches and shrubs to drown out the doubts and fears that were circulating within her.

But above all, she did not want to think of *him*.

William Sterling was a man of contradictions. His attentions and affectionate smiles made her feel as light and fluttery as a schoolgirl. But his announcement regarding Latham Hill and his own admission of danger on the moors gave her reason to pause. William Sterling was after something. He was searching, reaching for something . . . but what? She suspected that the answer lay with whatever was happening on Latham Hill. Was his kindness sincere, or was there some other reason? He had so many marks against him. But then again, did any of them even matter?

The women stopped at the crest of Wainslow Peak and stood in comfortable silence, looking out over the land.

Patience had climbed this hill nearly every day of her adult life, weather permitting. She reveled in the quiet peace that could be found at its crest. In late summer, she delighted in the breathtaking purple heather and the broad expanse of the unending sky, where sunlight played on silver clouds and the turtledove and willow warbler could be seen. Even the winter held its own beauty on this harsh terrain. Snow covered all, blanketing the earth with a dusting of diamonds and an unmatched silence. Normally, she used her daily walk to clear her mind, to help her find solace. In years past, she had come here to pray, to talk aloud to the Maker and dream of what her future would hold. But since her father's death, her visits to this precious spot had diminished. It had been more than a week since she last visited, and that was only to pass by on her way to Eastmore Hall to visit Charlie.

From the top of the hill, she looked down to the south and saw Rosemere and the hazy mist that surrounded the stone house, the smoke puffing from the chimneys. Beyond that to the right was Latham Hill.

Latham Hill. She could not have been more shocked to learn of Mr. Sterling's plans for the hill if he had told her he was going to live there himself. She knew she was not well-versed in the ways of the world . . . in the ways that men and women interact. She had been sheltered. Mr. Sterling, by his own account, had been many places, met many people. Whereas she knew her role and her world, he knew of things beyond.

"Remember how we used to climb this hill when we were

children?" exclaimed Cassandra, struggling to keep her hair free from her face in the mounting wind.

Patience felt a slight smile tug at her lips at the recollection. "Father would always get so angry. He wanted us to stay closer to the walls where it was safe. Remember that time we gathered all that heather and tried to dry it in the kitchen? Mary nearly had a fit." Her smile faded at the memory. "But that was a long time ago."

Patience moved to a large boulder, brushed the snow from it, and sat down. How different their lives were today. They each faced a future of uncertainty for different reasons. Only recently they had thought their paths were certain. But the ground had shifted beneath both of them. Nothing could be relied on anymore.

"How foolish we used to be, the two of us, always dreaming of great romance and adventure," Patience said.

Cassandra gazed down at the river. "And did we find it?"

Not even the angry wind could dislodge that question from their minds.

Patience wanted to stand on the crest of the hill and scream. Cry out to God. Beg for intervention. Beg to have her relationship with her brother restored. To have her mother back. To have her hope, her purpose back.

"You did not comment on the dinner last night. Did you have a nice time?"

Cassandra's question pulled Patience from her thoughts. It was odd that she had not shared the details of the previous evening with her friend, for the two women had always shared their deepest thoughts. But she was having difficulty putting thoughts into words, for she did not understand them herself. "I . . . I don't know."

"Did Rawdon tell you why he invited Mr. O'Connell to return?" Cassandra asked.

Patience looked down at the snow clinging to the hem of

her skirt. She had avoided telling Cassandra any details, hoping to spare her feelings, but she supposed there was no sense in hiding the truth. "Rawdon intends to expand the school. He wants to operate a boys' school from the west wing. He thinks it will be profitable. He has asked O'Connell to oversee the school."

"Where will you live?"

"Rawdon intends to build a cottage on the school grounds."

"Oh." Cassandra's voice fell in wistful thought. "And what of the girls' school? Surely you will remain as headmistress after you have worked so hard?"

Patience shrugged. "I do not know. Rawdon thinks I should marry and settle down."

"And whom does he think you should marry?"

Patience managed a little laugh. "I think you know the answer to that question."

Her friend nudged her arm. "And what do you think?"

Patience considered what she did think. The primary reason that Rawdon had brought Ewan back to Rosemere was to run the boys' school. But Ewan's behavior last night suggested that he was interested in more than merely employment. She shuddered at the memory of how close he sat to her and the way he tried to belittle Mr. Sterling.

For the first time in her life, Patience did not want to return to Rosemere. She looked down at it. It looked cold. Foreboding. Not the warm solace she once enjoyed. For within its walls were people who seemed to be strangers. Oh, the irony! People she loved, but who threatened her hopes for her future. People she would lay her life down for, but with whom she could not find peace. Everything was changing. Everything was different.

She looked over her shoulder at Eastmore Hall. Somewhere inside that massive home was William Sterling. He stood almost as a symbol in her mind. Of what, she was not certain. How she tried to suppress the flutter that danced within her heart at the thought of his clear blue eyes on the previous night.

Silly schoolgirl notion.

Patience adjusted the bonnet's bow beneath her chin. "We are still young enough to find adventure and romance, Cassandra."

Cassandra looked out over the land for a long time, then said, "I fear my heart will not. Cannot."

Patience waited, giving her friend the space and time to speak of the pain that weighed on her heart. But Cassandra did not say more. She did not need to. In the days since Rawdon's arrival, Cassandra had spoken naught of the betrayal. Today, her comfort was found on the moors, with no one to hear with the exception of her best friend and the short-eared owl watching from a tree.

The wind was exceptionally raw on the walk home from church a few days later, or perhaps it was the sour mood Patience was in that made it feel so. The icy mud and wet earth soaked through her kid boots as they returned to Rosemere, biting her toes and marring the hem of her gray mourning gown. Frustrated, she lifted her skirts a little more than what was proper. She only had one other half-mourning gown, and if this one was ruined, she hadn't the funds to have another one made. Or perhaps it was easier to focus on the frustration with her cold toes than other frustrations brewing within her.

Part of her had expected—had hoped—to see Mr. Sterling at church. Although she was not sure why, for it was not his habit to attend. But something in her still fell when his family pew was vacant.

In front of her, the girls walked in two pristine lines. Even before the carriage burned in the fire, they never took it to church.

Her father had believed walking to be the best exercise for the constitution. So they walked. But it was her brother, and not the girls, who caught her eye. She watched her brother's beautiful bride, hanging on his arm, barely seeming to notice the cold or the mud. Happiness beamed from her bright blue eyes, and she chattered on, making him smile.

The sight pained her, for even without looking at Cassandra, Patience knew that her dear friend was taking in the same sight. How much worse it must be for her. Of course, Patience had never loved in such a fashion and likely never would. But Cassandra knew the joy of returned affection. How it must hurt to see such a display.

Patience sighed. At least she would have the entire afternoon to herself to sort her thoughts. She had long enjoyed Sundays, but not for the reason her father intended. For her, it was a day free of work. Free of teaching. Patience knew she ought to find peace and draw close to God through worship. But that had never been a simple task. She believed in God, of course she did, but she had never had a relationship with God like her father's.

Once in Rosemere, Patience hurried to the study, her pace quickening to that of almost a run, as if to outpace her own thoughts. Once inside, she finally drew a deep breath. This room was always cold. As it was Sunday, no fire blazed in the room's grate. The old paned windows looked out over the grounds, allowing an abundance of afternoon light. She prepared to answer letters, but as she opened the writing box, the door opened.

"I hope I am not disturbing you." The Scottish brogue tinted the baritone.

Patience did not look up. She did not want to look up. She did not want to see Ewan. She resisted as long as she could. She wanted to hold on to the silence. Hold on to the solitude.

But they were already gone.

"You are not intruding, sir," Patience lied, sitting up straight, hoping her smile did not appear as insincere as it felt. "I am merely responding to letters."

He sat down in the chair opposite the desk and looked around the room, as if relishing memories of a time long forgotten. "How many hours did I spend in this room? Your father was a brilliant man. I am sure you miss him immensely."

The word *immensely* hardly seemed strong enough to describe the pain and emptiness that remained since her father's passing. But she did not have the luxury to dwell on that pain—or even recognize that pain—and it was probably best that way.

"I am so sorry I was unable to attend his funeral. I was away from home when your brother sent word. Otherwise I would have been here."

For the first time, Patience allowed herself to look at Ewan. Really look at him. The fine cut of his coat and detail on his waistcoat suggested that he had been doing well for himself. His hair was darker—no longer the copper hue of his youth, but closer to a nut brown—and the ends curled over his stiff collar. Not a handsome man, with pale brown eyes far too large for his narrow face, but his appearance had improved with maturity.

Patience tried to think of something to say. The weather. Or the morning's sermon. But the sight of him in such close proximity transported her to another time.

"I hope I do not overstep my welcome with what I am about to say, but I wanted to find a moment to speak with you. Privately."

She swallowed. "Privately?" She didn't like the idea. For the last time they had spoken privately, he had grabbed her about the waist and held her in an uncomfortable embrace. But the O'Connell who sat before her was no longer the awkward youth, but a man.

"Yes, in light of our . . . uh . . . past, I wanted to make sure you were comfortable with my presence at Rosemere."

The natural tone of her voice impressed even her. "Of course."

He crossed one leg over the other and leaned back against the chair, as calm and as relaxed as if they were discussing the previous night's dinner. "It was childish of me to leave in the manner I did, all those years ago. I never thought I would return to Rosemere, but after returning and seeing you, I feel like I must apologize for my behavior."

"If you feel the need to apologize, then I must add mine. I was young. And thoughtless."

"Good. Then we can put the past behind us?"

"Indeed." Perhaps it was the quiet of the moment or the desire to be free from bothersome worries, but she found a sudden bit of courage and decided to seize the moment. "I must ask you, Mr. O'Connell, why did you return to Rosemere?"

He studied the cuff of his coat, hesitating. "After all this time, it does feel strange to hear you call me Mr. O'Connell instead of Ewan."

"We are no longer children," Patience reminded him. "And times have changed. We have changed."

"True enough. And to answer your question, I am here because Rawdon contacted me and said he needed help. The Creightons have been nothing but kind to me, and I have long regretted how I abandoned your father. He may be gone, but at least in this manner perhaps I can repay his kindness."

He stood up and stepped toward her, his gaze unwavering. "And I hope to atone for past wrongs."

24

William stood at the gate to the vicarage. Thomas Hammond was just beyond this point. He wiped his damp palms on his breeches and tugged at his cravat. Angus whinnied and pawed at the frozen earth, as if pushing him forward.

Even six weeks ago he would have avoided this interaction. But present circumstances demanded it. The brooch he'd been carrying around was driving him to distraction, and knowing that Miss Creighton may somehow be involved in the puzzle was making him question all he thought to be true. He'd not found a private moment to speak with her at the dinner a few days prior, and, truth be told, finding another moment alone with her was unlikely, especially now that her brother had returned and O'Connell seemed intent on being her constant shadow. He turned his attention back to the vicarage. He knew full well that this conversation could only uncover old wounds, hardly heal them. But this was part of the man he was trying to be. Responsible. Make up for past wrongs. He needed to *know* about the past.

William secured Angus and stepped through the gate. The frosty grass crunched beneath his boots. A biting wind swept down from the gable, carrying with it a gust of the freshly fallen snow. He wiped it from his eyes.

When the servant answered his knock, William walked in and handed her his things. Immediately, the vicar was present.

"Ah, so you decided to call after all. I was hoping you might after running into you at Rosemere."

William nodded. "Might we talk?"

A smile creased the vicar's face. "Of course. Let us go to my study. We will not be disturbed."

William followed Hammond through the modest parlor and down a narrow hall, where he had to duck to miss the exposed beams. With every step William considered turning and running out on this conversation. For as much as his curiosity wanted to know what secrets the vicar could unearth, his pride begged otherwise.

So lost in his thoughts, he nearly jumped backward when a door to his left opened. The hall was dark—no windows lined its length—but he clearly saw Mrs. Hammond's sharp expression of disapproval. She scurried to her husband, took him by the arm, and whispered in his ear. Caught between wanting to give them their privacy and wanting to hear what she had to say, William stopped, keeping a respectable distance. He looked down at the bare wood floor, but not before seeing the man's gray head shake from side to side. He looked up only after he heard the soft sound of slippers retreating and a door close and a latch click.

The vicar stood for several seconds with his back toward William before turning to face him. "Please excuse my wife."

Feeling more uncomfortable than ever, William forced his feet to move. The vicar's study looked like one would expect. A small but cheery fire burned in the small grate on the far wall. Two square windows were carved into the thick plaster walls, and naught but a cross and a small painting of a woman with a lace cap hung on the space between. The vicar directed him to a seat, but William preferred to stand.

William was in no mood to exchange pleasantries, and there was no need to attempt to hide the reason behind his visit. "I suppose my visit is overdue."

The vicar took the chair behind the tiny desk, the fire's light hitting the sleeve of his severely cut black jacket.

William cleared his throat. "I need to speak with you about Isabelle."

"I figured as much."

William shifted his weight from one foot to the other. "And I need to find out what you know about this." He pulled the brooch from his pocket and leaned forward to place the jewelry on the desk. It sparkled and shone in the fire's modest light. "Have you seen it before?"

The vicar paused, picked up the piece, turned it over in his hand, and then returned it to the desk. "Yes, I know it."

The man's responses were slow and frustratingly short. "We did not leave this topic on good terms all those years ago. I am no longer trying to find Isabelle, but since finding this brooch at Rosemere, I do need answers. I implore you. Once and for all, please tell me what you would not tell me then so I might make peace with it."

The older man rubbed the whiskers on his square chin. His eyes seemed to darken, and he pushed his spectacles up farther on his nose. "Sit down, Sterling."

Optimism surged at the change in the man's tone. Perhaps finally he would hear the answers he sought.

The vicar's voice was low. "I regret the way things were left. But the reason we would not tell you where Isabelle had gone was for her good . . . and yours."

"Mine?"

"Yes." The vicar stood and moved to the window, his back to William. "Do you know why Isabelle came to stay with us, Mr. Sterling?"

"She was visiting for the summer."

"Yes, but that is not the entire truth."

The distinct feeling that he was about to hear news he would rather not hear seized him, making him feel ill. And yet he had come too far to stop.

"Isabelle was sent to us by her mother, who is my wife's sister. You see, Isabelle had been involved with a gentleman in Southampton, and when their indiscretion was discovered, scandal ensued. The young man refused to marry her, so her mother sent her to stay with us until the scandal passed."

William tried to remember, but no, Isabelle had never mentioned a past love. Ever.

Hammond said, "She came to us under protest. She was angry and defiant. And then she met you. After her history, you can imagine why Mrs. Hammond and I were so concerned at your relationship. You were both such vibrant people, and with Isabelle's troubled past, we did not want her to make the same mistake twice. Then, when you proposed, we were naturally concerned, so we sent word of the engagement to her mother. The news made it to the other gentleman, and within days Isabelle received a letter with an offer of marriage."

William was having trouble with the sequence. "This man proposed after I did?"

The vicar nodded. "I believe Isabelle was never able to let go of the other gentleman. After receiving his letter, she made her decision. She said nothing to us, just ran away during the black of night."

William felt almost dizzy. The news, which should have brought peace and clarity, only muddied his thoughts, stirring up emotions that time had muted. "So she did not love me as she professed."

"Remember, she was a troubled young woman. I do not believe she knew her heart. Which is why, when you tried to find her, we would not reveal her location. At the time, Mrs. Hammond and I believed that the other gentleman was a better choice."

Half angry, half remorseful, William could not bring himself to look at the man. His chest tightened, his lungs refused to expand, not so much from the news but from the buildup of eight years of wondering. Eight years of regret.

So it had not been him.

Isabelle had a secret past—one she never trusted him enough to tell him about.

He should feel relief. But instead a weight pushed down on him. What had happened to Isabelle in all those years? Was she happy? Did she ever think of him? He needed to know. "Where is she now?"

The vicar hesitated. "She died, Sterling."

The words hit harder than the blows that Rafertee's men had delivered. Heat crept up his neck, choking him. "Died? How? When?"

"She died four years ago of a fever."

William had to remind himself to breathe. To blink. "Why, then, did you not tell me as much? Let me make peace with it. How difficult would that have been?"

The vicar remained calm. "Because there is more to tell. And it is time you know the truth."

"Truth? What truth?" William jumped from the chair and paced the small room, growing increasingly aggravated. "Everything I thought was a truth I am learning was a lie."

"I understand you are angry. I would be too. But perhaps when you hear what I have to say, you might understand."

William continued to pace, his teeth clenched so tightly that his entire jaw was beginning to ache.

The vicar picked up the brooch. "After Isabelle married, we learned soon after that she was with child. The child—a baby girl—arrived five months later. You see, she had only been married five months when the baby came, and yet the baby was fully developed. Of good size and sound health. It was obvious. The child was not her husband's."

Beads of sweat formed on William's brow. *Isabelle bore a daughter.*

He squinted in confusion, then slowly, as the words came together in his mind, he knew. He had been with Isabelle in the months before she left.

"Her husband quickly figured out Isabelle's deceit and threw her and the child from his house. She took the child to her mother's, but the scandal was great, and her mother, too, would have nothing to do with them. When the little girl was not yet four, Isabelle wrote to us. She'd fallen ill, and Mrs. Hammond and I went to visit her in the days before she died. She asked us to care for the child, to keep the child free of scandal. And on her deathbed, she named the child's father."

William looked up and met the older man's eyes, his mind swimming with a certainty that he already knew what the man was going to say.

"She named you as the father."

The news should have been a shock. And it was. But he knew it was the truth. He could not deny it. Emotions swirled within him. Isabelle bore a child. *His* child.

He was a father.

Anger took hold. It bubbled low within him and grew with every passing second. "Why was I never notified?" William shouted. At a vicar. He should stop. "You knew this and you kept it from me! What gave you the right?"

"She asked us not to tell you." Hammond's voice was frustratingly calm.

"And why would she do that? Did she think I would not take responsibility? Did she not know that I loved her? That I would still care for the child?"

"She was ashamed. She confessed that she knew she was with child when she left you and married another. She had been blinded by what she thought was love for another and made a selfish decision."

"Wait." William held up his hand to stop the man. "She knew she was carrying my child and still she married?"

"It pains me to be the one to tell you."

William ignored the apology. "Did she think I would abandon *our* child?"

"To be fair, Sterling, the life you were living at the time Isabelle died was hardly one of a family-centered man."

"And what qualifies you to make that decision?" William thundered.

"Nothing, other than experience. For if you had decided not to care for the child, what then? Is it fair that the child be exposed to a life of rejection when she could be happy and well cared for in a girls' school?"

The words hit with a force that almost stopped his next breath. The vicar's words held merit. After Isabelle left, he had spiraled quickly into a dark, lonely place. Intoxicated every day. Up all hours of the night. Asleep all day. "Perhaps I would have acted differently had I known."

The vicar returned to his desk and sat down. He leaned forward, his voice still low and controlled. "Perhaps, but rightly or wrongly, I made a promise. And for the child's welfare, I kept it. Forgive me if I have wronged you. But I made the decision with the information I had at the time."

William forced his breathing to slow. Beads of perspiration lined his brow and dampened his shirt.

The vicar's voice was calm. "And that brings me to the brooch."

The brooch. William had almost forgotten about it.

"When the child entered our care, Mrs. Hammond and I placed the child at Rosemere, which is why you found Isabelle's things there."

"You mean to tell me that my child has been living on my own property for all these years?"

The vicar nodded.

William pressed a hand to his forehead and whispered, "Which girl?"

"Emma Simmons."

The girl's face flashed in his mind. Of course. He saw it clearly. Isabelle's olive complexion and mahogany hair. His own clear light-blue eyes with the Sterling black lashes. Anger flared afresh. "Why would you allow that poor child to think she had no one, that she was an orphan? That is cruel!"

At this, the vicar did not respond.

William leaned forward, his hands on the back of the chair, and willed his breathing to slow, the volume of his voice to lower. "Who else knows of this?"

"My wife."

William rolled his eyes. Suddenly Mrs. Hammond's cool behavior was almost understandable. "Who else?"

"Mr. Creighton, before he died, knew of the circumstance."

It was not Mr. Creighton who concerned William. "Does Miss Creighton know?"

"No. But I feel strongly that she should. After the fire, she had questions about Emma's family, but because of my promise, I could not provide answers." He clasped his hands on the desk in front of him. "But she deserves to know, as does little Emma. I hope you will do the right thing."

25

I'm a father.

William stepped out of the vicarage, out from the Hammonds' home. Snow swirled around him.

A father.

The reality muddled his mind. He'd been a father for years, and he never knew.

In a fog, William mounted Angus and circled the horse around. His daughter had been living less than a mile from his estate.

William didn't know if he was angry.

Or happy.

Or scared.

He'd raced Angus on the way over here, eager for answers. But now that he had every answer to every question, he wasn't sure what to make of them.

Isabelle. She'd betrayed him and rejected him. And then kept the greatest secret from him and took it with her to her grave. Why on her deathbed did she insist that he not be told? Was it embarrassment, as the vicar had said? Or something else?

Would knowing he had a daughter have changed the manner in which he had lived his life these last eight years? Apparently Isabelle had thought it would not have made a difference, and better for her to think that than accept William as the father.

He could not doubt his paternity. He knew the past; he knew full well his actions. And there was no mistaking the blue eyes and black lashes that had long marked the Sterlings. The deep dimple in the child's cheek was so like his mother's.

He urged Angus into a faster gait. The snow had turned to sleet that, driven by the wind, stung his eyes. The cold forced its way through the fabric of his caped coat, pricking his skin and chilling him to the core. He stopped at the top of Wainslow Peak and looked down toward the school. In the past few weeks, this school, this small school, had turned his life upside down. And his daughter was inside and had been for years.

Twilight was falling, and yellow candlelight winked from Rosemere's windows. Every breath he took burned in the chill air. He had two choices. Accept the child as his own or turn his back on her and continue the secret.

He realized he could ignore the news he had received—allow life to continue on as it had for Emma. She seemed content enough in Miss Creighton's care. But now that he knew the truth, could he doom her to a life alone, with no family? An orphan?

And what about his life?

How could he take on the responsibility of a child when he could not even manage his own affairs? He thought of Rafertee. The debt. The beating. Maybe even the fire at the Rosemere stable. How could he put a child at risk? And not just any child. This was his child. *His Emma.*

He turned the horse to the east, ready to head home to Eastmore Hall. A prize by any account. But increasingly, it had become a noose, growing tighter and more cumbersome by the day.

The tally of his folly, his gambling, had grown too large, too dangerous. He'd been fighting to save Eastmore Hall and the land, at times asking himself, *For what?* He now had a reason to fight. A purpose. His daughter. This was for her. An atonement for her lonely life up until this point.

He circled his confused mount, trying to determine the best course of action. He could not go to Rosemere. He was not yet ready to tell Miss Creighton and reveal his identity to his daughter. Instead, he needed to think.

Jumbled thoughts, a torrent of disorganized priorities, bombarded him. He should formulate a plan. But he'd never been good at such things. He just acted on impulse.

One thought came into focus—being worthy.

Worthy of his family's legacy.

Worthy of his daughter's esteem.

And another thought seemed to align itself with every other rational thought in his mind . . . worthy of Miss Creighton.

26

William was exhausted. His heart's pace had not stilled, his mind had not yet calmed. When Eastmore Hall came into view, he was surprised to see light spilling from the windows. It had been months since Eastmore Hall's windows had shone so. Something was not right.

With a swift kick to his horse's belly, he maneuvered down the narrow path and through the arched stone gate.

Lewis, as if waiting for him, stood under the portico and reached out to take Angus's bridle.

William dismounted. "What's going on here?"

"Riley and other men. They were working out at the site for the new mill when the snow began. Came back here to wait it out."

William stepped under the portico and wiped the sleet from his face. "Made themselves at home, did they?"

A twinge of self-conscious embarrassment surged through him. How many of them would see the state of Eastmore? With its sheeted furniture? Its cold rooms?

He rubbed his chin. Surely they would figure out his secret. And he was almost relieved.

William stepped into his own house. The grand foyer had been lit, and light and masculine chatter spilled out through the library's paneled doors.

The butler looked at him apologetically. "Welcome home, Mr. Sterling. These men seemed determined to wait out the weather here. I did not think you would wish me to turn them away."

"You are right, Cecil. Thank you for handling them."

Cecil took William's outside things. "I served them the last of the port. I hope I was not presumptuous."

"No, of course not. How long have they been here?"

"About two hours."

William shook the moisture from his hair, his clothing, and, with a deep breath, stepped into the library. His instincts were tingling.

Five men, each with a drink in his hand. Their loud laughter and disheveled appearance suggested they had been indulging far longer than the two hours the butler had suggested, or else they had been at it before they arrived.

It was Riley who first noticed William.

"Sterling! There you are! Where in blazes have you been? Been waiting for hours."

William stiffened as Riley slung his arm around his shoulder, heavy with the weight of uncontrolled movement. William scanned the room. He recognized Carlton, but the other men he'd not seen before. Yet they were in his house. And were they involved in his business venture?

He nodded in their direction. "Who are your friends?"

"This here's Cyrus Temdon. And this is Henry Groves and last is Charles Benson. All these fine men are going to help us with the mill as soon as the land softens a bit."

William eyed the men, who had been playing cards, his

annoyance growing by the moment. The men appeared sloppy. Foxed. Is this what Riley had meant by "taking care of the details"?

"Will, you need something to drink. Somebody get this man something to drink." He held up his glass, entertained by his own notion, and then pointed his finger toward one of the men.

"Thank you, no."

Riley's eyes opened wide and he tucked his chin down, as if unable to believe what he had just heard. "Sterling? William Sterling? Turn down a bit o' brandy?"

Riley leaned in closer, nearly tipping over until William shifted, allowing his partner to get his footing. "Listen, these blokes are good sorts, just fancy a pint or two. They'll be right in the morning, and then you'll see."

William grunted. "Look a little sorry to me."

"Best not let them hear you talk like that. Tend to be sensitive, that lot." Riley waved a pointed finger in the air. "Listen, I been meaning to discuss a matter with you."

William almost dreaded hearing the words. There was always something Riley wanted to discuss. "What?"

"The land that we are building on is top-notch. Top-notch, indeed. If only we had more room."

William frowned and folded his arms across his chest, unable to pry his eyes from the raucous game of cards and unwilling to have the same conversation they'd had on the moors. "What are you getting at?"

"Well, you know my thoughts on the Thaughley River. But what if we also had an outlet to the main road in town?"

William's response was curt. "Don't see how you can have it both ways. Besides, we've talked about this, Riley. Latham Hill is the only land I am willing to invest."

"Whoa, no reason to be so testy. Just making conversation." An easy laugh slipped from Riley.

Everything amused Riley when he had a drink or two. Everything was a joke. But William was hardly in the mood for such folly. His body ached from the ride, and his head pounded with the recent news. Normally a drink and company would soothe anything, but he was past those days. He just wanted answers.

Riley sauntered to the gaming table, and William sat like a stranger in his own home. Activity swirled about him, infusing the house with life and gaiety. Had he not in recent weeks been lamenting the lack of companionship? Mourning the days of parties and gatherings, weekend house parties and extravagant festivities? With these men in his house, the noise pummeled his ears. Their gritty laughter made the pounding in his head worse. Perhaps he'd grown used to the quiet and lonely evenings, but he knew there was more to his discomfort than that.

His thoughts were no longer on finding pleasure in the moment, in finding splinters of raucous distraction to divert his mind from the matters weighing on his soul. Call it maturity or perhaps even responsibility. He was no longer that same person.

He was a father.

While the merrymaking raged on, William racked his memory, trying to remember the details of the child. He tried to recall the happy, bright-eyed child he saw on his first visit to Rosemere, but instead his memory held tight to the recollection of what she had felt like limp in his arms. His heart thudded against his rib cage even though he sat perfectly still.

He wanted to see her. Wanted to know she was safe. Wanted to protect her. But his library was full of living, breathing memories of the past he needed to face and confront before he could be the type of father he wanted—no, needed—to be.

"Join us, Sterling."

William waved Riley off.

"Not like you to turn down a game of chance, now is it?"

"Been a long day." That really was not a lie.

"More like you have someone else on your mind."

William bit on the leading question. "Oh yeah? And who is that?"

"You've been spending a lot of time over at Rosemere, or am I mistaken? That sister of Creighton's is pretty. Is that the reason you are not interested in selling the land? Eh?" Riley took a long swig of brandy, then turned back to William and pointed a wobbly finger in his direction. "Ah, and I say that is a capital idea. Just what you need."

William studied his neighbor. Even though drink softened Riley's edge, experience had taught William that it also unearthed another side of Riley. Drink had the tendency to loosen Riley's tongue. Opinions flowed freely. Accusations and condemnation emerged with equal ease.

"You are mistaken. My only interest is in my horses."

Riley snorted a sarcastic chuckle and rolled his head to the side to face William, his dark eyes red. "Yes, yes, I know all about your horses. But you cannot keep secrets from an old friend."

Old friend, indeed. William shifted uncomfortably. "Maybe I will have a drink." He ignored the sly smile on Riley's face and helped himself to a glass.

"That's what I like to hear. So tell me. Miss Creighton, is it?"

William did not like the sound of her name on Riley's lips. She was pure. Good. And increasingly, Riley seemed to become a representation of things that were evil.

"I have nothing but the highest respect for Miss Creighton. She is quite capable in her profession. But that is the extent of my admiration."

"Oh, come on." A raw laugh sputtered from the man he'd considered a friend for so long.

William poured a drink, consumed nothing. His stomach soured at the thought of it passing his lips.

Miss Creighton. Emma. Rosemere. Eastmore Hall. They were inexplicably connected. He felt it within his core. And just hearing the smirk in Riley's voice made his muscles twitch. But he had to stay calm. This was his business partner, and regardless of what he thought of their actions on this particular night, he needed Riley. Well, at least he needed the mill and the financial security it would provide for him *and* his daughter.

"Come on. Why so serious? The building will commence soon. 'Tis time to celebrate!"

William rubbed his hand across his face. He wondered if the men were planning on spending the night. His preoccupation with his own thoughts made him agitated. The hour had grown late. The men, drunker.

After an hour or so, Lewis ambled in and no one besides William seemed to notice. He sat next to William.

William said, "I do not think they are leaving."

Lewis extended a booted foot and laced his fingers behind his head. "I think you are right." He nodded toward the man in the far corner. "Do you recognize that man?"

William squinted. He was sure he'd recognize a man with such a hooked nose if he'd ever seen him. "No."

"Are you sure? Look closely."

William shook his head. "Can't say that I do."

Lewis released his laced fingers and leaned forward with his elbows on his knees. "Cyrus Temdon."

He said the words with such an inflection that William thought surely he should remember who the man was. But try as he might, he still could not place him. He shrugged.

"You really do not pay attention, do you? He was the groom at Rosemere for about the last five years. Up and quit after Mr. Creighton died, remember? Left 'em in the lurch, with just old George and young Charlie. Now he's the groom at Ambledale."

Uneasiness crept in. Too much was happening. Too quickly. William stood.

"What are you doing?" demanded Lewis.

"Nothing. Just going to get better acquainted with my friend." William narrowed his eyes on Temdon. "After all, he's connected with my business, is he not?"

William ignored Lewis's attempt to detain him and strode over to the card table and stood back, looking at the men.

Temdon was slouched in a chair, sloppy with drink's effect, although William suspected that the man's normal demeanor could not be much sharper. A scraggly beard covered his thin chin, and his unkempt clothing suggested his appearance was never much of a concern. His rheumy eyes were mere slits in his flushed face. William plopped in the chair next to the man and watched him. And listened. The man never took his eyes off the cards.

Most of what he heard was a foolish man's musings. He sat and listened for a good twenty minutes. Waiting. Listening.

And then he heard, "We'll just burn it down again."

William snapped to attention.

The man and one of his companions laughed.

William leaned toward Temdon. "Burn what again?"

The intensity and volume of his question silenced the room.

A nervous chuckle slipped from Temdon's chapped lips as his eyes darted with apprehension to Riley.

Riley's face reddened, and his eyes cast a dagger toward Temdon.

William stood up, knocking his chair backward. "I asked you a question, Temdon. What do you mean, 'burn it down again'?"

The silence in the room was suffocating. Someone cleared his throat. William pushed past Temdon and walked over to Riley. Betrayal hung heavy in the air. He wanted to know the truth as much as he wanted to deny it. "To my knowledge, nothing has burned around these parts since the stable at Rosemere. So I repeat. Burn what down again?"

Riley's uncomfortable laugh and averted gaze gave William the answer he sought. His heart was beating at an alarming rate. His muscles twitched with anger. He broke his stare at Riley only when Lewis stepped behind him.

Riley, a pleading look in his eyes, extended his hands. "Come on, Sterling," he sputtered.

William could not wait for his halfhearted excuse. With both hands, William grabbed Riley by the coat and pulled him to a standing position. Riley cursed under his breath and grabbed hold of William's arms to steady himself.

"You'd better start explaining yourself, Riley."

"What did you expect me to do? You said the land was non-negotiable."

William tightened his grip on the coat. "And that gave you the authority, the right, to burn my property?"

Riley struggled to maintain balance. "It was only the stable."

"And what were you hoping to accomplish with that?"

"You said they would never leave. I was trying to get them to leave." Riley twisted, attempting to free himself. "Latham Hill is not big enough for our needs."

"There are women and children at Rosemere! You could have killed them!"

"There is no need to be so dramatic."

"Dramatic?" William pushed Riley away. "You burned my property! And you tried to frighten my tenants into leaving. One of the girls was injured. Seriously injured." William's hands balled into fists, but he stepped back to prevent himself from throwing a punch at anyone. As far as he was concerned, all of these men were involved. "I want you out of my house and off my property. And not just Eastmore Hall property. I want you off Latham Hill."

Riley lowered his voice, as if trying to shield what he was saying from the men in the room. "You don't mean that. You're just angry. This is just a misunderstanding."

"A misunderstanding?" William's voice thundered from every stone in Eastmore Hall's walls. "No, you lied to me! I believe the misunderstanding came when I trusted you with this business arrangement. Consider the arrangement terminated."

Riley stared at him as if stunned into silence.

"Did you hear me?" William shouted. "Leave at once!"

27

The door flung open with such intensity that it banged against the paneled wall. Patience was so startled she nearly jumped from her chair. She gasped at the sight of Charlie standing in the doorway, his complexion pale and his eyes wide.

Alarmed, Patience hurried over to the boy. "Charlie, dearest, what is it?"

The boy sniffed and wiped his nose with the back of his hand, his eyes fixed on Mrs. Lydia Creighton who was seated next to the fire.

"Charlie, this is Mrs. Lydia Creighton, Mr. Creighton's new wife." She explained who Lydia was, thinking that Charlie's uncustomary silence had to do with the presence of the stranger, but when the boy made no effort to greet Lydia, her concern grew.

"Lydia, would you be so kind as to give us a moment?"

The boy shrank against the wall as Lydia nodded, gathered her sewing, and left the library. Once she was gone, Charlie pushed the door closed and stepped close to Patience. "I heard something."

The earnestness of the boy's expression and the intensity of his whisper sent an icy finger tracing along her spine. Patience drew a sharp breath, alarmed at Charlie's strange behavior. She kept her voice low, half fearing the answer. "What did you hear?"

"I heard Mr. Sterling and Mr. Lewis arguing." Charlie gulped, his eyes nervously scanning the room before turning his attention back to her.

"And what were they arguing about?"

"The fire at the stable was not an accident."

A tremor shook Patience. "Of course it was an accident."

The boy shook his head, unblinking. "No, ma'am. I heard them talking about it myself."

"Whom did you hear, Charlie?"

His chin trembled. "Mr. Sterling."

At the name, a knife sliced through Patience. She felt the wind leave her lungs, along with all her silly schoolgirl inclinations. She shook her head. "Surely you are mistaken. Mr. Sterling owns this property. He would never purposely damage it."

"But I heard him, Miss Creighton. Him and Mr. Lewis, with some other men. They want to build a building."

The mill.

Patience pressed her lips together, wishing she could unhear the words she'd just heard. "What exactly did you hear? And start from the beginning, please."

"It was cold last night, so Mr. Lewis said I could sleep inside Eastmore Hall. They was up way late, Miss Creighton."

"Who was up late?"

"There was a bunch of men. Mr. Lewis said they was Mr. Sterling's friends with the mill, and I was to keep quiet and out of their way."

She swallowed a dry lump in her throat, realizing that he might be speaking the truth. She sat down in a chair and motioned for the boy to sit as well. But he only shifted from foot to foot, as if bursting to tell her what else he knew.

"Well then, go on," Patience prompted, her voice barely above a whisper.

"Said that he wanted us to leave the school so that they could build the mill here. Wants the school to go away so they can have the land next to the river."

She thought of the Rosemere land, which was the smoothest, most level land compared to the rocky and hilly terrain that surrounded it. Of course it was an attractive location. Close to the river. Close to the village and the main road. Was that the reason why Mr. Sterling had been so interested suddenly? She could not explain the tears gathering in her eyes or the pinch of emotion in her throat. At first she could not believe that Mr. Sterling could be in such a business as to burn the stable. He had been so prompt in beginning the rebuilding. But then the warnings of Mrs. Hammond were vivid in her mind. *A most unscrupulous man.* Was Mrs. Hammond right? Had she been foolish to fall prey to the charms of Mr. William Sterling?

"You're sure you heard it correctly?" she asked.

Charlie stammered, "I didn't see him say it, but I heard it through the walls. Then there was a lot of shouting, and I couldn't make out anything anyone was saying. Then they all left."

"And have you seen Mr. Sterling today?"

"No, ma'am. Was I right to tell you?"

"Yes, Charlie. You were right."

He sighed, as if relieved. "I can't stay there. Not no more. Can I come home?"

Patience looked down at her hands. How they trembled. She did not trust her legs. Nor did she want to sit down. She felt odd. Ill. She closed her eyes, waiting for the trembling in her lips to subside. She took a deep breath and blew it out.

There it was. Her answer.

Had Mrs. Hammond been right? Mr. Sterling could not be trusted. Whether or not Charlie heard the story correctly, how could he have been mistaken about the fire? Whatever he heard, the truth was that foul play was at hand. And Mr. Sterling was either aware of it or party to it.

She could hardly deny that her heart had harbored romantic inclinations toward Mr. Sterling. How quickly she recalled his clear blue eyes. The gentle timbre of his voice. How she warmed when he was near, and how he occupied her mind in the quiet moments of her day.

She had been presented the facts. Warned by people.

But why did her stubborn heart resist the warnings?

A knock sounded on her door.

She drew a shaky breath. It could be any of her students. Her brother.

The door opened, and her heart sank even more. *Ewan.*

Patience wiped a shaky hand across her brow. "Ew—Mr. O'Connell."

His brow creased. "What is the matter?"

She forced a smile. Her chin quivered. "Nothing is wrong."

"Your cheeks are flushed." He rushed forward and grabbed her arms. The nearness of him, the expression of concern on his familiar face, all contributed to a sense of suffocation.

With a sudden burst of energy, she wrenched her arms free and rubbed them protectively. "I said I am fine."

He dropped his hands, then adjusted his cravat. Without being invited, Ewan sat down in a chair near her, leaned back, and folded his arms across his chest.

She diverted her eyes and tried to ignore how in the afternoon light he looked so like the boy she had grown up with. The familiar way his too-long hair fell over his broad forehead. For a brief moment she found herself wishing things could be as they once were, when she could confide her troubles in him, and he would always know how to set things right.

She had misinterpreted Mr. Sterling's intentions.

Perhaps she had misread Ewan O'Connell's as well.

Patience walked over to stoke the fire, eager to be busy. "What can I do for you?"

He did not respond, and she paused at her task and turned to look at him.

"I wish you would sit with me."

She arched an eyebrow and blew out a breath. She felt sick—not the sick of an anticipating heart, but a sick dread. She nodded, wordlessly returning the poker to its holder, and sat down on the chair next to him. The overwhelming sense that something important was about to happen nearly stole the wind from her lungs. She waited for him to speak.

"You've changed."

She sucked in a defensive breath, but instead of firing back a clever retort, she pressed her lips together and looked out the window to the fading dusk and waited for him to explain himself.

"Will you at least look at me?"

She turned toward him and forced her eyes to meet his. Pale, brown eyes that, when she had been younger, she thought to be full of mischievous romance.

"I suppose we have both been changed," he said. "Time does that. I can only imagine that things have been quite harrowing since your father died. I can see you are troubled, and I'll not pretend that I have the right to know what it is. I thought I would never see you again. But when I saw your brother, and when he told me the circumstances surrounding the school, I knew the time to redeem myself had come."

Redemption? His words were delivering a cryptic message. A

gust of air slammed the window, sending in slivers of cold air, and she was grateful for the coolness. She pictured herself running for the door, but he leaned in closer.

"Miss Creighton. Patience."

Her Christian name sounded strange coming from him. Suddenly, she could not breathe. She jumped from the chair, but as she did, he rose too, and in one step, he was inches from her, had gathered her hands in his, and was holding them against his chest.

She diverted her gaze and inched back. But he held her hands tight.

"You bewitch me. You always have." She could feel the warmth of his breath on her skin. "I flatter myself to think that you feel the same way. I am proud of you, Patience. Proud of how you filled your father's shoes when your brother could not. But you need not bear this weight alone."

Ewan inched closer. She had nowhere to go. If she stepped back, the fire would surely light her skirt, and a heavy mahogany chair pinned her from her right. She pressed her lips together. She had no choice but to hear what he had to say.

His eyes were intent, almost pleading. She could not look away. "It is fate, do you not see? My heart first suspected it when your brother told me you had not married. And when he invited me here to help with the school, I dared hope that you would feel the same way."

She had to stop him. "Please, Mr. O'Connell, I—"

"And then I saw you again. Every bit as lovely as that day I last beheld you under the elm. My last memory of you was that day with tears in your eyes, and here I find you a strong and independent woman."

She was no longer hearing his words. In a panic, she shook her head. "Don't, I—"

"But surely you cannot deny this force that has brought us

together." Excitement quickened his words and heightened his color, refusing to allow her to reject him. "I wanted to wait, but heaven help me, I cannot. I no longer speak as a youth, but as a man, with full possession of my heart and mind. Do me the honor, Patience. Do me the immense honor of becoming my wife."

When his rush of words finally silenced, Patience was unable to look away from the pale brown eyes that had implored her so many years ago.

She had accepted that she would be a spinster. Or she *thought* she had. William Sterling awakened feelings in her heart that she had never known could exist. Before she could process the feelings within her, here was Mr. O'Connell, not Mr. Sterling, making an offer of marriage.

Tears pooled in her eyes. For when her heart was so clearly set on another, how could she accept?

But in light of the accusation she'd heard regarding Mr. Sterling, how could she refuse?

She could not get her lips to articulate her thoughts, nor was she sure she wanted them to. She stared at Ewan, mouth hanging open, watching his changing expression as he interpreted her silence.

Slowly, he released his fingers from around hers. Many years ago, when she did not answer, tears had filled his eyes. But today, anger was apparent.

"There is someone else, is there not?"

Her chin quivered, but she said nothing. The warmth that had softened his eyes vanished, leaving behind a cold, steely expression. Then he said, low and with menace, "Sterling."

"Don't be ridiculous."

"I will not press you for an answer. I know that I have just returned, that I caught you off guard. But promise me this. Promise me that you will at least consider it."

Her breathing slowed and she could only whisper, "I will."

28

Willliam paced the alleyway of the stable in front of the foaling stall. The mare circled in restless agitation, nipping at her swishing tail and neighing loudly. A wild look widened her black eyes.

"Should be any time." Lewis folded his sleeve high on his arm.

William nodded and looped a length of rope around his shoulder. After all these months of planning, the time for the first foal was about to arrive. The delivery had to be successful. Slaten's offspring had to be strong. There was no other choice.

In the silence of the dark stable, waiting as they were, he shook off his exhaustion. Two days ago he learned he was a father. And two days ago he'd learned of Riley's betrayal. Both were a shock, for different reasons, and ever since he'd been unable to find a moment's rest.

He hung the rope on a nearby hook and let his hand linger against the cold metal. The fire had not been an accident. It had been a ruse on Riley's part to force the Creightons from the land with the assumption that he would not be able to rebuild the stable. And the fact that Riley's action had injured his daughter only fueled the anger within him. He had foiled Riley's plan by rebuilding the stable, but he had been counting on money from the mill. Money now gone.

With a quick glance at the laboring mare, he stepped outside for a breath of fresh morning air. Ever-present mist shrouded his view. He looked out toward Wainslow Peak. Its height and clinging foliage blocked any sight of Latham Hill beyond it.

He looked off toward Rosemere and could just make out the chimney line above the trees. He tried to reconstruct the image of the child, his child, who lived there. He could see only Isabelle's olive skin. His own clear eyes. He wanted to run to Miss Creighton, explain everything. But if he were Miss Creighton, would he want to release a sweet child to the care of a man who had gambled away everything?

The best plan would be for the child to remain at the school. He had no way to care for her properly at Eastmore Hall. But he could not allow her to go on living under the belief that she was an orphan. He wanted to be more than merely financially responsible. He wanted to be a father, a true father. He was not a man prone to emotion, but with so much that he had to make right, he felt overwhelmed, almost lost.

His gaze fell on the overgrown path leading to Sterling Cemetery, where his mother and father lay under ancient elms. He'd tried it his father's way, relying on his own strength for success and self-worth. With so many decisions to be made, he would try it his mother's way.

He stood in the open, empty yard in front of Eastmore Hall and lifted his face to the churning sky. Was God up in the heavens, beyond the mist and clouds? And if he called out to God, would He respond? With his face upturned and his hat brim away from his face, the raindrops fell on his cheeks and lashes. "God, if you hear me, I need help." He wiped the rain from his face and looked heavenward. "I want to make it right. Help me know what to do."

L

Lydia swept into the study, her hair in an intricate twist and books stacked in her arms. Her face formed a pretty pout. "Patience, dear, whatever is the matter? You look as if you have seen a ghost."

Patience looked up from the letter she was writing. "Oh, no, no. I am well. A headache is all."

"Well, it is no wonder." Lydia began stacking the books on the shelves. "I am surprised we are not all sick in bed on account of this weather. I do not know when I have been so cold. And this endless rain and snow! Is the weather always like this here?"

Patience tucked the half-written letter away. "We often get snow this time of year, but this winter has been unusually harsh."

Lydia paused from her task of shelving books long enough to click her tongue and cast a quick glance out the window. "It has been weeks since the fire, but I can still smell smoke. It is as if it still clings to everything in this house."

Patience watched Lydia shelve the last of the books. How young and full of life she looked. Patience swallowed a twinge of envy at the girl's—no, woman's—pale yellow silk dress with dainty half boots made of ivory kid leather. Her glossy hair, the color of straw, was neatly smoothed and curled against her head. Patience lifted her hand to smooth her own wayward black hair from her face, wishing she'd taken more pains with it.

But what did it matter? Now that the stable was nearing completion, William Sterling had not been by for days.

Either way, it was of little consequence.

"I've been meaning to ask you a question, Patience."

Patience pushed her childish thoughts aside. "Yes?"

"It is about your mother." She took timid steps toward her, reminding Patience of the first day Lydia came to Rosemere. "I hope I am not being too forward."

Patience tensed, anticipating unpleasant news. But any topic would be a diversion from the unwelcome storm of her own thoughts. "Of course not. She is your mother too, is she not?"

Lydia scurried to close the door and then returned. "Is she . . . well?"

The question was an odd one. "Yes. I mean . . . no. Ever since Father's death, she's been . . . melancholy."

Lydia's face twisted in contemplation, and she pressed her lips together thoughtfully. "I do hope you do not think me impertinent. But since my arrival, I have been unable to discern her opinion of me. At the dinner when your neighbors were here, she seemed so happy with me, but ever since—"

Patience drew a deep breath. "You will have to forgive her, Lydia. She has had a hard time with my father's death. No doubt Rawdon has mentioned that she has changed."

Lydia toyed with the lace trim on her sleeve. "Truthfully, he has said little on the matter. When I questioned him about it, he said only that things are the way they are. And that is why I have come to you."

"I see." Patience didn't want to talk about her mother, but at least they were not talking about a burned stable. Or her brother's plans for the school. Or Ewan O'Connell. Or, heaven help her, William Sterling.

Perhaps it would be nice to have another friend to talk with. And if she could not trust her sister-in-law, whom could she trust? "I wish I knew how to help her. I could barely get her out of bed for months following my father's death." Patience bit her tongue, stopping short of sharing her recollection of how hard it had been to see her mother so forlorn, especially in her own grieving state. Patience did not wish to paint a picture of her mother as being sad. Instead, she would continue to promote her mother as she knew she could be. Kind. Loving. "She is getting better by the day."

"I am familiar with what it can be like to bear the weight of one's grieving. Oh, I will not go into details, but I can tell you I have had my share of pain." Lydia offered a weak smile, and Patience wondered if she should inquire. But before she could decide, Lydia's face brightened. "I am glad to hear she is on the mend, for I have news to share, and I was not sure how she would take it." She hurried over to Patience and took her hands. "Will you hear my news? I need to know if you think such news will upset your mother."

"I cannot imagine that anything you have to say to my mother could upset her."

"Oh, but it is big news, and if I thought she was not pleased with my union with her son, it could be quite disastrous. Perhaps if you give me your opinion, it will help me decide how best to proceed."

Patience prepared herself to hear her sister-in-law's news. Heaven knows she'd already heard enough in one day that she should be shocked at nothing. Interest piqued, Patience braced herself. "You may tell me anything."

Lydia wrung her hands as she stood there, her eyes bright. "I am with child, Patience."

Patience had been wrong. She had been prepared to hear any-thing . . . but that.

Patience sank down in the chair, hiding her alarm behind a smile. Suddenly, it made sense. How pale Lydia had been in the morning. Her dizzy spells. The appropriate words seemed to slide from her lips without much intention. "I am so happy for you and Rawdon. How are you feeling?"

Lydia smiled and pressed her hand to her middle, and it was only then that Patience noticed the small bump on her slight figure.

"I am doing well. I was so worried, for my older sister was quite ill, but I have managed to be fine." Her hand flitted up to her hair, then back down over her midsection. "I have to admit, I feel relieved to have been able to tell you my news."

Guilt pressed on Patience's chest. She may have a hard time accepting Rawdon, but her sister-in-law had given her no reason to mistrust or dislike her. "I am glad you told me."

"Should I tell your mother?" Lydia's concern was obvious. "It is big news, indeed. And sudden. Of course, she will notice for herself soon enough, but she has dealt with so much in the last couple of weeks. Do you think it will be too much for her? I do so worry for her."

Patience was skeptical. She wondered how much of Lydia's concern was fear for her mother and how much was fear of their mother's disapproval. But either way, it was not her place to make a judgment. There were so many children bustling around Rosemere. But they were other people's children. She'd always thought that the first infant at Rosemere would be her own.

But it was not to be. She was unmarried. The first child would be Rawdon's.

Patience chided herself at the foolish tears gathering in her eyes. It was not the time for selfish regret. "My dear Lydia, it would be unfair of her to be anything but excited for this new addition to the family! A baby is always a cause for joy. I think this is the best medicine for Mother."

Her sister-in-law rushed forward and embraced her. A spark of connectedness shivered through Patience. But her face ached with the effort it took to smile. "Does Rawdon know that you were going to tell me?"

Lydia nodded. "He does. He said he thought you would probably have figured it out, since you are so observant."

An embarrassed chuckle rattled from her chest. She'd been so preoccupied with the happenings that she had noticed little. On many fronts. "Well, he was wrong. I had not suspected a thing. But I am glad."

Lydia smiled. "Good. Then Rawdon and I will tell her later today. Thank you for your advice."

Patience watched as Lydia hurried from the room in a swish of yellow satin and rose-scented water. But then, as she was about to reach the threshold, she turned. "Oh, how could I have forgotten?" Her expression changed from that of an expectant mother to that of a young schoolgirl in seconds. She hurried back and lowered her voice in a whisper. "I came to speak with you earlier today and saw Mr. O'Connell leaving this room."

Patience regarded her sister-in-law's wide eyes and mischievous grin. Questions disguised themselves in her statement, and unsure of what Lydia was about, Patience folded her arms across her chest protectively. "Yes."

Lydia wrinkled her nose and giggled. "Rawdon told me of your past with Mr. O'Connell. I do hope you do not mind his telling me, but now that we are sisters, I doubt you will. He told me that you parted ways in an abrupt fashion when you were both much younger. It seems as if fate is reuniting you." Lydia's eyebrow raised, and a smile parted her lips.

Patience felt uncomfortable under her sister-in-law's scrutinizing look. She recognized a leading question when she heard one, and no doubt Lydia wanted to know details. Considering what she was already aware of, she likely knew that Ewan meant to propose. Again. Even though Lydia had been so forthcoming with her personal secret did not mean that Patience was ready to do the same. Not yet.

"Yes, he was here."

Lydia looked at her expectantly. "And? Did he say anything of interest?"

"No."

"Oh." Lydia headed for the door but turned back with a teasing smile. "Well, I feel certain he could well have something interesting to say soon."

And with that she quitted the room.

29

William watched the gangly, long-legged colt in the stall. Hours old, he was already on wobbly, knob-kneed legs and nursing from his mother.

"All that waiting and now the lad is here," Lewis said.

William always found it amazing when a new horse was born, but it had been so long since he'd last witnessed a birth that he found it amazing all over again.

He'd expected something to go wrong. For that was his fate of late. He'd expected the horse to be stillborn. To have a deficiency. To have something happen to his mare. But nothing of the sort occurred. The foal was even a male. 'Twould bring a greater amount, and in light of what happened with his textile prospect, he needed money more than ever.

Lewis draped his arms over the stone wall of the stall and looked down at the foal. He scratched his disheveled hair. "Good-looking animal."

They had moved mother and baby to the stall next to the

birthing stall, and William had been shoveling up the soiled straw. "Let's hope he takes after his papa."

Lewis reached over to pat the mother on the neck. "Good girl," he cooed, and they watched as the foal again began to nurse. "He'll be strong."

William thought about his brief prayer. Had God heard him? Perhaps. But he could not breathe easy. Not yet. "I am going to write Bley to let him know the horse has been delivered and is here. Give him the opportunity to speak for him before he is weaned. I'll take the letter to town. There should be time to get it posted today."

"Are you sure you don't want me to take it to town?"

"No, you finish up here. Been a long day. I could use a ride."

The men worked in silence until William finished with the stall, then he hurried to the library. How many times he had sat here to pen a missive, but never had it seemed more crucial. To Bley, it would probably seem like just a courtesy note. But to William, it signified much more. If Bley would endorse him as a breeder, find success with one of Slaten's offspring, his plans stood a chance.

William rode to town, but instead of taking the shortcut over Wainslow Peak, he rode out to the main road. After posting his letter in Darbury's main square, he'd planned to head straight back to Eastmore Hall. But a flash of pink and green caught his eye.

Lydia Creighton was on the opposite side of the street, peering in the window of the milliner's shop, looking more suited to the streets of London than the sleepy town of Darbury. A pink gown hung from beneath her dark green, velvet pelisse, and a jaunty red feather plumed from her black cap. True to fashion, she was not out alone but with her maid, who was carrying a brown package beneath each arm.

He thought he'd be able to turn down the alley next to Griffin's

End and escape without being seen, but she turned, and when she did, a smile lit her face.

He'd been seen.

She waved her gloved hand in the air. "Mr. Sterling! Oh, Mr. Sterling!"

He froze. It was too late. To leave now would be rude, and if he expected to raise Emma, he not only needed to be on good terms with Mr. Rawdon Creighton but with his wife as well.

He walked across the street and bowed. "Mrs. Creighton. Pleasure to see you."

"Mr. Sterling. Just the man I was hoping to see."

He looked past her. "I am surprised to see you without your sister-in-law."

"Oh, I am sure you know Patience. So busy with the school, she barely has time for herself. So I thought I would treat her to a new bonnet. What do you think?" She surprised him by opening one of the boxes there in the street and holding a straw bonnet with an emerald green bow. "Should be becoming with her dark hair and green eyes, do you not agree?"

He was hardly an expert on women's hats, but he supposed the straw bonnet with a wide brim was nice enough. He allowed his mind to imagine what Miss Creighton would look like, her black hair and full lips.

Without giving him an opportunity to respond, she tucked the bonnet away. "In fact, I am pleased that I have met you here. You see, I am hosting a dinner tomorrow at Rosemere, just a small gathering, and Mr. Creighton and I would be honored if you would attend."

His interest was piqued. Miss Creighton would be there, surely. He could talk to her about Emma. And about . . . other things. "I'd be delighted, Mrs. Creighton."

"Good." She rewarded him with a good-natured smile and

returned the hat box to the solemn-faced maid. "You shall be in attendance, and I have invited the Hammonds and, of course, Mr. O'Connell will be there."

William thanked her for the invitation, tipped his hat, and walked back across the road to Angus. He shifted and adjusted his collar to guard against the wind. With the twinkle in her eye and the coy smile on her lips, he was certain Mrs. Lydia Creighton was up to something. He could prove nothing, and he knew little of her other than her talent for drawing silhouettes, but there was a motive behind her innocent invitation to dinner.

William retrieved his horse, mounted, and guided Angus back down the main road. He paused only slightly as he passed the main gate to Rosemere, with its formidable stone walls, intricate iron gate, and bits of ivy. His daughter was in there. He needed a plan. He'd formulate one tonight and then reveal all tomorrow.

Patience wove through the rows of easels as the girls stood in the library, looking out to the frozen moors. How she had loved painting as a young girl. She'd never had much talent for it, but she had enjoyed studying the details of nature and trying to capture the beauty.

She placed her hand on Ivy's shoulder as she passed. "Lovely," she exclaimed. But as she turned, a sharp cry echoed from in the house, a door slammed, and something crashed to the floor. The girls gasped and looked toward Patience, then a whisper circled among the students. Patience brushed past one of the other teachers, giving her instructions to oversee the children, then hurried from the room.

She entered the main hall, and Rawdon, face flushed and hair disheveled, was running down the stairs, taking them two at a time. His lips were pinched together in a fine line. When his eyes landed on Patience, he pointed his finger at her. "Of all of the unreasonable women," he sputtered, "she is the most ridiculous."

He stomped down the main hall, and for a moment Patience only stared after him, stunned at the emotional display. She wondered about following him. Their conversations since he had returned to Rosemere had been short. Terse. But regardless of what had transpired, he was still her brother.

Her only brother.

She decided to follow him and found him in the library, by the sideboard, pouring himself a glass of brandy. He shot it down his throat and poured another.

Patience slipped quietly into the room. She wondered if he was referring to their mother or his bride, but she didn't have to wait long to learn the answer to her question.

"I thought that she of all people would be pleased to learn she would be a grandmother."

Patience sat on the settee and folded her hands on her lap. It appeared as if he had finally realized the change in their mother's personality in a most personal way. "What happened?"

He replaced the decanter stopper and paced the room. "I still cannot figure it out. Lydia told you our news, and we went to tell Mother. I don't know what happened. Mother flew into a rage and accused Lydia of trapping me—as if Lydia could be capable of such a thing. I tried to speak reason to her, but she would not listen. The next thing, Lydia locked herself in our room and is refusing to come out or let me in."

Patience was mystified. "Why would Mother make such an accusation? And after showing Lydia such favor?"

Rawdon shook his head. "Something is different about her. Am I insane? Surely you see it too. She is different." He studied his hands. "I hardly know her."

Patience nibbled her lip. Her brother finally saw what she had been seeing for months. She had thought that once her brother acknowledged the problem, she would feel better about it. That the burden would get lighter, but instead, it felt like a heavy rock, weighing her down. No. It did not make the burden lighter. It only made it more real.

"Mother has been through a lot over the last several months, Rawdon. I am sure she is simply overreacting to the news. You will see. Give her a day or two. I am sure she will come around."

Rawdon's black eyebrows rose. "Oh, I see. You are siding with her."

"I am not siding with anyone. But I do think you need to accept that Mother is not herself right now." Patience remembered her sister-in-law. "How is Lydia?"

Rawdon threw up a hand in exasperation. "I have never seen her so angry. Truth be told, I never thought her capable of such a temper. She demanded that we return to London right away." He snorted. "But where does she think we are going to go? All of our plans are—have always been—to invest her dowry in this school. I am not about to leave because of my mother's irrational rant."

His words sent selfish panic stabbing through her. If Rawdon were to leave, would Mr. O'Connell stay behind? Would he continue to run the school? She forced the feelings in her to settle. Rawdon was finally talking to her in a meaningful way. In a way that suggested their fragile relationship might indeed be strong once again, as it had been before their father died.

She chose her words carefully, as if each one might sway him. "I could talk to Mother, make her understand that—"

"Make her understand what? She cannot treat my wife in this manner. I will not tolerate it."

"Have compassion, Rawdon. Mother is frightened."

"Frightened? Of what?"

"Consider all the changes that happened in a short time. Father died. The stable burned. You brought home a new wife." She surprised herself that she was defending her mother. "And you left. For months. We did not know where you were. Or if you'd ever return."

He threw out his arms defensively. "So it is my fault?"

"No. I did not say that." Her voice remained low. "But consider the toll that this has taken on her. On all of us here."

He stared out the window, his lips pressed into a hard line. He rubbed his hand against the back of his neck. "What do you mean?"

"We were unsure if you were returning. We'd had no letter, no word. So we had to move forward as if you were not. What choice did we have with all these children? So you must understand how difficult it is for us when you come home with all of these changes. Lydia has been nothing but charming, but consider what this has done to Cassandra. And then Ewan's return. And your decision for a boys' school, a new cottage . . . it is all too much."

He pursed his lips, and his face contorted with annoyance.

"So be patient with Mother." She hesitated. "And with me."

At this, he finally looked right at her. She wanted to tell him everything. How angry she was with him. How she ached for Cassandra. Her brother was a matter-of-fact person, rarely swayed by emotion and with little tolerance for sentiment. But how could she continue to carry around the weight of her anger with him? It was tearing at her, and with all of the other worries on her mind, she wanted her brother—the brother she knew and loved—back.

"Patient with you?"

"When you left, I threw everything I had into the school. You weren't here. Mother was ill. And you come home with all of these changes. You even called me nothing more than a governess, a nurse. You have not even asked my opinion! And I have been the headmistress ever since you left. I am not angry, Rawdon. I am hurt. I know you are more acquainted with things of business than I am. But be patient with me too."

Rawdon looked down. "I apologize. I did not realize. I thought I was protecting you."

For now, just the mere recognition that all those months had been difficult was enough to alleviate some of the pressure building within her. "I will talk to Lydia. She is understandably upset. Once everyone has had an opportunity to calm, a different light will shed itself on the matter. You will see."

Rawdon muttered, "I do not see how."

"Please. Trust me." As if drawing strength from her own words, Patience added, "Everything will be all right."

30

Patience stood in the west wing where the family's bedchambers were. She looked at her mother's closed door. Across the hall was Rawdon and Lydia's door. In her hands she balanced a tray of tea, the teapot steaming. She blew out her breath. Her mother must have been upset to have treated Rawdon, her favorite, in such a fashion. But the dismay in her brother's eyes haunted her.

She turned and shifted the tray to rest against a hip. She knocked softly on the door.

Patience held her breath, waiting for a response, but none came.

She knocked again, louder this time. "Lydia? Lydia, dearest, it's Patience. May I come in?"

Again, her request was met with silence. She frowned, torn with the decision of whether she should try again. But just as she was about to turn to take the tea to her mother, she heard soft footsteps on the planked floor. The latch clicked and released, and the door swung open a crack.

The patter of feet retreated, and with her hip, Patience pushed the door open.

When she entered the room, Lydia was seated on the tall bed, her feet dangling over the side, making her look more like a child than a grown woman.

With careful balance, Patience pushed the door closed with her foot. "I brought you tea."

Lydia sniffed and studied her hands in her lap. Her muffled response was barely audible above the crackling fire. Patience set the tray down on a table.

The lackluster afternoon light fell across Lydia's fair hair and stooped shoulders. Neither the fanciest hair dressing nor the most shimmering silk could mask the young woman's pain. Her eyes, normally bright, were red-rimmed. The tip of her nose glowed crimson, and the space under her eyes was puffy. A twinge of regret shot through Patience at the sight of the young woman. She should have been more welcoming.

Perhaps she could start to make things right.

"I . . . I brought you tea." Even to her own ears, her voice sounded forced.

Lydia did not look up. "Thank you."

"Shall I pour you a cup? It is hot and strong."

Lydia did not respond, but Patience went ahead with pouring the tea, more so to keep her hands busy in the awkward silence.

Oh, God, give me the words to say.

She handed the tea to Lydia, who stretched out trembling hands, nearly splashing the steaming liquid on her gown.

Lydia kept her eyes focused on the teacup. "I take it you talked to Rawdon."

Patience nodded.

Lydia sniffed. "It was a mistake to come here. I see that now."

"You mustn't let Mother make you feel unwelcome. She has

not been herself for quite some time. She meant nothing by it, I assure you. Besides, you are Rawdon's wife. You belong here."

The words, once out of her mouth, struck her with profound meaning.

You belong here.

And Lydia did belong here, just as much as she did. She was family. Patience needed to start treating her as such. Patience sat next to her sister-in-law, trying to think of comforting words, and was almost relieved when she finally spoke again.

"Who did Rawdon betray?"

Patience was startled. "What do you mean?"

"Your mother said that he betrayed someone here. Who was she talking about?"

Cassandra.

Patience hesitated, and Lydia pushed herself off the bed and walked to the window.

"I do not expect you to tell me." Lydia's statement was more a stream of thought than an attempt to communicate. But then she turned with a renewed energy. "There was another, was there not?"

Patience sucked in a deep breath and tried to find a way to bring comfort without either betraying her friend or overstepping her bounds. "Whatever his past, I know my brother. Probably better than anyone. And he loves you, Lydia."

But Lydia would not give up. "There was another, was there not?" she repeated. "You might as well tell me. I will certainly find out sooner or later."

The directness of Lydia's question convicted her.

Patience lowered her eyes and nodded.

Lydia's sharp intake of breath surprised her. The afternoon sun revealed her silhouette through the delicate fabric of her dress. Lydia's protruding abdomen was evident. Patience's heart ached for her sister-in-law when she realized the thoughts that must be going through her head.

Funny how her heart could ache for both Cassandra and Lydia in the same moment.

"It was Miss Baden." Lydia's words were soft but held such a demand that they could not be ignored.

The women locked eyes.

Lydia looked away. "Your silence has given me my answer."

Tears streamed down Lydia's pale cheeks. Patience stood and walked over to her and took hold of her hand. "My brother loves you, Lydia. Whatever his past, he loves you. I have watched him."

Lydia's shoulders shook with sobs. Patience wrapped her arms around the young woman. "And for what it is worth, dear Lydia, I am glad you are here. Please forgive me if I have been unwelcoming. I was wrong. You belong here at Rosemere, and you have a sister and a friend. You have me."

Lydia pulled back from the embrace. "What of your mother? She said I tricked him into marrying me. She called me a Jezebel. A Jezebel!"

Patience winced at the word. Yes, she could hear her mother say it. "My mother is unhappy, but it has little to do with you and more to do with her inability to accept the loss of my father. Give her time."

Lydia managed a weak smile.

Patience retrieved the abandoned cup of tea. "Here, drink this while it is hot."

Lydia sat down and took a sip of the tea. Knowing of Lydia's eager anticipation for that night's dinner party, she said, "You must relax. You have a dinner party tonight. Or have you forgotten?"

A tiny spark flashed in Lydia's eyes. "Oh yes. I had forgotten."

"Everyone will be expecting you to create your silhouettes again."

"I daresay my silhouettes will be the last thing on Mr. O'Connell's mind."

The teasing glance in her sister-in-law's eyes concerned her. She had hoped to offer her sister-in-law a distraction from her distress, but this was not exactly what she had in mind.

Her sister-in-law took another sip. "He seems quite smitten."

"Our romance ended long ago, Lydia. It is best left in the past."

A frown creased her forehead. "Is it? Perhaps your heart belongs to another?"

Patience stood up. She was ready to discuss Lydia's romantic life, but hers was off limits. "I must go check on the girls."

"I did not mean to offend, Patience, really. But there is information I must tell you."

Patience whirled back around. "What?"

"I have invited another guest to the dinner. And he has accepted the invitation. William Sterling."

She hesitated for only a moment, then hurried from the room.

Patience felt flushed. Uneasy. For how could she discuss her heart when she herself did not understand it? She hurried down the corridor and flew down the stairs. She paused at the landing and looked down at the new stable.

How much had changed in her life. Pretty and new, the little stable stood almost as a testament to change. Things would not—could not—stay the same. The fire—and the events leading up to it—robbed her of the security of her past. She would have to be brave and strong and let go of the things that were familiar.

She turned to continue down the stairs when movement from the window caught her eye. Near the tree line, two figures were talking next to a garden wall. She squinted, clearly making out Rawdon's black hair, his shoulders. But who was that next to him? *Cassandra!*

A feeling of dread washed over her. She felt almost faint. She watched, not knowing what to do. Should she look away? Forget she saw them? They appeared to be doing nothing inappropriate.

But then why did her heart protest so? Lydia's tear-stained face flashed in her mind. What was her brother doing?

But then Cassandra took two steps back. Her eyes were fixed on the ground. Rawdon, dressed in a sharp blue coat, gray breeches, and black boots, gestured toward the house, and Cassandra followed his gaze, causing Patience to dart away from the window for fear of being noticed. When her pulse calmed, she looked back out the window. They were standing farther apart. Rawdon's palms were outstretched. Cassandra shook her head and then covered her hair with the hood of her dark brown cloak and walked toward the house.

Heart still pounding, Patience leaned her back against the cool stone wall. She drew a deep breath. She would not jump to conclusions about what she saw. And yet the pain in her sister-in-law's eyes haunted her.

Rosemere was alive. Everywhere Patience turned, emotions bombarded her.

The house that had for so long been her shelter was no longer the protector. Instead of keeping pain and strife out, it kept them locked in.

In the early afternoon, she taught French to her young pupils, but she merely went through the motions. Her mind was fixed on what she had seen outside, near the garden wall. She snapped at a child whose attention was waning.

What was wrong with her? Why could she not rise above these thoughts?

Her mind's eye replayed the stolen moment she'd observed between Rawdon and Cassandra. Anger she could not explain lurked below the surface. She knew she was jumping to conclusions.

But how could she not? As soon as she was free, she marched up to Cassandra's room and pushed open the door.

"We must talk," Patience blurted out, pushing the door closed with such force that the window pane rattled in its frame.

Confusion twisted Cassandra's face.

"I saw you down in the garden with Rawdon." She took a step closer. "How could you do that? I know you do not care for Lydia, but Rawdon is a married man, Cass!"

Cassandra's mouth fell open at the blunt accusation. "You don't know what you are talking about," she snapped. Her reprimand was more forceful than Patience had expected.

"But I saw you with him, and I cannot stand by and watch you get hurt without speaking my mind."

"You are mistaken, Patience." Cassandra's nose tipped upward. "I should think you would give me more credit not to toy with a married man's affections."

"But I saw him. I saw you—"

"You saw us saying good-bye."

"Good-bye?" Patience felt numb. "I don't understand."

"I am leaving, Patience."

It was then that Patience noticed the gowns strewn across the bed.

Cassandra folded a gown over her arm, preparing to put it in her trunk. "Like I told you before, I don't belong here. I have been offered a position in Manchester."

"Of course you belong here! This is your home!" Patience reached out and grabbed her arm. "Will you stop?"

Cassandra expelled a breath and rolled her head around to look at Patience. "Be reasonable. I cannot stay here. Rawdon has made his choice."

"But you are a teacher here. You can't just leave."

Cassandra's nostrils flared, but her eyes remained dry. "Patience.

Please consider my situation. Do you know what it is like to see him, day after day, with another? And not only that, but to know that he has pledged himself to her and started a family with her?" She shoved her dress into her trunk, the force with which she performed the task the only indication of her frustration. "He told me of the child."

"But do not allow him the satisfaction of seeing you leave because of it."

"Patience, it is too late. I have already written to accept the position. They expect me within the week."

"But Manchester? That is too far!"

"It is not that far. You will be able to visit."

Patience shook her head. "How could you not tell me of this?"

"I received the offer only yesterday. And I tried to find the right time to tell you. But I could not find the words."

"How can you be so calm? You are getting ready to leave everything you love! And he forced you to it. How can you not be angry?"

Cassandra shook her head. "What makes you think I am not angry? Patience, I gave that man my heart, and he betrayed me. But if I act in that anger, if I let myself stay in that place, I am only hurting myself."

Patience stared at Cassandra, searching for a compelling reason to give her friend to stay at Rosemere, but could find none. "I could never forgive a man for treating me in such a way."

"Could not? Or would not? God tells us to forgive when we are wronged. Even if it is difficult. If I choose to be angry, if I choose to not forgive him, then I am in disobedience. God allowed this to happen. I do not comprehend why, but He will not leave me here, Patience. This is part of His plan for my life. If I stay here, if I stay angry, I might miss the plan that He has for me."

"And you think His plan is taking you away from Rosemere?" Patience shot back. "Away from those who love you?"

"I do. Please do not ask me to stay. My heart is broken, Patience. I need to heal." Despite the tears gathering in her eyes, a smile appeared. "Who knows what adventure awaits me."

Tears fell down Patience's cheeks. Cassandra reached out and smoothed her sleeve. "There could be a dashing stranger waiting to sweep me away." Cassandra smiled. "This is my path, Patience. I need to follow it, just like you need to follow yours."

Patience sat on the bed. "Why is everything changing? What is happening? This is not how things were supposed to be."

"Do not be mistaken about me, Patience. My heart is broken. How will I face a day without you? But if I choose to do nothing but bury my anger and pain, I will be miserable. I need to give it all to God and be free."

Patience thought of her mother, how her mother could not let go of the anger, the pain. She looked at Cassandra. How she would hate to see her sweet friend dissolve into such pain.

"I believe you are at the start of your own great adventure," Cassandra said.

Patience lifted her head but remained silent for several moments, then said, "Mr. O'Connell proposed this morning."

The words should have been a surprise. Should have been shocking, but instead they hung thick in the air.

Cassandra's voice was soft. "I do not know this for certain, but I think your future is not with Mr. O'Connell. I believe your future is with quite another. Do not let your anger, your frustration, blind you."

Quite another.

Patience wiped the tears from her cheeks with the palm of her hand and let Cassandra draw her into an embrace. "I will miss you, dear Patience, but you and I will always be together in spirit, regardless of how far apart we may be."

Patience looked up when she heard a knock on her bedchamber door. Without an invitation, the door opened, and Lydia, with her lady's maid directly behind her, walked in.

"Lydia!" Patience exclaimed, genuinely pleased to see that her sister-in-law's face had regained its rosy hue. "What are you doing here? I thought you would be getting dressed."

"Oh, I have been ready for ages. But with all the conquests you have at present, I thought Fiona could do your hair."

"My hair?" Patience shook her head in protest, almost a little apprehensive of the French-speaking servant who always trailed Lydia. Instinctively, a protective hand flew to her black tresses. No one besides Cassandra or Mary had touched her hair in years. "No, no, thank you."

Lydia waved a dismissive hand in the air. "Do not be silly." She scurried behind Patience and gathered her hair in her hands. "With not one but two men vying for your charms, we must put your best foot forward."

"Lydia!" Patience scolded, her eyes flicking to Fiona and back to Lydia.

"Oh, do not worry yourself. Fiona can be trusted completely." Lydia smiled affectionately at her servant and waved a hand excitedly. "Isn't it divine?"

Patience shifted uncomfortably. "I do not know, Lydia. Mary will be in here any moment to dress my hair. I think—"

But Lydia ignored her plea, and in flawless French instructed the girl on how to dress Patience's hair. Patience watched her reflection as the young girl, with amazing speed and accuracy, swept her black hair up off her neck and embellished it with pearl pins.

After the maid had completed her task, Patience stared at her reflection.

Satisfied, Lydia released her servant and stood behind Patience. She looked in the mirror. "Delightful."

Patience smiled. "It does look pretty, doesn't it?"

"Perfectly elegant."

Perfectly elegant. Patience was pretty sure that nobody had ever called her "elegant" before, but looking at her reflection was like looking at someone else. She touched the top of her hair just to make sure she was actually seeing the true reflection.

Lydia went to the wardrobe. "Oh dear." She riffled through the clothes. "All these mourning clothes." She dove into the back and pulled out a gown of light lavender. She smiled.

"Mother would never approve," Patience said.

"You must look toward your future tonight, Patience, for I believe your future is near."

She held the gown up beneath Patience's chin.

"Who will win your heart, Patience? Will it be the clever and intelligent Mr. O'Connell? Or the dashing and dangerous Mr. Sterling?"

At the sound of Mr. Sterling's name, a shadow seemed to gather over her thoughts, and yet, at the mention of his name, her pulse quickened. "You shouldn't say such things. Mr. Sterling has given no indication of any feelings."

"Oh please, Patience." Lydia dropped the gown on the bed. "The man cannot remove his eyes from you the moment he walks in. And honestly, how many times must he check the status of the stable?"

Patience felt a flush on her cheeks. She had allowed herself to hope that she had not been imagining such things, and to hear her sister-in-law say them aloud did give her reason to wonder. She nibbled her lower lip and returned her attention to her reflection.

"And back to my question, Patience. Who will win your heart?" A cunning smile curved Lydia's lips. "I daresay you already know."

31

William looked at his reflection.

He was a father. The more he thought about it, the more the idea filled him with optimism.

He didn't necessarily *look* like a father. He looked like the same man he'd always been. And yet he was certain he was changing.

Initially, the idea that a child—a girl, no less—would belong to him was frightening. But as the days passed and the idea settled, he grew comfortable with it.

And it made the decision to sell his land—or at least a small corner of it—that much easier.

He adjusted the snowy folds of his cravat and smoothed his thick hair into place. Tonight he would talk with Miss Creighton and inform her that he is Emma's father. He patted his pocket, just to make sure the brooch was still there.

The door opened and Lewis stepped in. "Angus is ready."

"Good. How's the foal?"

"Strong. Ornery. Good sign. Any word from Bley?"

William shook his head and retied his cravat. "No. Doubt he's had time to read it yet, if it has even arrived."

"It's still early to tell, but that horse looks fine. Won't be long before the other foal arrives. Good grief, how many times are you going to tie that?"

William passed a look of annoyed indifference and looped the fabric through.

"Wouldn't be a certain reason why you are looking extra dapper, would there? Pretty lady at Rosemere, if I am not mistaken?"

William ignored his reference to Miss Creighton. "Hand me that letter, will you?"

Lewis walked over and picked up the letter on the table. He handed it to William, who promptly tucked it in his pocket. "What is it?"

"I have decided to sell Rosemere to Rawdon Creighton, if he'll have it." William had expected the words to sound strange, but when he spoke them, they almost sounded reasonable. Responsible.

All sense of humor fled from Lewis's expression. His eyes narrowed. "You're serious?"

"With the mill deal fallen through, it is too risky to rely on only selling the horse. Even if Bley bought it, it would hardly cover my debt. At one point, after my father died, Edmund Creighton asked if I would be interested in selling. And I am. I don't see any other way around it."

William omitted the detail that he had a long-lost daughter. And he also left out the detail that the headmistress of the school had captivated him beyond explanation. "I am going to try to sell Rawdon Creighton the Rosemere land and Latham Hill."

"Are you sure you have thought this through?"

"I'm sure."

"I mean, are you sure you are doing it for the right reasons? You aren't letting your, er, feelings for a certain young woman play into your decision?"

William shot a warning glance at Lewis, who shrugged.

William fussed with his cravat—again. He'd not try to hide his regard for the headstrong headmistress. Not from a person who knew him as well as Lewis did. "Creighton told me of his desire to expand the school, and if his father had enough money to offer to buy the land, one would hope that money is still available. If Creighton is as eager to see to his father's work as he claims, he should jump on the offer."

"How much will you sell it for?"

"Enough to get out from under the debt. Buy a few more broodmares. Reinstate the staff."

"Well then, I will be eager to hear what he says."

"Ready yourself to travel, for if he agrees to the arrangement, I will have you go pay Rafertee as soon as the funds can switch hands."

William arrived especially early to the dinner at Rosemere. With the clouds hanging thick in the sky, the night would be dark. Even the light from the full moon would not permeate their murky curtain.

With all the excuses he had used of late to visit Rosemere, both he and his horse knew the path over Wainslow Peak quite well. The letter with the offer to sell the Rosemere land and buildings was in his pocket. Rawdon Creighton was a sensible man. The price was reasonable, considering the value of the property. How his father had stubbornly fought to keep the estate intact. His father would likely say William had failed, for to his father, land meant security. But at least the money from this sale, should Creighton choose to take him up on the offer, would fund so many things that could lead to Eastmore Hall's prosperity once more. To future generations, he would either be regarded as the man who divided the property or the man who made it thrive.

After arriving at Rosemere, William stabled his own horse before turning his attention to the house. It was so alive. Yellow candlelight winked from the windows. Children's voices wafted on the wind. Once inside, he handed his things to George and inquired after Rawdon Creighton.

George's voice was as gravelly and raspy as ever. "He is in the study."

"Is he alone?"

"I believe so."

"Good. I will show myself in."

George stepped back, allowing William space to move down the hall. William knocked on the door before pushing it open. Creighton was sitting at the desk that Patience frequently occupied.

"Ah, Sterling." He closed the ledger on the desk and leaned back in the chair. "I was not expecting you until later."

"I have business to discuss with you and thought it best to tend to it before the other guests arrive."

He looked surprised. "Business? All is well, I hope?" He waved a hand toward a chair in front of the desk.

"Definitely. But knowing of your plans to expand the school, I have an offer to extend to you." William sat down and adjusted his coat. "I have come up with a plan that I think will be beneficial to us both."

William had thought the words would be harder to say, but the desire for his future burned stronger than his regret. "In the past, your father has inquired about purchasing the Rosemere property and Latham Hill. You yourself mentioned plans for improvements and a new building. I wondered if you would have any interest in purchasing both the Rosemere and Latham Hill properties outright."

Creighton sat up straighter. "Well, that is an idea. I thought you were set on building a mill on the land. Saw the men working there myself not two days past."

"Turns out there were business practices afoot that I could not, in good conscience, align myself with. I realize the plot of land is not large, but it would include the property that abuts Rosemere and runs down to Thaughley River."

Creighton studied his tented fingers. "That is a nice bit of land."

"Knowing your intention to build, I thought it would be ideal. The hill will be an ideal setting for a cottage, and it is close enough to the school to be practical. I understand the strength of the tie your family has to this land. It is difficult to part with it, but at least parting with it to the Creightons seems more appropriate than selling it to a stranger. I've put my terms in here." William slipped the letter from his pocket and placed it on the desk. "Give it thought. Since your name was transferred to the lease after your father's death, legally, we should be able to settle such a matter quickly. If you do not purchase the land, I may be in a situation to sell it once your lease expires."

Just then O'Connell, without knocking, entered the study. O'Connell's pale eyes narrowed as Creighton and Sterling looked expectantly at him. "Good evening, Sterling."

William cleared his throat. "You are well, I trust?"

"Tolerably." He turned his attention back to Creighton. "The ladies are ready."

"Then let us not keep them waiting."

32

At dinner, Patience sat next to Mr. O'Connell. Again.

She didn't want to, and yet he had managed to occupy the chair intended for Mr. Hammond.

Patience glanced up at Mr. Sterling. The desire to be by his side, to feel his strength support her, distracted her so much she barely noticed when Mr. O'Connell spoke to her. So many questions for Mr. Sterling made it impossible for her to concentrate on anything else.

"I hope you are not unwell."

She jumped at O'Connell's voice, so close his breath tickled her ear and sent little shivers down her back. She inched away and put her fork down. "I am well."

"You've barely eaten."

"I'm not hungry." And that was the truth.

"You should eat. You'll fall ill."

Patience shot him an annoyed glance, to which he seemed oblivious.

In a sudden action, Rawdon, at the head of the table, stood. "I have an announcement," he said, his eyes bright and his smile broad. His words quieted the room. Patience leaned forward and looked at Lydia, who stared at her husband, eyes wide with excitement.

What could her brother possibly have to say in such a dramatic fashion? Across the table, Mr. Sterling shifted, glanced in her direction, and then turned his attention to Rawdon.

"I have news that I think will please everyone here." Rawdon waited for the excited chatter to again dissipate before continuing. "Or, rather, I have arrived at a decision. Just this hour, prior to dinner, Mr. Sterling approached me with a most intriguing offer. Knowing that I wish to expand the school and that I am interested in building a cottage, Mr. Sterling has offered to sell Rosemere and the land extending over Latham Hill to me. I did not require much time to arrive at my decision, for it is already made. Mr. Sterling, I accept your offer and your generous terms." He laughed, a merry laugh, the merriest that Patience had heard from him since his return.

Patience felt her jaw drop in the most unladylike of manners. All around her, voices chattered, but she fixed her eyes on William Sterling. He looked shocked at first, then a cautious smile curved his full lips, and he glanced at her. A strange expression replaced his normally confident grin. He looked at her almost as if to gain her approval on the decision.

Patience was pleased. Wasn't she? But his change of heart confused her. Why, after all these years, would he sell? Her father had tried in vain for decades to purchase the land and building that had become their home. She turned expectant eyes toward him, trying to decipher the meaning she saw there.

She was finally distracted when her mother dissolved into tears. But for once, there was happiness in her tears. Margaret Creighton stood and rushed to embrace her son, as if their argument from earlier in the day had been forgotten.

Patience looked back at Mr. Sterling. His expression conveyed something . . . but what?

Ewan bounced eagerly at her shoulder, reminding her more of a zealous puppy than a grown man. "Isn't it wonderful, Patience? This is it. This is what we have worked for. This is our dream!"

She was so flustered by his linking the two of them together that she barely noticed when Ewan stood up next to her.

Patience's blood turned to ice. She sensed what he was about to say even before his pouty lips formed the words. She tugged at his sleeve as discreetly as possible, imploring him to sit back down, but with a shrug he pulled his arm away.

Heart racing, she sank back against the chair, wishing it would swallow her completely. She could not tear her eyes away from him. Seconds slipped by, slowed by dread.

"In the light of this good news, I have some of my own." Ewan turned to her, latching his eyes on hers. She shook her head, trying to communicate the need to stop, but his smile was too wide, his intentions too plain.

He reached for her hand. Her legs wobbled as he pulled her to her feet. She looked at Lydia, silently pleading for an intervention, but her sister-in-law only stared at them with her mouth hanging open.

Once standing, Patience focused on the uneaten veal on her plate. Every ounce of blood in her body seemed to sink to her toes. She felt certain she would faint before this humiliation passed.

After all were once again quiet, Ewan said, "This is a day for news, is it not? You must all know that I asked dear, sweet Patience, friend of my youth, for her hand in marriage. She has not yet given me an answer, but in light of this excitement, I find I can wait no longer."

He took her other hand in his and pulled her closer. "This news is a fresh start not only for the school but for us."

Her mouth went dry, and she felt certain everyone could hear the thudding of her heart. She forced herself to look at him.

His eyes were eager, his chest puffed proudly. "Patience, dear. Give me your answer in the presence of our friends and family, once and for all. Will you do me the magnificent honor of becoming my wife?"

Her arms felt as if they were made of lead . . . as unmoving as the stone peaks that surrounded this land. She opened her mouth to speak, but her chin quivered. No sound would come. Every eye in the room was on her.

She dared not look at her brother.

Or Lydia.

Or, heaven help her, William Sterling.

Her foolish fairy-tale dreams. Why had he come into her life? Mere months ago she would have accepted O'Connell's offer as a practical decision. She had given up the dream of ever finding romantic love. She would have accepted a loveless marriage in exchange for the stability a life with a man as constant as Ewan would have brought her. But since her heart had glimpsed the emotion, the anticipation of seeing him, the dream was once again alive.

And the man who incited such feelings in her, William Sterling, bore witness to the entire farce.

Ewan tugged her hand, as if to not only pull her closer but to extract an answer from her. Force her to say the words she was not ready to say because he had put her on the spot in such a public forum.

She stumbled back, nearly knocking her chair to the floor. Her cheek twitched. Tears blinded her vision. "Forgive me. I . . . I cannot."

His expression of shocked disbelief was the last thing she saw before she turned and ran from the room.

And she did not stop.

33

Patience ran up the stairs to the dark west wing and stumbled down the corridor. Tears streamed unchecked from her eyes. Uncontrollable sobs racked her body. It was as if the emotions of everything bad that she could not handle rushed at her with equal force.

She jiggled her door handle. It would not open fast enough. She thrust it open and slammed the door behind her. Her father's death. Her mother's distance. Her brother's betrayal. The stable burning. Cassandra's impending departure. Ewan's ridiculous ploy to make her respond to him favorably in front of others. It was not to be borne.

She fumbled in the dark for a handkerchief, but gave up and fell across her bed. The bedclothes were cold and foreign. How she wanted to be anywhere but here! She would, eventually, have to face the people downstairs and account for her ridiculous behavior of running out like a child.

But no one's opinion mattered as much as that of William Sterling.

After the initial onslaught of tears subsided, she was left with a few stray tears and a throbbing headache. She sniffed and wiped her face on the sleeve of her forgotten, elegant dress. How foolish she had been. Getting dressed up for a man who would never think twice about her. He'd been nice to her because he wanted to sell them the land. Nothing more.

She lifted her hand to begin removing the pins from her disheveled hair, fighting the urge to burst into tears once more. Once her hair was free and flowed around her shoulders, she curled up in a ball in the still darkness. Perhaps, if fate were on her side, sleep would envelop her.

Then came a soft knock on her door.

She did not respond.

The knock sounded again. "Patience?"

Mother.

Of all the people who might come to see her, her mother was the one person she could not send away.

She sat up on the bed. "It is not locked."

The door opened, and her mother slipped through and closed the door behind her. She placed the candle she had been carrying on a bureau, and in the faint light, Patience could imagine that it was her mother the way she used to be, coming to check on her and tuck her in at night. By this light, the graying of her hair was not as noticeable. The wrinkles in her skin not as pronounced.

Patience did not speak. For what would she say?

"It has been months since I have been in this room."

"You used to hear my prayers each night." Patience had not intended her words to sound like an accusation, but the look of hurt on her mother's face indicated that she interpreted them as such.

Her mother sat wordlessly next to her on the bed, and as each moment passed, the discomfort seemed to dissipate.

Her mother stared into the blackness. "When you were born, your father insisted upon naming you Patience."

Patience swallowed, thinking the statement odd, but in the shadowed room and her darkened state, she simply listened.

"I wanted to name you Mary, after my mother, but your father would not hear of it. He said he wanted to name you with a virtue so that every time you heard it you would be reminded of God's providence." She looked at Patience. Her smile seemed weary. "You know your father and his ideas of self-improvement." She looked down at her hands, as if reliving moments of long ago. "I do not need to remind you that you were not a patient child. Nor a patient youth. You were so eager to see what was around the next corner. To embrace the new instead of enjoying what you have today."

She took Patience's hand in her own. "Before your father died, we talked of you. He admired your strength, but we laughed at how you seemed to have completely missed your namesake. And when I see you, Patience, I believe you have begun to understand."

But Patience did not understand. Her mother's words did not make sense, and her head ached so that she could not seem to decipher their meaning. She fell back against the bed.

"I have not been there for you, Patience, and I am sorry for it. My heart is so weary."

As is mine. The words hovered on Patience's lips, begging for release, but stayed frozen, unsaid.

"You have been so strong. And I . . . I have . . ." Tears trickled down her mother's cheeks, communicating more than a thousand words ever could.

Patience sat up and wiped her hair from her own wet face.

Her mother sucked in a breath and then blew it out. "Your father is dead, but just as you have told me so many times, our lives . . . yours, mine, and Rawdon's . . . are not over. And I gather, from your words downstairs, that Mr. O'Connell does not fit into the rest of your life."

Patience moved her head from side to side. "He does not. My opinion cannot be altered." She closed her mouth. She knew the full reason why he did not fit in her life. There was no room left in her heart. "Is he upset?"

"After you left, he quitted the room in quite a fury. I have not seen him since."

"Do you think that is the real reason why Rawdon brought him here?"

"I think your brother is concerned for your welfare. As am I."

"Well, now that Rawdon will own this property, we do not have to worry. The school will continue on as it has been. And if he expands it, it can only be successful. And our family will, no doubt, continue to live here as we have always done."

Patience expected that fact to bring her more comfort than it did.

Her mother smoothed her hair. "I must correct you. This is where I shall live out the remainder of my years. You, my dear, are meant for other things. Your father had grand plans for this school, and he would be proud of the work you have done here, how you have kept it going with little to no help. How you handled the stable's burning."

Patience looked up. Her mother had not mentioned anything to her about the school in ages. Nothing of the work she had done. A welcome warmth spread from her middle to her limbs, momentarily pushing out the cold and dread.

"But this was your father's dream, Patience, and you have contributed to it. Do not let it blind you. Do not sacrifice your personal happiness for someone else's dream."

"But it is my dream, it is—"

"I am simply saying not to fool yourself into thinking that there is nothing else for you."

Overwhelmed by the glimpse of the mother she had missed for so long, Patience put her arms around her mother. "I have missed you so."

Her mother seemed to understand, for she kissed Patience on the forehead. "I know, dear. My heart has been heavy. But you said something that stuck with me. Father would not want me to continue in this way. I see you working, fighting. Rawdon is dealing with the loss in his own way. And I want to live again."

$\mathscr{L}$

As dawn broke over the moors the following morning, Patience stood outside, her shawl pulled tight around her. The drizzle from the gray canopy of clouds dampened her shoulders and face and hair. Emotion tightened her throat and tears threatened to spill.

Standing next to the carriage, Patience took Cassandra's gloved hands in hers. "Promise me you will write as soon as you are settled."

Cassandra sniffled, her smile trembling only slightly. "The minute I arrive."

She wanted to say anything to convince her friend to stay, but Patience knew all too well that once her friend had made up her mind, she was unwavering. "Are you sure you will not say good-bye to Mother?"

Cassandra squeezed Patience's hand. "It is better this way. I have said my good-byes to the other teachers, but I think, in light of my reasons for leaving, the less said, the better."

Cassandra stepped toward the open carriage door, but then stopped and turned. "Do not dislike the new Mrs. Creighton on my account. And, Patience, there are two men who are both in love with you. Do not let your anger blind you to what may be waiting for you."

And with that, Cassandra accepted George's hand and stepped into the carriage. Patience watched her through the tiny carriage window as she settled into her space and turned to wave a farewell.

Patience smiled back and waved, but inside, her heart was grieving. Crying. The carriage rumbled down the drive and disappeared through the iron gates.

She shivered. The dampness permeated her plain dress, and she brushed a lock of hair, still in a curl from last night's festivities, away from her face. She turned back to Rosemere and studied it with a sigh.

With the exception of Cassandra, everything and everyone she loved was tucked safely inside these walls. Her girls. Her staff. Her family.

But her heart did not find peace. For there was something missing.

Had she never met William Sterling, she might never have noticed. Ever since that day when he lay motionless and still in George's bed, she had felt a stirring in her heart. Every emotion concerning him was heightened, and now that she had rejected another, she understood why. She was in love with William Sterling.

With most of the house still asleep and the early-morning darkness blanketing the grounds with its silence, Patience retrieved a lantern, her bonnet, and a crimson cloak and went for a walk before the weather grew too intense.

The freshness of the morning air beckoned her. It was as if it carried with it the wind of change, a promise of a new beginning, and by simply being out in it she would find clarity of thought. The rain had turned to snow and fell in uneven patterns, gathering like a velvet carpet on the frozen ground. The air invigorated her. The wind stung her eyes. As uncomfortable as it was, the sensations made her feel alive. With a sigh, Patience climbed Wainslow Peak's smooth incline. The wind was strong here but carried with it the spicy, earthy scent of the frozen moors. It felt comforting. Like she belonged.

She could finally breathe. She filled her lungs. Today all would start anew. Whether Mr. O'Connell would stay after his display the previous evening, she did not know, but regardless, she could start fresh, throw herself into her work. Maybe even embrace the idea of a school for young men. Develop a relationship with a sister-in-law who could become a dear friend. And for all the practicality in her plan, perhaps she could leave room in her heart and mind for a little dream.

William was up before the sunrise. How could he sleep?

The dinner at Rosemere, which at first held such promise, quickly fizzled. It had taken every ounce of restraint he possessed when he heard O'Connell's proposal and beheld the humiliated expression on Miss Creighton's face. Even now, he could not shake the memory of it. He'd wanted to confront O'Connell, but the man disappeared shortly after Miss Creighton left the room. The other guests departed immediately after dinner.

After a sleepless night in bed, he rose early, before the dawn. Without a formal staff, there was always work to be done. He lit a lantern and headed for the stable.

Inside, the familiar sweet scent of hay and the comforting sounds of the horses soothed him, but only a little. When he stepped back outside into the bleak morning, gray streaks of light spread like ribbons over the steely sky, and he breathed in the scent of cold and snow. He was about to pick up a bucket when he looked toward Wainslow Peak.

A glimmer of light caught his attention. A fire? A lantern? It moved, then lowered and was still.

He squinted, unsure of what to make of it. The knowledge that Rafertee's men had been on that path not so long ago nagged him. He shifted his weight and looked again.

Rafertee's men, he decided, would hardly light a lantern. He went back in the stable, tossed the rope he had been carrying to the side, grabbed his coat from over the stall wall, and began the long trek up the hill.

The sound of the wind through the barren branches drowned out all other sounds of the morning, and with every step, his heart seemed to beat harder. For as he drew closer, he knew he saw a person. The only ones he had ever encountered on the hill prior to this were a nearby farmer and someone from Rosemere. As he got closer, his anticipation grew.

Could it be? But why this early? And alone?

Had he only imagined that her eyes had been on him at times at the gathering the night before? No, he was certain he had read her correctly. Her encouragement had been clear. And the fact that she rejected O'Connell, and in such a public manner, gave him reason to hope.

As he was deciding how best to proceed, he stepped on a twig and it snapped. The woman gasped and turned.

A thrill rushed through him, unsettling him, yet infusing him with strength. In the light from the lantern was Patience Creighton.

He stepped free from the brush. "Do not be alarmed, Miss Creighton. 'Tis only me."

She jumped to her feet, the expression in her eyes turning from fear to recognition. A nervous laugh escaped. "Mr. Sterling! I did not expect to see anyone here. Not at this early hour."

"I was in the stable and saw your lantern." He stepped closer. "I was concerned something was wrong."

She smiled up at him. "I know you warned me of being out on the moors while it was dark. One of our teachers departed this morning for Manchester, and after saying farewell, I thought I would take advantage of the silence to clear my mind."

"I did not mean to interrupt your solitude. I should leave you—"

"No, no!" Her words were immediate, and she raised her hands to stop him. As if suddenly realizing the haste of her response, she smiled and dropped her hands. "That is to say, there is no need to leave on my account. Please, join me," she said as she returned to her seat.

He sat next to her on the boulder, acutely aware of how close she was—the way the breeze blew a long lock of ebony hair across her cheek, the redness of her nose in the morning chill.

"Are you all right?" he asked.

"Oh yes, I am fine. Thank you."

Always proper. Always polite. But he noticed how the light illuminated the tear tracks on her smooth cheeks, and her eyes were wet and rimmed in red.

Perhaps she misunderstood his question. "I meant to inquire if you were all right after last night. I . . . The situation you were in last night was a difficult one, Miss Creighton. O'Connell is intolerable."

Her smile faded and she sat in silence, looking out at the awakening valley below, and then she switched the topic. "I was surprised . . . pleasantly surprised . . . to hear that you sold the land to my brother. Such news would have so pleased my father."

"In truth, Miss Creighton, that house should belong to the Creighton family. It is long overdue."

"I remember my father trying almost every spring to purchase the house and the land from your father, but to no avail. He always said he would not give up." She paused. "Rawdon has great plans to improve the school. He plans to expand to a school for young men and—"

"And you, Miss Creighton? What plans do you have?" Perhaps it was the faint hint of the morning light, of a new beginning, that made him bold. Or the vast open space. Or the intimacy of the dawn. But at this precise moment in time, he had little desire to speak of her brother. Or of schools. He wanted—no, needed—to know about her.

She tightened her shawl and diverted her eyes. She stuttered her words. "I . . . I plan to continue on as I have been."

"Without Mr. O'Connell?" He needed to be sure.

Even in the morning's shadow, he thought he saw the stain of a blush on her cheek. She studied the fringe on her cloak. "Yes. Without Mr. O'Connell."

The acknowledgment sent a rush of relief through him, energizing him and emboldening him with an unusual fervor. Words jumbled within him, waiting to be spoken, but she spoke first.

"I must know, what was it that made you decide to sell the land?"

Her question could have been innocent enough. She turned her eyes to him. But he sensed she was asking a far different question than the one merely on the surface.

He let his shoulders slump a little and stretched out both legs. How he wanted to share all. Unburden his heart and declare all wrongs. But where would he begin? "Everything is not as it seems, Miss Creighton."

"What do you mean?"

The truth was difficult, but if the lapses in his judgment had taught him anything, false pretense could cause more damage than revealing the truth. "I did want to see the house in your family's possession, that is true. But the whole truth is that I need the money."

"Oh." She nibbled her lip. "But you rebuilt the stable for us. I thought the money wasn't—"

"You needed it. That is to say, the school needed it."

She stood up and walked away from him, the cold air putting even more distance between them. She stood with her back to him, the moors spread out before her. "I . . . I've heard a report that the fire in our stable was not an accident."

He felt both anger and embarrassment at her statement. Where she heard it was not important. What she thought about it was another matter entirely. "You heard correctly. It was recently brought to my attention that foul play did have a hand in the fire."

Miss Creighton's eyebrows drew together.

"But why did you not say as much?"

William hesitated. Did she think he had a hand in the deed? "If I had known earlier, I certainly would have."

She whirled around to face him. "So you sell my brother land that is targeted?" Her voice remained soft. Calm.

"You are painting an inaccurate picture, Miss Creighton. The people who were responsible for the fire were attempting to coerce me. I only regret that you and your family were brought into it."

"But how can you be certain they will not try again?"

He sat for several moments, his eyes locked with hers. If, by some miracle, she returned his regard, she deserved to know the truth about him. All of it. "Do you recall how I said that I had plans to build the textile mill on Latham Hill?"

She nodded.

"Apparently my colleagues had their sights set on the plot of land where Rosemere sits. I told them repeatedly I would not sell. They thought that if the stable burned, I would be unable to fund repairs and you would leave the land for more suitable accommodations. Then I would not have qualms about selling the land and Rosemere."

Her voice held skepticism. "If that is the case, then why did you sell it to my brother?"

"Because I have debt, Miss Creighton. Significant debt that I cannot repay. The sale of the land will conclude my responsibility in that matter."

The words were out. His shame was out.

She looked away, again scanning the moors. He slid off his coat. "Here, put this on. It is too cold."

"But you will be cold," she protested.

"I will be fine."

She slid the heavy woven work coat over her shoulders. She looked so fragile. So small. So perfect.

He pulled the brooch from his waistcoat pocket. His fingers felt cold and thick as he held it out to her. "Do you recognize this, Miss Creighton?

She reached out and took it from him, her bare fingers briefly touching his. "Why yes! This belongs to one of my students." She looked puzzled. "Wherever did you find it?"

The jewel glimmered in the lantern's light as she turned it over. He cleared his throat. "I saw it in your study after you left me the other day."

She frowned. "How did it come to be in your possession?"

"I took it. I had to be certain."

"Certain?" Her confusion was obvious. "Of what?"

William was finding it difficult to look her in the eye. "I know whose brooch that is."

"You do? Well, that is wonderful! I have been trying for weeks to learn more about this student's family."

He lifted the lantern from the ground and held it close. "Turn it over and look at the engraving."

She turned the brooch over to catch the light. "EAS."

"Elizabeth Ann Sterling. My mother."

Miss Creighton shook her head. "But I don't understand. Why would your mother's jewelry be in Emma's things?" She tucked the brooch in her pocket. "Please tell me."

"Perhaps you had better be seated."

William waited for her to sit back down. "Several years ago I was involved with a young woman named Isabelle Simmons, a niece of Mr. and Mrs. Hammond's."

"I remember her."

"Eight years ago I was very much in love with Miss Simmons. I made an offer of marriage, and she accepted. But when a gentleman from her past learned of our engagement, he made an offer as well. She chose him."

Miss Creighton cocked her head to the side but remained silent.

"Regarding the brooch, I had given it to Miss Simmons just days before she left Darbury. I never saw her again, and to be quite honest, I had forgotten about the brooch until I saw it in your study.

"What I did not know, Miss Creighton, is that when Isabelle left Darbury, she was with child. *My* child. And when her husband learned of her deceit, he forced her from their home. Isabelle passed away four years ago, but before she did, she placed her daughter in the care of the Hammonds, who in turn placed her at Rosemere."

Miss Creighton stared at him, her eyes not leaving his face. "Emma."

"Yes." He paused, trying to interpret her expression, and when he could not, he continued. "I am not proud of my actions after Isabelle left. I made many bad decisions. Did things I am not proud of. Isabelle had made Mr. Hammond promise not to reveal that the child was mine, and Mr. Hammond, aware of my decline, decided not to tell me."

"What made him change his mind?"

"I am trying to change my course, and I believe Mr. Hammond

recognized that. He and I agree that no child deserves to not know her father."

A cautious smile played on her lips. "Well, I, for one, am pleased. I think you will make an excellent father." She swallowed, and he thought he saw tears in her eyes. "I see the resemblance. Your eyes are like hers. And you both share the dimple in your cheek when you smile."

Excitement surged through him. "With your blessing, I would like to tell her as soon as possible. I have a lot to make up for."

"Of course. This is the best news, Mr. Sterling."

"And I will reimburse the school for the tuition."

"But her bill is paid. We receive money regularly. Every month."

William frowned. Hammond did not say anything about who had paid for the child to attend the school. He would find out and repay them.

"Mr. Sterling, I have to say that Emma is special to me."

"I know. And I am glad my daughter was not alone during these years. I am anxious to get to know her, Miss Creighton. But this will be quite a shock for her."

"Yes. But surely you do not intend to take her away from Rosemere."

The woman's love for the child was evident. Miss Creighton had been selfless and had been his daughter's family when he could not be. "You have cared for my child in a manner in which I never could. I shall never take her from you."

William tried to interpret her silence, but her breathing seemed to quicken and she sank into his coat. Now was the time. He needed to tell her the rest. Tell her how she had captured his thoughts. His mind. His heart—

A shout sounded from Eastmore Hall. Horses neighed. More shouting. They both stood up to look down at Eastmore.

William tried to see through the branches down to the

courtyard. He saw nothing, but alarm took hold. Another shout. Was it Lewis calling him? Then the frantic neighing of the horses told him all was not well.

He did not want to leave Miss Creighton, but every instinct screamed for his return to Eastmore. "Excuse me. I must see what that is. I cannot imagine what it would be at this hour."

"Can I be of assistance?"

"No, no, Miss Creighton. Please, return to Rosemere. Quickly."

He bowed slightly, then headed back down the hill. Shouts carried on the wind. Horses neighed.

Something is not right.

34

William reached the clearing in front of the stable, his mind having played out every possible scenario. But even his imagination had not prepared him for what he saw. In the courtyard stood Lewis, dressed only in linen shirt, breeches, and boots, hair disheveled, his hands up in the air.

Then he saw him. Jonathan Riley. Intoxicated. Sloppy. Pointing a pistol directly at Lewis.

"What are you doing?" William shouted, stepping between Lewis and the gun. "Put down that pistol. Have you gone mad?" He stepped to one side, hoping to distract Riley and get closer to him.

Riley's inebriated words slurred into each other. "You sold the land."

The gun now was pointing right at him. William's heart thudded. The land. He'd forgotten about Riley.

Riley spat out each garbled word. "I know about it. You deceived me!"

"You burned my property!" William hurled the words back. "Don't be a fool. Put down the pistol. We'll talk about—"

"No!" Riley shouted, eyes wild, staggering back a step in his intoxication. Riley recovered his balance and widened his stance. He tipped his head forward like a bull ready to charge.

"Ewan O'Connell was at Griffen's End last night. Told me everything. How you seduced Creighton's sister. How you master-minded the entire plan."

When Lewis stepped to one side, Riley swung the gun in his direction. "Don't move!"

Lewis stopped and kept his hands in the air.

Keeping his head still, William looked for anything he could use as a weapon. A rope next to the stable door. A pitchfork leaning against a rail.

William tried to make eye contact with Lewis. Riley was drunk. They should be able to overpower him . . . if only they could get the pistol from his hand. Lewis finally blinked with the slightest nod.

A scuffle, a rustling sound made William turn. Standing in the clearing was Patience Creighton, her eyes full of fear, in the tight grip of Cyrus Temdon. Anger exploded within William at the sight. One of Cyrus's dirty hands was on her arm, and the other was around her waist. His work coat was still about her shoulders. She winced when Temdon adjusted his grip on her arm.

William whirled back around to Riley. "This has nothing to do with the Creightons. Your issue is with me, not with her."

A greasy laugh slid from Riley's mouth. "That was a happy accident, finding her, don't you agree?"

"Release her, Riley!" When he did not respond, William changed his tactic. "What is it that you want? You must have come here with an idea."

"You have cost me a great deal of money, *friend*. I am tired of your games, your excuses. I offered to buy the land, pay you a good price, and you betrayed me and offered it to Creighton. I want that land, Sterling. I think you know me well enough. I am a man who knows how to get what I want."

"Fine. I'll sell you Latham Hill, but the land that Rosemere sits on is bound in a lease. I've told you that. It cannot be sold now. It would do you no good. Not now."

"I think that Rawdon Creighton will reconsider that lease when he realizes who his sister has been cavorting with."

William sucked in a deep breath. He needed a diversion. Something to distract Riley long enough to make a move. Long enough to get the gun away from him.

Angus. It might work. Angus was in the pen and had wandered to the far side.

William whistled. As if on cue, the horse trotted around to the paddock gate next to the stable, distracting Riley just enough so that he turned his head.

William seized the break in Riley's concentration. He lunged at Riley, knocking him to the ground. William slammed his fist against the man's jaw, and the pistol flew from Riley's hand. Both scrambled for it. Riley grabbed it first, but William pushed the barrel away.

"Give me the gun!"

They continued to grapple on the ground. Riley was sloppy. Uncoordinated.

William freed the pistol from his hand and kicked it away.

William stood up and pulled Riley to his feet. He steadied his target and again slammed his fist into Riley's jaw. His neighbor staggered backward. William punched him again. And with this blow, Riley crumpled to the ground.

Chest heaving, William whirled around.

Patience.

The skirmish with Riley had happened so quickly that Cyrus had not yet responded. His eyes were red with drink's effect. William scooped up the pistol and walked toward Cyrus. Lewis was beside him.

"Release her, Temdon." William pointed the pistol right at Cyrus.

Like a cornered animal, Temdon licked his lips. His eyes shifted from William to Lewis and then back to William. Then he shoved Patience away from himself with such force she fell to the ground.

William did not move or take his eyes from Temdon. "Get off my property. And if you ever set foot on this property or that of Rosemere, be prepared to meet this pistol again."

William heard Patience scurry behind him, but he kept his eyes on his enemy.

Lewis moved toward Temdon, who bolted in the opposite direction. Lewis chased him.

William turned and saw that Riley was still in a heap.

He tucked the pistol in the waist of his breeches and put an arm around Patience. She did not pull away. Instead, she leaned into him. His anger intensified when he looked down and saw her frightened eyes and the tear tracks cutting through the smudges of dirt on her face. "Are you all right? Did he hurt you?"

She looked up at him and offered a weak smile. "You warned me that the moors were dangerous. I should have listened."

But her attempt to lighten the mood was lost on him. For nothing could be more serious—more important—than to keep her safe.

The expression in her eyes would be the undoing of him. He touched her face and tried to rub away the smudge of dirt on her cheek.

She drew in a shaky breath and tears filled her eyes again. "What happened?"

He stepped even closer, so close that he could not tell if she leaned into him, but suddenly, she was against him. Her body, so delicate. She was trembling. He wrapped his arms tightly around her and pressed his lips to her smooth forehead before resting his cheek on the top of her head. "Oh, Patience."

Strong emotion gripped him, commandeering his senses and all rational thought. She deserved a suitor who was steady. Smart. Wise. He was no good for her. But why did it feel like she completed a place in him that had been empty for as long as he could remember?

The harder he tried to step back, the stronger her lure. The sensation of her in his arms had the power to reach within him and unlock the part that had remained closed off for so many years.

His raspy words came out in but a whisper. "So help me, I promise I will never allow anyone to hurt you again."

She pulled away. Her hands covered her mouth. So many questions were written in her expression. "I . . . I don't know what to say."

He took her hands in his own and looked down at her face. Her beautiful, lovely face.

He could feel his own eyes fill with tears. Not from just the effect of this moment, but the effect of every moment leading up to it. Slowly he put his hands on her shoulders and ran them down the rough wool of his coat that she was wearing.

He leaned close and whispered, "Believe me, Patience Creighton, when I say that I promise to see to it that you never have need to cry again."

William was pulled from his trance when he noticed Lewis running toward them, unshaved cheeks ruddy from the cold.

"Well, that was a fine 'good morning.'" Lewis adjusted his shirt and shoved a shock of hair from his forehead. "I don't think we'll be hearing from Temdon anytime soon. Miss Creighton, are you all right?"

Patience tightened William's coat around her shoulders and nodded.

"Good. Do you want to go for the magistrate, or shall I?"

William wanted to be the one to bring Riley to justice, but he could not leave Patience. Not after what she had been through.

A sharp wind gusted from the moors, and Patience leaned in close. Instinctively, he put an arm around her and drew her closer. He looked over at Riley, who was still sprawled out on the ground, unconscious, and, considering the state of him, would likely be out for a while longer.

"Prepare the carriage. We'll return Miss Creighton to Rosemere and then we will visit the magistrate."

35

Patience hurried to the window, hoping to catch a glimpse of William as he departed from Rosemere to transport Riley to the magistrate, but the courtyard and the drive were empty. He was gone.

Her shoulders slumped. She never wanted to be apart from him again.

In the solitude of her bedchamber, with great reluctance, she removed Mr. Sterling's—William's—coat from her shoulders. It smelled of him . . . the scent of sandalwood soap . . . of the outdoors and leather.

The events of the morning had blurred, seeming more like a dream than reality. Her fear after being snatched by Cyrus Temdon had lost some of its clarity. Its horror. And yet this coat, hugged now in her arms, was a tangible confirmation of the morning's happenings, of her protector making all things right again.

Upon their return from Eastmore Hall, William explained to Rawdon and the rest of her family what had occurred. But it was what he didn't say that touched Patience. For as he spoke of the morning's happenings, he kept his hand tenderly and protectively on the small of her back. With such a public display, there could be no doubt of his intentions.

Now she just needed to hear him say the words.

Lydia knocked, opened the door, and peeked in. Her eyes were big and her cheeks were flushed. She scurried in and closed the door. "I still cannot believe it. Mr. Riley is a wretched, evil man! You must have been so frightened! Tell me everything, again, and don't you dare omit a single detail." She sat on the bed. "Here, sit down."

Patience sat next to Lydia and thought about how much Lydia felt like the sister she had never had. "Well . . . after Miss Baden left, I—"

"Oh, for mercy's sake"—Lydia waved her hand in dismissal— "Mr. Sterling told us all that already. What I want to know is what of Mr. Sterling?"

Patience smiled. For how could she not smile? He'd defended her. Embraced her. Pressed his lips to her forehead and promised her that she would never again be in fear.

But Patience did not need to say a word, for Lydia prattled on about how brave Mr. Sterling was. How handsome. How noble. Yet Patience heard little of it, so lost was she in her own recollections.

Lydia motioned for Patience to turn. "Rawdon was so angry. I don't know who made him angrier, Mr. Riley or Mr. O'Connell."

The mention of Mr. O'Connell drew Patience from her thoughts. "Mr. O'Connell?"

"His behavior last night was atrocious! Unforgivable! Rawdon tried to confront him immediately after the dinner last night, but Mr. O'Connell had already quitted Rosemere, and he never returned. He stormed out of the dining room immediately after you left. Then, first thing this morning, a letter arrived stating Mr. O'Connell would be returning to London. Permanently."

At the news, Patience knew she should feel compassion for her brother now that his plans had been thwarted, but all she felt was relief. Freedom. It was like waking from a nightmare and knowing it is finally over. She'd been so worried about another confrontation with Ewan, and now that obstacle was gone.

And William Sterling did care for her! She had not misinterpreted his attentions.

Her heart felt as if it might burst at the happiness she felt for little Emma. William Sterling—Emma's father. Suddenly, the mystery of the name—Isabelle—that he shouted out that frigid dawn after George found him in the stable made sense. It was Isabelle Simmons, Mr. Sterling's past love and Emma's mother.

Patience could look to the future with confidence. There could be no denying the events in their lives that had brought them both to this place. Whatever their differences in circumstances no longer mattered. Mr. Sterling had made clear his affections for her.

And Patience understood that her great romance was spread out before her. Her heart had made its choice.

At the close of the day, pink ribbons were strung across the broad expanse of the darkening sky. Twilight was settling over the snow-covered moors.

After depositing Riley with the magistrate, William returned to Eastmore Hall to make himself presentable. He had left Patience with a promise that he would see her soon. He bathed, shaved, and dressed in fawn breeches, navy coat, and snowy cravat. With a jump in his step, he hurried from the house, saddled Angus, and made his way to Rosemere.

On the ride over, William tried to plan what he would say. But his anticipation was too great. His world was about to change.

Suddenly there seemed to be order. A clear purpose. How wrong he'd been, all those years, chasing folly.

George let him in at Rosemere, and with sure and steady steps, he hurried to Miss Creighton's study and knocked on the door.

"Come in." Her voice was soft.

He opened the door, and his chest swelled with emotion when he saw them, Miss Creighton and Emma.

Light seemed to dance in Miss Creighton's eyes. "Mr. Sterling. You're here at last."

At last. Yes, at last. It seemed he'd waited a lifetime to reach this point, for as he walked into the room, his future became focused.

Everything that mattered from this point forward was here. In this room. Not horses. Not Rafertee. Not shame or unfulfilled expectations. Everything that mattered was *here*. And he would spend the rest of his life making himself worthy of such a gift.

Miss Creighton's words brought him back to the present. "Are you ready to . . ." She nodded toward Emma, as if asking his permission.

He nodded.

Miss Creighton gathered the child in her arms and leaned close. "Emma, I have wonderful news to tell you."

Emma eyed him before turning her clear blue eyes toward Miss Creighton.

The similarity struck him. Her eyes were like looking at his mother's portrait or even in a mirror at his own. Her mahogany hair was the exact same hue as Isabelle's. Her skin the same tone. How he'd never seen it before was remarkable.

Miss Creighton said, "Do you remember how you needed to stay here every holiday because we did not know where your mama and papa were?"

The little girl nodded as she looked back at William.

Miss Creighton squeezed the child's hand, a smile on her face. "We have found your papa."

The child frowned, as if uncertain whether to believe her. "Where is he?" Emma tore her gaze from William and looked up at her headmistress.

"Why, dearest, it is Mr. Sterling." Her eyes met his. "Mr. Sterling is your father."

William hadn't realized he was holding his breath until he nearly needed to gasp for air. He'd rehearsed what to say, but the child stared at him with such curiosity, he could not tell if she was pleased.

He finally found the words, and he stepped toward her and knelt on one knee. "Emma, I . . . I am your papa. I regret that I have been gone for so long. But I am here now. And you will never be without a papa again."

Emma looked at Miss Creighton, who gave her a nod of encouragement. The child slipped from Miss Creighton's lap and approached him slowly. Cautiously. "You look like me."

Relieved, William laughed. "Yes. Yes. And you look like me."

She nodded and looked back to Miss Creighton before turning her attention again to him. "What shall I call you?"

"Father. Or Papa," he added when the memory of what he had called his own father as a child rushed to his mind. "Whichever you prefer."

A smile dimpled her cheek. "Papa."

When he looked up at Miss Creighton, tears glistened in her eyes. It was then he realized his own eyes were misting up, his vision was getting blurry, his chest was tightening.

The child reached out and touched his hand. "Are you sad, Papa?"

The words were so soft. So sweet. And he would spend the rest of his life getting to know her and making himself worthy of her.

He took her tiny hand and pressed his lips to it. "No. I am not sad. I am happy, Emma. Very, very happy."

Emma looked back at Patience, wide-eyed innocence and honesty in her expression. "Where am I going to live?"

Miss Creighton glanced at William. "You will continue to live here for the time being."

"But whenever you are ready," William quickly added, "you may come live at Eastmore Hall."

"The big house past the hill?"

He looked nervously at Miss Creighton. "Yes. And you may pick whichever room you like."

Emma's eyes grew wide. "A home . . . just like the other girls."

Miss Creighton smoothed the child's hair. "Just like the other girls."

Miss Creighton hugged Emma. "You may go and join the rest of the girls and get ready for bed. There will be plenty of time to get to know your papa, I promise."

Emma turned to her and curtsied to William, who gave a slight bow in return.

"Good night, Papa."

Her voice was so soft. Innocent. She stepped closer and motioned for him to lean in closer. She put her tiny hand on his shoulder and placed a kiss on his cheek.

That simple act of trust, of affection, unnerved him, yet at the same time filled a void that he had not even realized was there. "Good night, dear Emma."

His eyes followed her as she left the room. "She is perfect," he whispered.

Miss Creighton smiled and said, "How I have grieved for that child all these years. You will be an excellent father to her, I am sure."

His heart was full. It was as if he was being given a chance at something he never thought possible.

William tried to think of appropriate words to say. But his throat was dry. Miss Creighton was the woman who had cared for his daughter these many years, whose strength and dedication surpassed that of anyone he'd ever known. He stared at her black hair. The smoothness of her skin. The slope of her nose. But her beauty extended beyond that. Her heart was beautiful.

He'd thought that seeing Emma and her strong likeness to her mother would bring back thoughts of Isabelle. But in fact, it was quite the opposite. When he met his daughter, he saw Miss Creighton's influence. Her quiet mannerisms. Her polite sweetness. And none of Isabelle's recklessness. None of her loud laughter or wild ways.

He knew, without a doubt, he had to make Miss Creighton his. "I never finished what I was going to say to you on the moors this morning."

A flush rose to her cheeks, and he heard the slightest intake of breath.

What thoughts were churning within her?

"I shared with you the folly of my past, Miss Creighton . . . Patience."

At the use of her Christian name, her eyes met his. Boldly. Unwavering.

He continued, "I know you know my flaws. I have made poor choices. I have gambled and lost. But through all that, God did not turn away from me. He even has given me a child. I thought after losing Emma's mother that I would never love again. But I have another confession."

He stepped closer, half fearing she would look away or turn and run. And yet she did not move. Did not step back. If anything, she seemed to lean in toward him, a simple act that infused him with confidence.

Sudden desperation seized him, like a man given a second

chance at redemption. He forced his hands to remain at his sides, and yet her intoxicating scent of rosewater teased his senses. The nearness of her awakened a part of his soul that he thought long dead. He could reach out and touch her hair, her shoulder. And if he did, how would she react? Would she pull away?

His pulse raced at the thought, his own words barely audible above the thundering of his heart. "And will you hear my confession, Patience?"

Patience swiped her hair from her face, letting her trembling fingertips rest on her cheeks for a few moments.

She nodded.

He took her hand in his. The lace of her sleeve brushed his fingertips.

He studied the small white hand in his large rough one. How long he had believed he did not deserve such happiness. But out of past regrets grew a hope for the future. A hope for a family. Hope for love. She only needed to say yes.

She looked down, and as she did, a black lock of hair fell across her forehead. On impulse, he smoothed the lock back into place. He had not expected the feeling of such intimacy in that simple gesture.

His heart now controlled his voice. "I have made mistakes, mistakes that make me undeserving of so many things. But in a short time, so much of what I thought I believed to be true has been proven wrong."

Her black lashes fanned on her flushed cheeks as she lowered her gaze. Was she frightened? He touched his forefinger to her chin and gently tilted her face so that her eyes met his.

"I do not know what the future holds, but it is meaningless if you are not in it."

Her chin trembled, and she pulled her hand away. He shifted. Fear that she may not return the same sentiments crept into his mind, speaking louder and more powerfully with each second that passed. "Have I upset you?"

Tears filled her eyes, making them appear even larger and more vibrant. No longer was she the steady, controlled headmistress who had so calmly dealt with a fire, an injured child, and so many other crises. Instead, she was vulnerable and endearing, and the realization made his heart ache for her all the more.

Every moment that passed tortured him, yet he would not rush her or push her for a response. His eyes were drawn to her quivering lips, and each shallow breath that passed her parted lips entranced his senses.

Finally, a smile. The tears that had filled her eyes finally burst free and slid down her flushed cheeks. "I am not upset, William."

His face was inches from hers. Mirth spread through him, at first as a slow ember and quickly exploding to a raging fire. Gently, ever so, he took her face in his hands and wiped the tears away with his thumbs.

Her body seemed to weaken under his touch. She rested her hands on his chest, and she melded against him as if nothing could keep them apart. Her eyes flitted from his eyes to his lips, and that was all the encouragement he needed.

He lowered his lips to hers, not fully prepared for the impact that would have. For at the touch of her lips on his, a fierce longing surged through him. He slid his arms around her, drawing her closer, feeling her tremble. She did not pull away. Instead, she snaked her arms around his neck, lifted her face to accept his kiss, and returned his affection with equal passion.

Having difficulty controlling his own emotions, he pulled away and smoothed her hair away from her face. How he wanted to remember this moment, the way she looked, the way she felt in his arms, for he was certain that this moment, maybe more than any other, would define him from this time on.

"Patience"—he ran his hand along the smooth contour of her cheek—"dearest Patience. Will you do me the honor of becoming my wife?"

A smile as beautiful as he had ever seen brightened her face. "Oh yes, William. Yes!"

He needed to hold her. Make sure she was real. Relief mixed with happiness at her utterance of that one word. *Yes.* He pulled her to him with increasing possessiveness, and she moved into his embrace. "I love you, Patience. And I will spend the rest of my life showing you how much."

36

William walked over to where Lewis was saddling Angus.

"Is it all there?" Lewis asked, adjusting the stirrup.

William tapped the leather pouch in his gloved hand. "Yes, all here."

"Must be a good feeling." Lewis looked at William, squinting in the bright morning sun.

"It is." William handed the pouch to him, and Lewis tucked it in a saddlebag. "It's all there, plus extra, in case Rafertee has any hard feelings about it."

Lewis stepped into the stirrup. "Don't you worry. I'll see it gets there, safe and sound."

William nodded. "I know you will."

As Lewis settled in the saddle, William's chest tightened. How he wanted to be the one to deliver the payment to Rafertee's men, to finally be free from the debt's weight. But he had other matters at hand, and Lewis, good and faithful Lewis, would not let him down.

"I'll be back in three days' time, four at the most."

"Godspeed."

"Take care of that colt." Lewis tipped his hat. "We want him healthy and strong when Bley comes to claim him."

"Don't you worry." William watched as Lewis rode down Eastmore's drive to the main road, then he turned back to the stable.

William paused long enough to notice how the sun's light reflected from the paned windows of Eastmore Hall to the ground below. There was not a great deal of money left from the sale of the Rosemere land and Latham Hill, but there was enough to reinstate a staff, begin repairs on the grounds, and make it a worthy home for Patience and Emma.

He walked toward the stone stable, where smoke curled from the chimney at the building's east end and animals roamed the pens outside the building. One of the animals was the newborn foal, who now, almost two weeks old, was already testing his bounds. The letter in his pocket confirmed that Mr. Bley would indeed be purchasing the animal. He had sent money as proof of his good faith. The letter said he would arrive in two days to check the animal and assess the other broodmare.

William chuckled as he thought of the promise he had made to Lewis. Yes, he would take good care of this animal. And with the other broodmare ready to deliver any day, it appeared that his plans for horse breeding might grow legs after all.

He hurried to the stable and to one of the back stalls. There was Delilah, surrounded by Emma, Patience, and Charlie.

"Look, Papa!" exclaimed Emma as she finished tying a pink ribbon around Delilah's neck. "Isn't she lovely?"

William swept the child up in his arms, and she giggled with delight. He looked down at the animal. "Well, it is an improvement, I suppose."

He planted a kiss on the girl's soft cheek before she wiggled back to the ground. "I brought a blue ribbon for the baby horse. Where is he?"

William laughed and jerked his thumb toward the door. "He's out in the pen."

He stepped back to avoid being run over by the two excited children.

"Mind the mud!" Patience called as she watched the children run from the stable. She placed a hand on his arm.

Her presence and the openness of her affection made his heart swell with unending joy. He took her warm hand in his cold one and tucked it in the crook of his arm.

Patience leaned into her betrothed. His presence made her feel safe and warm, wanted and loved. He smiled down at her. The tenderness in his eyes, the sincerity in his smile, brought a heat to her cheeks on this cold March morn.

"Perhaps we had better go see what they are up to," he said and nodded toward the door. "Besides, I am sure the last place you would want to spend time is in a stable."

How she wanted to tell him that she didn't care where she was as long as she was by his side, but instead, she leaned her head against his shoulder as they walked into the fresh morning air.

Outside, the children were at the fence, trying to call the foal over, with no success.

William's rich laugh rumbled from his chest. "They can try all they want, but that one is stubborn."

The sight of Emma laughing and playing brought Patience a sense of peace. "Emma seems at home here, William."

He covered her hand with his as they walked the path to Eastmore Hall. "I am glad, for it is her home. And it will be yours soon."

The intimacy in his expression brought a tremor to her heart, and she drew a deep breath. She looked up at Eastmore Hall, so large, so intricate. In the time she had spent here in the past few days, it had become less intimidating. Less daunting.

"Yes," she breathed. "Home."

"Will you be sad to leave Rosemere?"

Patience thought about how she did feel. She had recently believed that the school was her calling. Her mission in life. She had thought she could never leave the school. But her brother was in charge, and his plans for the school and for his growing family were solid. And with the school so close and the girls so dear to her, they would never be far away.

It was as her mother said. She had completed her part in her father's dream. And now she would have dreams of her own.

Patience drew a deep breath and looked up at William. "No, I am not sad. For I know where I belong."

William cocked an eyebrow. "And that is?"

She smiled. "Right here at Eastmore Hall. With Emma. And with you."

William pressed a kiss on her forehead. "And I with you, Patience. And I with you."

READING GROUP GUIDE

1. Mr. Hammond knew that William was Emma's father for many years, but he chose not to divulge this information to William until he felt the time was right. Do you agree or disagree with Mr. Hammond's decision to keep Isabelle's secret? Why or why not? How do you think William's actions would have been different if he'd known the truth earlier?

2. During the Regency period, if a woman was not married by the age of twenty-five or so, she was already considered a spinster. Does this surprise you? Patience believes herself to be a spinster and thinks the opportunity for a husband and children of her own has passed her by. How do you think this belief affects her decisions through the course of the story?

3. Which character (male or female) in the book do you identify with the most? In what ways are you similar to that character?

4. When Lydia arrives at Rosemere, Patience initially resents her new sister-in-law's presence. Over time, however, Patience begins to feel friendship for Lydia and eventually enjoys her

company and accepts her as family. Have you ever had a relationship that you initially resented but that ended up being a very positive one?

5. Do you think William will be a good father to Emma?

6. William finds it difficult to forgive himself for his past mistakes, and over the course of the story he works hard to redeem himself. What do you think William learned through the course of the story? How has he changed by the end?

7. How would the story have been different if Rawdon never returned from London?

8. When Cassandra learns that Rawdon has married another, she decides to leave Rosemere, the only home she has ever known. If you were Cassandra, would you have made the same choice? Why or why not?

9. In what ways is Patience different at the end of the novel than she was at the beginning? In what ways does she remain the same?

10. Now it's your turn . . . what's the next chapter of this story? Does Patience continue to teach at Rosemere after she and William marry, or does she leave the running of the school to Rawdon? Do Patience and William start a family right away? Are William's plans to become a horse breeder successful, and if so, what impact does this have on their family? If you were the author, what would be next for William and Patience?

ACKNOWLEDGMENTS

My writing journey would not be possible without the support of some truly amazing people.

To my husband, Scott, and my daughter . . . thank you both for going on every step of this journey with me. Your daily encouragement, enthusiasm, and love inspire and motivate me.

To my parents, Ann and Wayne—you have prayed for me, cheered for me, and you have always believed in me and my dreams. Thank you.

To my mom, Ann, and my sister Sally, who are my wonderfully insightful "first readers"—thank you for taking the plunge with me and sharing my passion for stories!

To my editor, Sue Brower, and my copy editor, Jane Haradine—you ladies challenged me to stretch beyond my comfort zone, and this story is stronger because of it. And to the marketing, design, editorial, and sales teams at Thomas Nelson . . . you guys constantly amaze me.

To Tamela Hancock Murray—I am so blessed to be able to call you not only my agent, but my friend. Thank you for being my cheerleader!

ACKNOWLEDGMENTS

To my dear writing accountability partners, Carrie, Melanie, and Julie—thank you for your daily encouragement and friendship. And to my writing "sister," Kim—I am so grateful for you and for fun brainstorming sessions, solid advice, and good laughs.

Each one of you is a blessing to me!

ABOUT THE AUTHOR

Photo by Forever Smiling Photography

Sarah E. Ladd received the 2011 Genesis Award in historical romance for *The Heiress of Winterwood*. She is a graduate of Ball State University and has more than ten years of marketing experience. Sarah lives in Indiana with her amazing husband, sweet daughter, and spunky Golden Retriever.